To. Laurie,

With love from Mum & Dad.

October 1976.

OTHER PUBLICATIONS BY THE SAME AUTHOR

BOOKLETS

Maori Carving, 1941, 2nd edn 1950
Maori Designs, 1943, 2nd edn 1960
Maori Art, 1946
Maori Carving for Beginners, 1949
Maori Carving Illustrated, 1955

BOOKS

Maori Houses and Food Stores, 1952
Carved Maori Houses, 1955
The Book of the Huia, 1963

MAORI LIFE AND CUSTOM

by

W. J. PHILLIPPS

A. H. & A. W. REED

WELLINGTON SYDNEY LONDON

First published 1966
Second impression 1969
Third impression 1973

A. H. & A. W. REED LTD
182 Wakefield Street, Wellington
51 Whiting Street, Artarmon, Sydney
11 Southampton Row, London WC1B 5HA
also
29 Dacre Street, Auckland
165 Cashel Street, Christchurch

Publication of this work has been assisted by the Maori Purposes Fund Board, whose help is gratefully acknowledged

ISBN 0 589 00207 4

Printed and bound by
The Continental Printing Co. Ltd, Hong Kong

To

My Children

BILL, BRIAN, AND JOY

CONTENTS

ILLUSTRATIONS

MAP

Jacket: The picture on the jacket front is from an oil painting by Marcus King, and is reproduced by courtesy of the National Publicity Studios.

FOREWORD

AS MUCH OF THE MATERIAL for this book was prepared by its author during his long term of service as a member of the staff of the Dominion Museum, it seems fitting that his contribution to New Zealand ethnology should be briefly summarised in biographical outline.

It was at the early age of thirteen that Mr Phillipps showed an interest in his future lifework by taking a course of lessons in chip carving which was in vogue as a hobby at that time. From this useful practical beginning he was well prepared to commence more serious study when at the age of sixteen he became an assistant in the biology laboratory of the Otago Museum. The dominance of the spiral design in Maori carving attracted his attention and this interest brought him into fruitful contact with H. D. Skinner who was then a student of biology with ambitions later fully realised in the field of anthropology. Mr Skinner was also at that time collecting and studying material from the midden sites of Otago and he and Mr Phillipps joined forces in making their own collections of artefacts.

After discharge from war service overseas in 1915, Mr Phillipps took up school teaching in 1916 and was appointed to a temporary position in the Dominion Museum a year later. He retired in 1958 after over forty-one years continuous work in the Museum.

He was first responsible for supervision of the fish collections and ichthyological research, but in 1926 as his interest in ethnology was undiminished he took charge of a display of Maori material set up in the Dominion Farmers Institute because of danger of fire in the overcrowded premises of the old Dominion Museum building. He received further inspiration and much help from the late Elsdon Best and shortly afterwards published his first ethnological papers. As the Museum staff grew Mr Phillipps was relieved of his biological work in order to devote more time to ethnology, and the period 1947–60 has seen a remarkable output of papers. Most of these have been published in the *Polynesian Journal* and similar publications, in which about eighty titles will be found. On a more comprehensive scale he has written two books on Maori carved houses and storehouses and several semi-popular booklets on Maori carving, art and design.

For nearly thirty years he was the senior member of the scientific staff of the Dominion Museum and had considerable administrative responsibility as Deputy Director, which involved periods as Acting Director as well. The Museum has benefitted from his work not only in reputation for Maori ethnology, but also from the methodical way in which Mr Phillipps has built up the large collection of illustrations of which the nucleus was founded by Augustus Hamilton and Elsdon Best. Artists employed from time to time at the Museum have co-operated skilfully and acknowledgment of their work appears elsewhere.

It is recognised that efforts in many directions and by many people, both Maori and Pakeha, have helped to keep alive the tradition of Maori decorative art. This is a valuable public service, and there is no doubt that the distinctive contribution made to it by Mr W. J. Phillipps will always be recognised as significant and important.

R. A. FALLA

Dominion Museum,
Wellington.
15 June 1966.

INTRODUCTION

MANY OF THE MAIN ELEMENTS of Maori culture were introduced from Polynesia, while other elements were developed in this country over the years. There is no doubt that the best and most reliable evidence on the Maori of former days is provided by his material culture, and in particular by the objects and appliances he used in everyday life. Legends and traditional stories may vary over the centuries, and even from tribe to tribe, but objects belonging to the past can speak to us and tell their own story.

The year 1950 will be remembered as the date of publication of the monumental work entitled *The Moa-hunter Period of Maori Culture* by Dr Roger S. Duff. Before this date we were aware that the Maori or pre-Maori population of New Zealand had hunted the moa, as evidenced by moa bones in the vicinity of old oven sites of Otago and elsewhere. The book, carefully documented and compiled on available archaeological evidence, supplied the first clear-cut picture of an early Polynesian people who hunted the moa in the vicinity of Blenheim and caught whales in Cook Strait. These early inhabitants of New Zealand, doubtless descendants of Kupe or some of the first canoes to reach the South Island, buried their dead chiefs in graves, together with their precious adzes and necklaces of cut whale's teeth, and supplied food for the spirit in the form of whole moa eggs. The new conception gave us a fresh insight into the conditions of one of the main Polynesian settlements in early New Zealand.*

Another work of importance to North Island pre-Maori material culture is the book by G. Leslie Adkin entitled *Horowhenua*, published in 1948. Most important is the chapter "Outline of History and Successive Inhabitants", in which the author tells us that the "earliest occupants of Horowhenua of whom there is any trace were the ancient Waitaha – a people of relatively high material culture, who were eventually driven out by the Ngati Mamoe". The latter was also a pre-Maori tribe. Adkin's work was an important landmark in obtaining a general understanding of Maori life.

In this work I have to acknowledge personal indebtedness to the late Elsdon Best with whom, over a period of fourteen years, I was associated as a member of the staff of the Dominion Museum, Wellington. From Elsdon Best I received not only first-hand information, but also much good advice Later I studied with interest and benefit that great work *The Coming of the Maori* by Sir Peter Buck (1949).

In the more challenging climate of New Zealand, pre-Maori and Maori people were compelled to cast aside any Polynesian languor they might have possessed, and to tighten up their economic and social systems. Family groups or hapu became more closely knit, and kinsfolk joined in one to become a tribe or iwi. The pa became an integral part of the new way of life, welding the people into close defensive units. The highest honours, and the best that land and sea could supply, were reserved for those of breeding and high lineage. First came the ariki or sacred high chief, the eldest son of an eldest son, who traced his direct descent from the gods and was held in deep respect by the rank and file. Next came those nearest to the chief in rank and lineage, and after these the experts, the tohunga of various grades, priestly diviners, tattoo artists, carvers, and warriors, some even combining many of these qualities in their own persons. Then there were the food providers, fishermen, and fowlers, who also

*Dr Duff has recently found similar burials in Tahiti.

may have been identical with the highest classes. In the lowest grade were the slaves, who usually had to perform the menial work of the community and whose lives might be forfeit if the occasion demanded, e.g. the opening of a new carved house.

In this connection the importance of the term rangatira must also be mentioned. It is usually applied to a chief, sometimes to an eminent woman, to a person of noble birth, a master or mistress, or in fact to anyone highly respected in the community.

The Maori was a daring and courageous person, quick to learn and to imitate, hospitable, and possessed of a good sense of humour. His fears were the fears of the unknown, spirits of the night, sacred things, sacred places, and forebodings and dread of the powers of tapu.

In these pages I have endeavoured to give a balanced picture of the many-sided temperament of the Maori. He had initiative and executive ability, and these qualities enabled him to make devices and ingenious inventions to aid him in his struggle in an environment in which iron and steel were unknown.

The physique of the people was of a high standard, and their height approximately the same as that of the Pakeha. Women usually had a large and well-developed breast, shoulders, and upper arms. The beautiful Polynesian eyes of the Maori have often caused favourable comment. There was, and still is, a haunting lustre which seems to linger in the dark eyes of children and adolescents. The number of full-blooded Maoris remaining in New Zealand today is relatively small, but there are large numbers of half-castes, quarter- and eighth-castes.

The three main requisites for everyday life are food, clothing, and shelter. In the present work this dictum is applied to the Maori people.

Seafoods are placed first, for in any picture of Maori life it would seem that food from the sea, together with lakes and rivers, would be greater in bulk than food derived from the land. The only exceptions to this statement would occur in tribes such as the Urewera, living in areas remote from the sea. It may not be too much to say that the ancient Maori was largely a fish and shellfish eater. Kumara kept in storepits would be expected to last the winter, but it appears that in most localities kumara could not be stored much longer than the spring. Then would come the growing period when other foods must be sought. Although the pataka or elevated storehouse contained no kumara, fish, food of all kinds, relishes, birds from the forest, dried seaweeds, etc. were stored there. It was raised from the ground, and was fitted with a sliding doorway, in order that its contents could be aired continually.

In his clothing the Maori evolved new ideas, and made great innovations. To protect himself against rain and cold, the construction of a rain cloak with flaxen tags which would shed water was necessary, while a rapaki or loincloth of varying degrees of thickness was worn as a kilt. Pounding stones were used to beat the hanks of flax fibre required by the weaver. The stones were round in section, elongated, and fairly heavy.

Shelter, the last of the essentials, is treated at length. To the sun-loving Polynesian people shelter was of paramount importance in a temperate zone. New types of houses were evolved. Most of them were small, with the floor beneath ground level, and earth heaped up on the sides to contain the warmth within. Such houses were essential to communities living in a state of near nudity, for it is traditional that in going about their daily duties both men and women wore only a kilt. The exceptions would, of course, be high-born individuals of both sexes.

Tools, implements, and appliances of all kinds, together with weapons and canoes, come next. They are followed by art and design, basketry, music, toys and pastimes, religion, and the life cycle. The object has been to produce a readable account, with abundant illustrations, emphasising a number of important points not dealt with by previous writers.

No book describing new aspects of Maori life and culture could be written without help and assistance from many kind friends. First of all, gratitude is expressed to the

Director of the Dominion Museum, Dr R. A. Falla, for his continued interest and support during the preparation of this work. For useful suggestions in connection with the presentation of the text thanks are offered to Dr Falla and to Mr J. M. McEwen, Secretary of the Maori Affairs Department, who also contributed the chapter dealing with the Maori language.

To my publishers, and in particular Mr A. W. Reed, Mr J. H. Richards, Mr D. W. Sinclair, and Mr F. A. Davey, sincere indebtedness is acknowledged for their appreciative interest and for the excellent manner in which this book has been produced.

Those to whom my special thanks are due include also the following: Dr Gilbert Archey, Auckland Museum; Dr R. S. Duff, Canterbury Museum; Mr M. J. G. Smart, Wanganui Museum; Mr and Mrs P. R. Ranapia, Te Kaha; Mr C. R. H. Taylor, sometime Librarian of the Alexander Turnbull Library; Mr E. G. Schwimmer, late of Maori Affairs Department; Mr R. W. Halbert, Gisborne; the late Mr G. L. Adkin, Wellington; Mr R. H. Traill and Mrs W. Dawson, Stewart Island; Mr R. A. L. Batley, Moawhango; Mr J. B. Palmer, Suva; Mrs Peter Beckett, Middlemore, Auckland; Mr Peter Beckett, formerly of Paraparaumu; Dr Allan North, Te Whaiti; Mr C. S. Curtis, Newlands; Mr W. T. Ngata, Secretary to the Minister of Maori Affairs; Miss Susan M. Davis; to the artists Miss Sheila Traill (Mrs Natusch), Mr Gordon White, Miss Lavinia L. D. Buswell and Miss Stella M. Bagnall; and to all of the Dominion Museum staff. To many other friends of past years, Maori and Pakeha, I send greetings and grateful thanks.

W. J. PHILLIPPS

LIST OF ILLUSTRATORS

A list of artists and the illustrations for which they are responsible, is given below.

1

DISCOVERY OF NEW ZEALAND

THE TRADITIONAL STORIES of the discovery and settlement of the islands now known as New Zealand are of absorbing interest. Much room for speculation exists about the era when man first set foot in this land. The Polynesians were traditionally seafaring people who traversed great ocean spaces in their voyages of exploration. It is possible that they first knew of a southern land by observing that the long-tailed cuckoo makes an annual migration southwards from Samoa, and from the Cook and Society Islands. The migration would then have been on a much larger scale than it is today, and would constitute a challenge for exploration southwards. The long-tailed cuckoo arrives in New Zealand in October, departing again in February. Also godwits migrating south are said to fly low over some islands.

The possibility that drift voyages were the cause of the first settlement of New Zealand has been advanced by Andrew Sharp* who does not accept the literal interpretation of traditions of organised voyages. In this

Ancient Voyagers in Polynesia, 1956, revised and reissued as *Ancient Voyagers in the Pacific*, 1963.

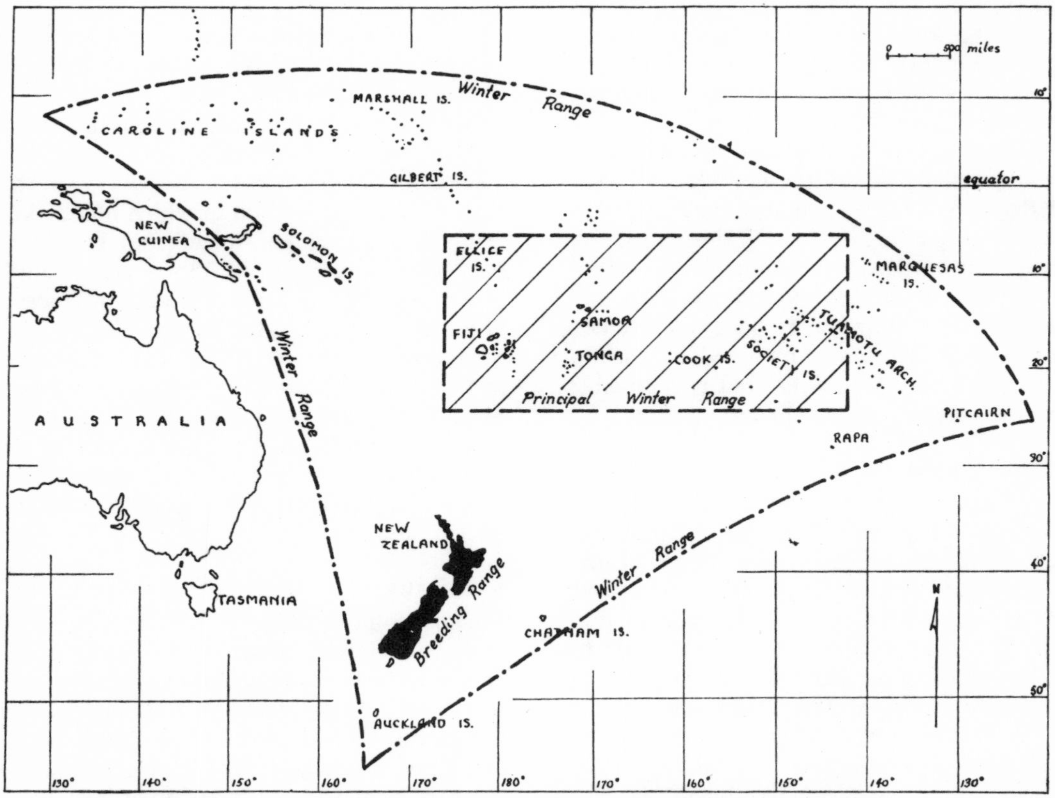

Breeding range and migration of long-tailed cuckoo (after C. Bogent, 1937).

connection it may be noted that there is a South Equatorial current which would carry canoes westwards across the Pacific and thence, during certain seasons, obliquely southwards from the Cook Islands to New Zealand.*

Kupe and Ngahue

The accepted story of the discovery of New Zealand is from limited North Island sources and deals with the coming of Kupe and his companion voyager Ngahue in the vessels Matahorua and Tawiri-rangi. They were double canoes, or of the outrigger type. Kupe is said to have arrived in New Zealand forty or forty-one generations ago, i.e. some time between the years 900 and 1000 A.D. Kupe's voyage originated in Hawaiki and the islands of Tahiti, Raiatea, and Huahine. After discovering greenstone, Kupe is said to have sailed north to Hokianga and thence back to Hawaiki, where he imparted the knowledge of his discoveries to his descendants. Recent researches seem to indicate that there may even have been more than one Kupe.

Quite possibly New Zealand was inhabited by Polynesians before the coming of Kupe. Dr Roger S. Duff's account of the Polynesian moa-hunting group living at Wairau, on Cook Strait, shows that they did not know greenstone (or at least they did not use it to any great extent), but appear to have been traders and hunters. The date, obtained by carbon 14 analysis, was 1150 A.D., but it is possible that the original settlement was earlier.

Toi and Whakatane

The North Island legend of the next visit to New Zealand concerns Toi, who arrived about eight generations before the arrival of the Great Fleet. Whatonga, Toi's nephew, was lost at sea, whereupon Toi decided to find him. Touching at Rarotonga, he decided to sail from there southwards to Aotea. Toi eventually settled at Whakatane and built a pa there. Meanwhile Whatonga returned to his home and went in search of his uncle. He sailed by way of Rarotonga, and finally landed at Whakatane, where he found Toi living with the local people.

Maui

But if we turn to South Island traditions, we find a different story. They are not so well verified as those of the north, as the people with knowledge were sparse and the investigators few. James Cowan, who met and talked with numbers of the older men of Ngai Tahu in the South Island, was informed that their traditions gave the name of Maui as the first Polynesian explorer to discover New Zealand. He is said to have arrived in a canoe called Maahunui about two centuries before Kupe, his home being a south-sea land called Mataora. It is probable that there were several Mauis in Polynesian history, one of whom was Maui the voyager. The first land seen by Maui was the Kaikoura Range, which in the figurative manner of the Maori is known as Te Taumanu o te Waka a Maui, meaning the thwart of Maui's canoe.

Maui is said to have returned to his homeland where, according to Cowan, he composed a song of triumph about his discovery. In this song for Ika roa a Maui in which he invoked Tangaroa, the name Aotea (roa) is said to bear the significance of "long clear light". The North Island name for Maui's canoe is Nuku-tai-memeha. Herries Beattie, in *Our Southernmost Maoris* (1954), tells of Maoris in Otago and Canterbury who believed that Maui had visited New Zealand, and mentions a number of other Maori place names. Maui, the navigator, is said to have visited New Zealand in 400–450 A.D., when Tutumaiao settled here.

Rakaihaitu

We now come to the great voyager who is said to have followed Maui in the South Island and to have founded an important tribe. His name was Rakaihaitu, or Rakaihautu. He appears in several of the older South Island traditions and whakapapa, not all from the same source. His era was about 850 A.D., and his canoe was called the Uruao. He was

*David Lewis in *Journal of the Polynesian Society*, 75, 1966, p.85, has demonstrated that a catamaran can be navigated from Rarotonga to New Zealand without the use of instruments of any kind, proving, as he says, that "major traditional voyages are navigationally quite feasible".

the father of the Waitaha tribe, which must not be confused with a much later Waitaha of the North Island. The name Rakaihaitu is known only to South Island Maoris and in the extreme north of the North Island. His lines of descent average forty generations. A Nga Puhi genealogy shows thirty-five generations. It is possible that the Wairau community of Blenheim belonged to his tribe.

The Fleet

According to a well-established tradition, a fleet of canoes arrived in New Zealand from Polynesia some twenty-one generations ago, about 1350 A.D. The best known were Te Arawa, Takitimu, Aotea, Mataatua, Tainui, and Horouta. They were probably double or outrigger canoes (most likely the former) and there is some evidence for believing that a substantial house or large hut was built above the level of the thwarts in order to give additional space and comfort. The people who sailed in these canoes were of hardy Polynesian stock. Apparently their landing was welcomed by the earlier migrants and in some cases they may even have been revered as gods. Every Maori of note proudly traces his descent from one or other of the Maoris who came to New Zealand in the "Great Fleet". In all the canoes of the Fleet brought into New Zealand some seven or eight hundred new settlers. If there were already 20,000 inhabitants in each island, they would constitute a small minority; but the earlier settlers would be dispersed over large areas, and it would naturally be politic to welcome new arrivals from the homeland.

Every conquering nation speaks poorly of the vanquished, so full credence cannot be given to Maori traditions of the tangata whenua, the people of the land.

Summary

Traditional sources may be reconciled with modern archaeological discoveries. First, the legendary stories of Maui, common in varying forms to all Polynesia. Maui, as Sir Peter Buck tells us, was probably an early navigator and explorer who lived so long ago that he formed a link between the supernatural and the natural, between gods and men. The conception of fishing up an island is a Polynesian figure of speech for its discovery. Legend tells us that Maui fished up the North Island but he appears most closely associated with the South Island. Perhaps he did discover the South Island on a drift voyage along the South Equatorial current.

Recent researches have shown that some 800 to 1,000 years ago or even more the South Island climate was much warmer. It is possible that in that period the South Island would be preferred to the North, and that Wairau therefore became the great whaling and moa-hunting centre.

After this came Toi and Whatonga to the Bay of Plenty. With their crews they married wives of the tangata whenua. It seems that at this time the North Island was inhabited by partly nomadic communities of the type which later journeyed from both islands to the Chatham Islands, and became known to us as Moriori. With the coming of the Great Fleet of 1350 A.D., more Polynesians landed in the North Island. They exploited nephrite (greenstone from the South Island), became builders of fortified pa, glorified warfare, built many canoes, manufactured new weapons, and evolved new religious conceptions which were grafted on to older beliefs. Most important of all they introduced the kumara and several other agricultural plants from other parts of Polynesia, and were able to raise flourishing communities which depended completely on the products of land and sea.

The early culture period has been designated "Moa-hunter" by Duff. It extends from the first human settlement until the arrival of the Fleet. A new culture period commenced in 1350 A.D. with the arrival of the Fleet and extended to the arrival of Captain Cook in 1769. This has been designated as the Classic period of Maori culture.

2

THE MAORI LANGUAGE

by J. M. McEwan

Oceanic Family

Of all of the existing families of languages, the one which was spread over the greatest continuous area of the surface of the globe, before the expansion of English, was that known as the Austronesian, Malayo-Polynesian, or Oceanic family of languages. Austronesian languages are spoken from Madagascar, off the African coast in the west, to Easter Island, approaching the coast of South America in the east, and from Malaya and Hawaii in the north to New Zealand in the south. From these boundaries must be excluded the Papuan languages of part of New Guinea, and the Australian Aboriginal tongues.

The languages which comprise the Austronesian family are Indonesian, Melanesian, Polynesian, and at least in part, Micronesian.

Maori

Maori is, of course, a Polynesian language and belongs to the East Polynesian branch, which also includes Hawaiian, Marquesan, Tahitian, and Cook Island Maori. The West Polynesian branch includes Samoan, Tongan, Niuean and the languages of the Ellice Islands and other small islands further to the west. These two groups, whilst closely related, have important differences in both grammar and vocabulary, so that a Maori would have much less difficulty in following Hawaiian than he would Tongan, notwithstanding the far greater distance from Hawaii to New Zealand. He would have even less difficulty in following Tahitian and Rarotongan.

In comparison with other Polynesian languages, the two striking features of Maori are the extraordinarily rich vocabulary and the well-preserved word forms. The majority of Polynesian languages have lost various consonants, which have become replaced by the hamzah, or glottal stop, but of the eleven consonants which the parent tongue obviously possessed, Maori has lost only *s*, which has been replaced by *h*.

In vocabulary, however, with over 30,000 words, Maori must lay claim to being the richest language in Polynesia. This is probably due to the fact that migrations to New Zealand took place from various islands and also to the great distances separating various tribes, some of whom retained words which others lost. Thus there are fourteen words meaning the head of a man, only a few of which are found in any one language elsewhere in Polynesia.

Like its related tongues, Maori is full of imagery and poetic language. It is rich in proverbial sayings which condense a world of wisdom in a nutshell. There are few languages more suited to speech-making, and few people more addicted to it. Being an almost completely isolating language, it is flexible to an amazing degree. That is, instead of relying upon inflexions added to a word to change the meaning, the principal words, such as nouns, verbs, adjectives, and adverbs, remain unchanged, differences of number, tense, mood, or function being conveyed by the use of particles, or by the position of the words. Thus the one word *pai* is used to mean "good", "goodness", "well", or "to please", without any change of form. As in English, compound nouns may be formed from any of the principal parts of speech.

Pronunciation

The Maori alphabet consists of the five vowels a, e, i, o, and u, and ten consonants h, k, m, n, ng, p, r, t, w, and wh. The vowels are all pure vowels pronounced as in most languages other than English. As a rough approximation it may be said that they are pronounced as follows:

- *a* short as in *a*bove, or long as in f*a*ther;
- *e* short as in t*e*n, or long as in the correct pronunciation of the French word f*ê*te, or as "*a*" in the broad Scots pronunciation of c*a*ke;
- *i* short as in p*i*ty, or long as in él*i*te;
- *o* short as in *o*bey, or long as in h*o*me as pronounced in broad Scots;
- *u* short as in p*u*t, or long as in fl*u*te – *never* pronounced as the *ew* in *new*.

The consonants are pronounced approximately as in English, but particular notice should be taken of *ng* and *wh. Ng* is pronounced as in si*ng*ing and *never* as in fi*ng*er. For some reason its appearance at the beginning of a word, such as *ngaio* is apt to trouble a European, but even here it has exactly the same sound as in si*ng*ing. It is commonly said by some that *wh* is pronounced as *wh* as in *wh*ere, or by others as the consonant *f*. In fact both are wrong. This sound is correctly produced by saying *f* without allowing the bottom lip to touch the top teeth.

Accent

In correct Maori the accent is on the first syllable of each word, with a secondary accent on the third syllable of words beginning with the prefix *whaka-*. It is important to realise, in pronouncing place-names, that many of these are compound words. Thus most place-names beginning with O are a compound of *o*, meaning "the place of", and the name of a person. The second syllable in such names should thus be accented. Otane means "the place of Tane", Ohiro means "the place of Hiro", and so on. In correct Maori Oamaru should be pronounced with the accent on the first *a*, the name meaning "the place of Amaru".

3

FOOD OF THE SEA, LAKE, AND RIVER

Fishing

The Polynesians of New Zealand were expert fishermen. They had to be, for winter was a lean time, and additional supplies were always needed for the food stores. Nothing that the sea could provide was overlooked. It was stern necessity that drove them out to take whales with their primitive harpoons.

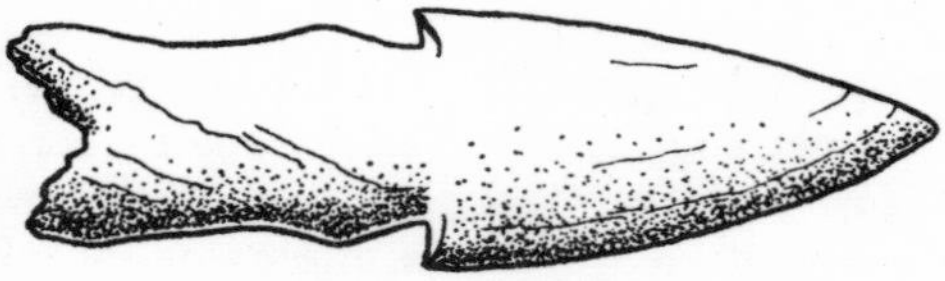

1. Harpoon barb (Bollons Collection).

It is probable that more fish food was eaten than that secured both by fowling and by agriculture. Almost every known device for securing fish was used at one time or another by these neolithic fishermen.

Maori fishing methods may be divided into three groups: net fishing; line fishing; and the use of traps of various kinds.

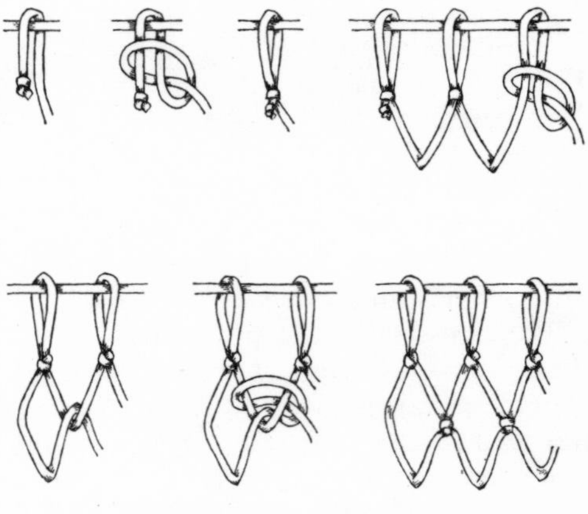

2. Maori netting (after Sir Peter Buck).

Nets

Nets were well made and were usually tapu until they were used. The first fish caught was thrown back into the water, while the tohunga addressed Tangaroa, god of the sea and of fish, telling him of the gift. After this the net was noa (common) and might

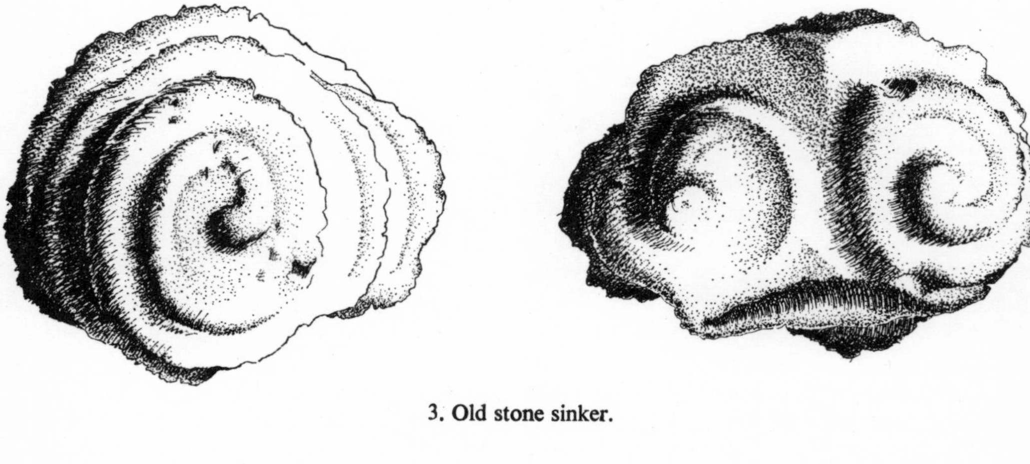

3. Old stone sinker.

be used as required. Fishing nets seen by the first European settlers are said to have been a mile or more in length, requiring 500 people to handle them.

Coastal fish were best secured by seine fishing. This method of fishing was carried out on a large scale. Such nets were usually composed of three main sections, the two outer being coarsely plaited, and known as whakaihi. The middle and most important section was carefully woven, and was known as the konae. Various sub-tribes or families would be held responsible for the manufacture of each part of the net. The joining of the sections of a new net was done under strict tapu, and all important subsequent seine fishing was carried out under direction of a priest or tohunga. The term kaharoa was generally used to refer to the seine net.

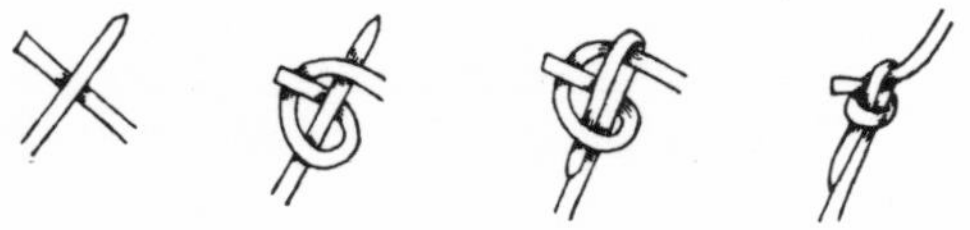

4. Knot for joining the netting strip (after Sir Peter Buck).

By use of the netting knot, small mesh bags were constructed to hold smooth water-worn stones. These were used as sinkers, sometimes for fishing lines and traps, but more often for nets. They were made quickly and easily from unprepared strips of common flax, and were serviceable for a limited period. They had to be kept dry when not in use, otherwise the fibres of the flax decomposed quickly. This procedure would be most useful when permanent grooved stones, or mahe, were running short or when time did not permit permanent mahe to be prepared.

The matarua was another common form of fishing net. It was circular in construction. seven or eight feet in diameter and two or three feet deep. It was stretched by two or three hoops, and open at the top for nearly its whole extent. The bait was fastened on the bottom and the net was then let down into the sea. By means of this funnel net large numbers of fish were taken on rocky coasts. It was referred to in the account of

5. Enclosed stone sinker (Bollons Collection).

Captain Cook's first voyage, and was apparently in common use all round the North Island in pre-European times.

Net-floats were made from the extremely light wood of the whau (*Entelea aborescens*). The floats were fashioned either in the form of a human figure or to resemble a hand with three fingers. They took the place of the cork floats in modern nets. Sometimes dry leaves of the raupo (*Typha muelleri*) or gourds were also used as floats.

Modern control of fishing methods applicable to rivers and estuaries have compelled Maori fishermen to utilise European nets for taking whitebait and other fishes. Formerly Maoris on their own tribal territory could block streams and by means of suitable traps take as many fish as they required. Whitebait are for the most part the young of a small freshwater fish, the New Zealand minnow, *Galaxias attenuatus*. The adult deposits its eggs in the estuary. Eggs or larval fish are washed out to sea to return as whitebait.

Line Fishing

Line fishing was widely practised. In the manufacture of fish hooks, bone, wood, stone, and shell were all used, and the processes employed in the manufacture were slow and tedious.

Bone hooks were most common. They were sometimes manufactured from human bone. The shape was first drawn or scratched on a piece of flat bone, holes were drilled around the shape, and then the piece extracted and further shaped by grinding stones.

In general form many fish hooks were peculiar in that the point came close to the shank. Old people believe that these hooks were more effective than others. When Europeans arrived in New Zealand, the Maori soon learned the advantages of metal, and fashioned many iron fish hooks in the shape of those formerly employed.

Trolling hooks with a paua shell face were much used for kahawai and kingfish, and these too were modified as iron became available. Instead of spinning in a circular fashion, the trolling hook worked in a reciprocal manner, winding and unwinding itself as it moved across the surface.

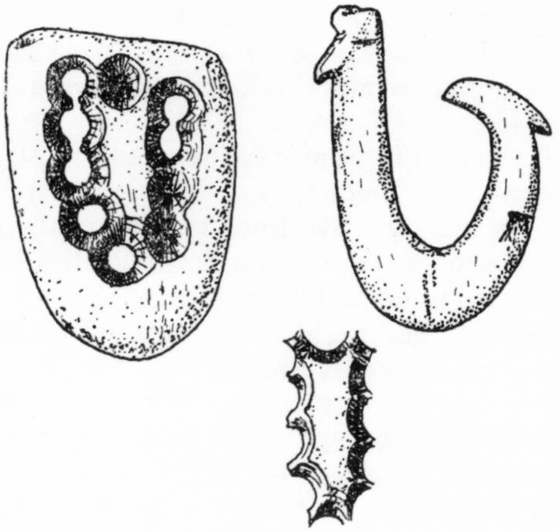

6. Making a fish hook.

An alternative method of making bone hooks by cutting out an interior portion from a flat piece of bone made it easy to obtain the correct shape. In the South Island in particular, the centre piece was drilled out rather than cut, but in the North drilling may not have been used to the same extent. An interesting suggestion has been made that the drilling method of hook making belonged to

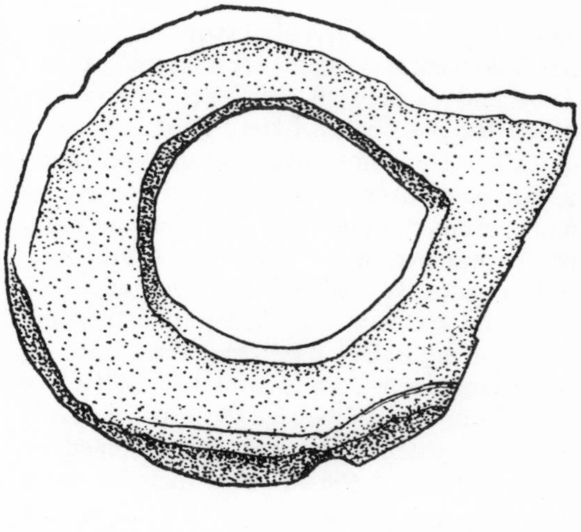

7. Bone hook in process of being made (Bollons Collection).

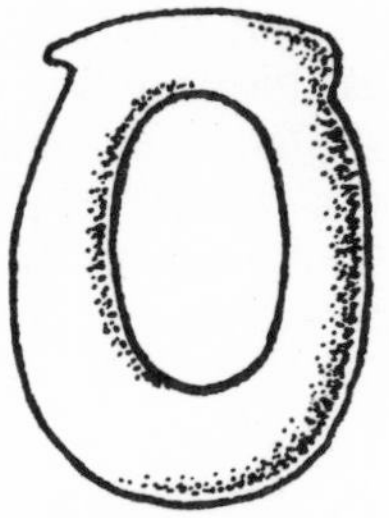

8. Shell hook in process of being made (Bollons Collection).

the earlier Polynesians, and the cutting method to the later arrivals.

On seashore middens from Hawke's Bay northward, small shell hooks, averaging in size one and a quarter inches by one and three-quarter inches, may be collected. In order to utilise baited hooks to best advantage, and to prevent tangling, a wooden spreader or pekapeka was often employed. The spreader consisted of a wooden stem with several branches, each branch holding a short line to which a hook was attached. The wood from which the pekapeka was made was usually manuka.

Trolling hooks resembling the Polynesian pearl-shell shanks of bonito hooks were largely used by Moa-hunter people. The shanks were of stone or bone, the line being attached below and above. Points vary in pattern, most being plain; but others were notched and barbed. Many bone points were perforated below to facilitate binding to the shank. The shank was also perforated above. The holes were useful for binding the line to the upper part of the shank.

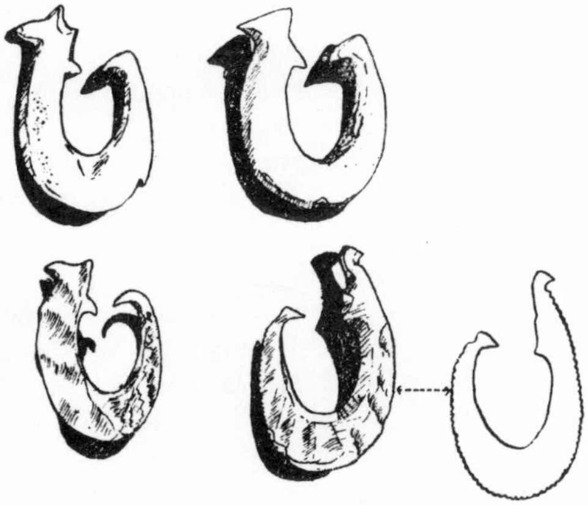

9. Shell hooks (matau), Hawke's Bay.

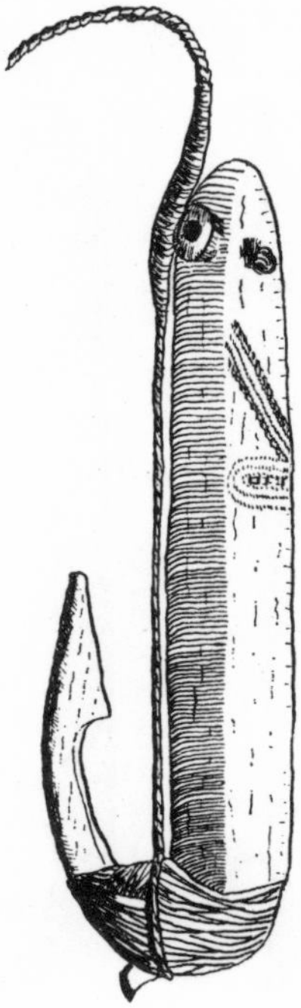

10. Stone shank, line and point attached.

Barracouta hooks, known as okooko, were in common use in pre-European times. The barracouta is largely a surface fish, somewhat curious and unafraid. At some periods of the year large shoals congregate, probably prior to spawning. The bait was the red, wooden shank of the fish hook which had a bone barbed hook attached to it. At the upper back of the shank was a grooved portion which served to make a tie for the fishing line. A stout stick some three or four feet long was

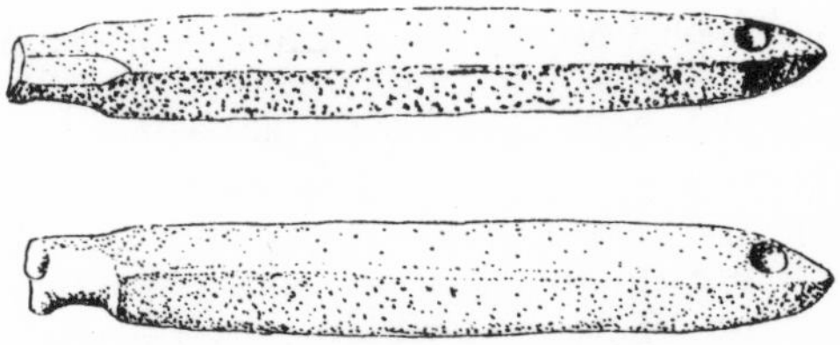

11. Stone shanks for fish hooks (Bollons Collection).

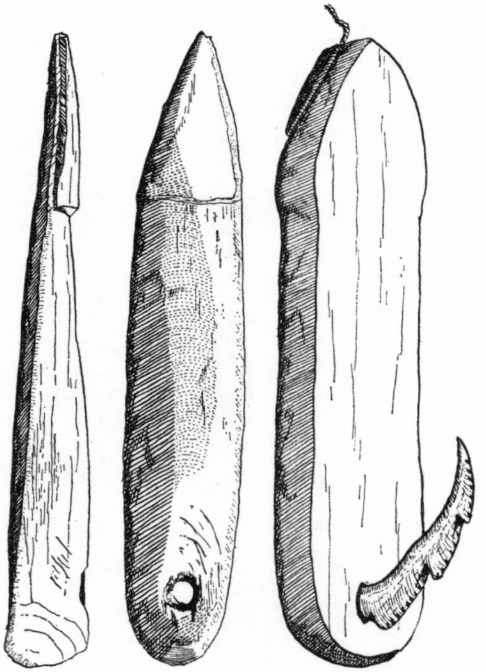

12. Barracouta hooks.

selected and to this the line, measuring only about three feet, was attached. Then the fisherman paddled to the shoal and lashed the water with his seemingly clumsy hook. The barracouta snapped at the hook and great numbers were taken.

Composite hooks with wooden shanks were also drawn behind canoes. They were baited to take albatross. Although such hooks are found in all large museums, little is known of the methods of using them. The wooden shank would help to float the bait on the surface.

Koko

An interesting method of fishing is practised on the East Coast and parts of the Bay of Plenty. It is termed koko, or prodding with a pole, and requires two men, one with a hand net and the other with a pole about nine feet long. The koko method can be used only where there are suitable channels along the rocky seashore. The pole startles the fish and moves them from their hiding places, after which the hand net is brought into play. The kehe or granite trout is the principal fish caught by this method. It feeds on smaller forms of seaweed which grow in rocky channels close inshore, and its movements are influenced by the seasonal growth of the marine algae.

13. Albatross hook with carved wooden shank.

Crustaceans and Shellfish

The sea crayfish or koura was caught by diving and spearing, in much the same way as that used by the modern underwater fisherman. There was also a trap, which was known as the taruke koura. It was oval in shape, flattened below, and with a relatively small opening above. It was baited with the head of a hapuku, and weighted with sinkers. The trap was secured by a stout rope, and its position indicated by a buoy placed above it.

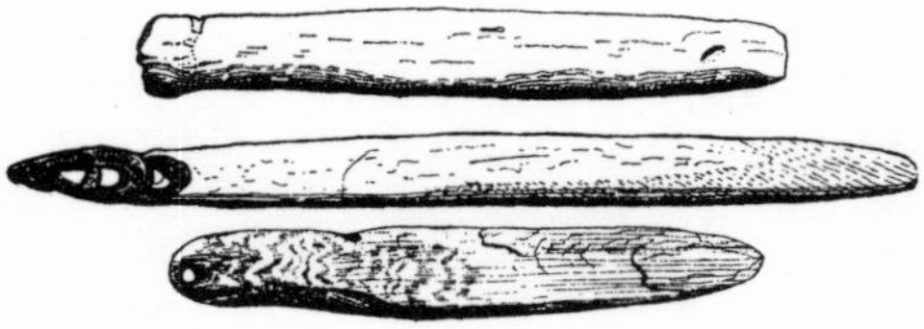

14. Ripi paua.

The paua lever, or ripi paua, was part of the domestic stock-in-trade of Maoris living in rocky coastal localities. The paua were levered from the rocks by means of these tools and were placed in a form of basket termed kawhiu. Ruku paua, as the task was termed, was a pursuit in which persons strove to surpass each other, as they also did in the taking of crayfish off the rocks in the spring months.

Eels

North Auckland Maoris used a stick and a relatively short line to take eels in streams. The bait was a large grub known as mokoroa, which lives in the puriri trees growing in that vicinity. By a series of simple loops around the body of the grub it was attached to the end of the fishing line, called pakai-kai.

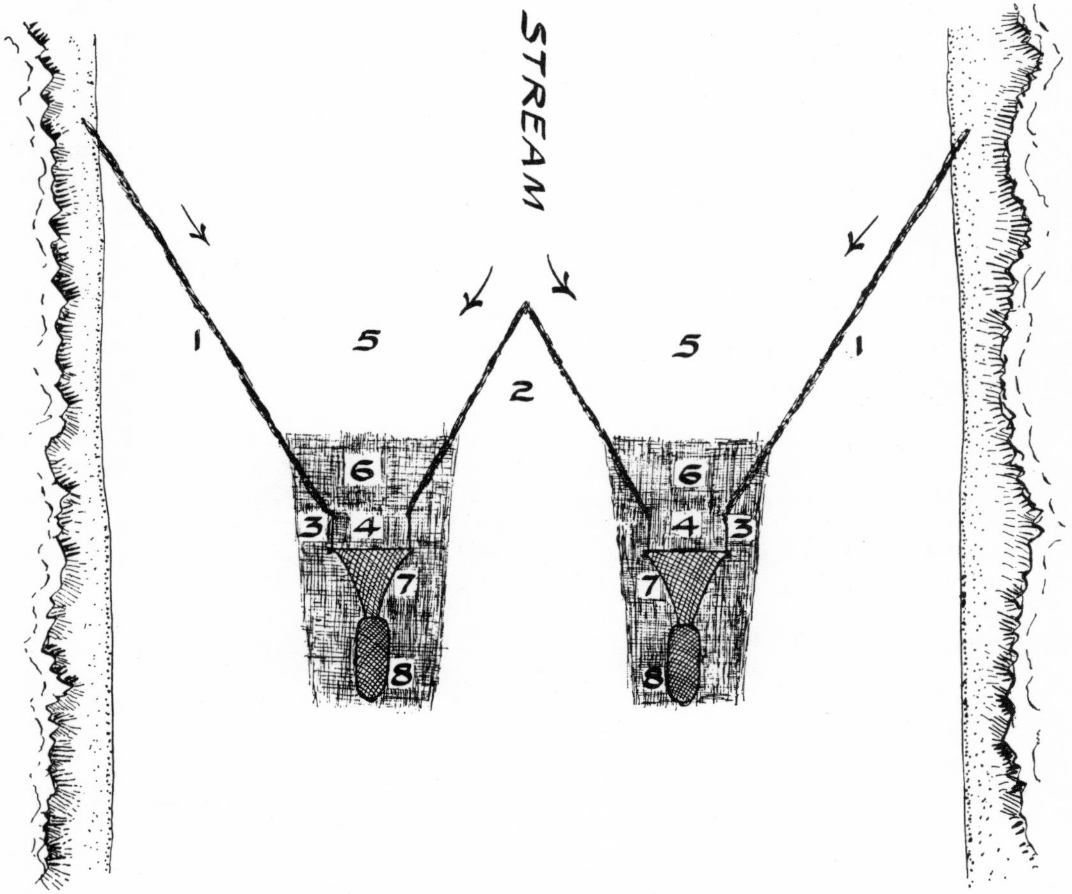

15. A pa taurenui having two ngutu, as used in taking eels moving downstream. 1. Paikau. 2. Tuki. 3. Tapangutu. 4. Ngutu. 5. Waha. 6. Whakareinga, whakatakapau, whariki (scour mat). 7. Purangi or leading net. 8. Hinaki (eel pot). (After Best.)

The pakai-kai was attached to a stick of supplejack, or kareao, seven feet long. In tying the string to the stick, a knot called whakapahuhu was used which consisted of a binding tied several times around the stick and then secured under the last one or last two bindings. Pakai-kai is defined as the string which ties the bait to the hook, and is actually the fishing line.

16. Whakapahuhu knot. A=Pakai-kai.

Sometimes a stone sinker was used to lower the line to the bottom. The fisherman moved his line gently in the water and in a low monotonous chant he called the eel from its hiding place. The eel swallowed the bait, and was drawn gently to the surface, where a man was waiting with a landing-net. The following chant was used during the operation:

Tuna-tuna, para para, kopu kopu,
Kai mai ra ki taku matire,
E mui a ana, e rangoana,
Tukia i to puku nui takia i to puku roa,
Mau ka ahu mai ahu mai,
Kia u.

To take eels in bulk in rivers and streams, a pa tuna or eel weir was constructed. The downstream outlet was frequently in the form of a V, with the foot of the letter left open. The guiding fences of the weir concentrated the main rush of water through the V with its opening at the point. A hinaki or trap consisting of two parts – a funnel-shaped guide net, or poha, and the main trap, or hinaki – were placed at this point. The illustration shows the poha, or guide net, attached to a circle of manuka reeds. The net was made from raw flax and was open at the back where it was inserted into the hinaki. A typical hinaki has a funnel opening below and a cap at the other end, enabling the fisherman to remove his catch with ease. The slim stem of the mangemange, a climbing plant, was frequently employed in the manufacture of hinaki, as also were manuka stems and other climbing and creeping plants. Eels were also speared at night, and special pronged spears were used for this purpose.

Joined leaves of the kanono or manono, *Coprosma australia*, were wrapped around the bodies of eels which were being prepared for the oven. The resulting food was greatly esteemed by Maoris of Hokio, near Levin, where this custom was still in use a few years

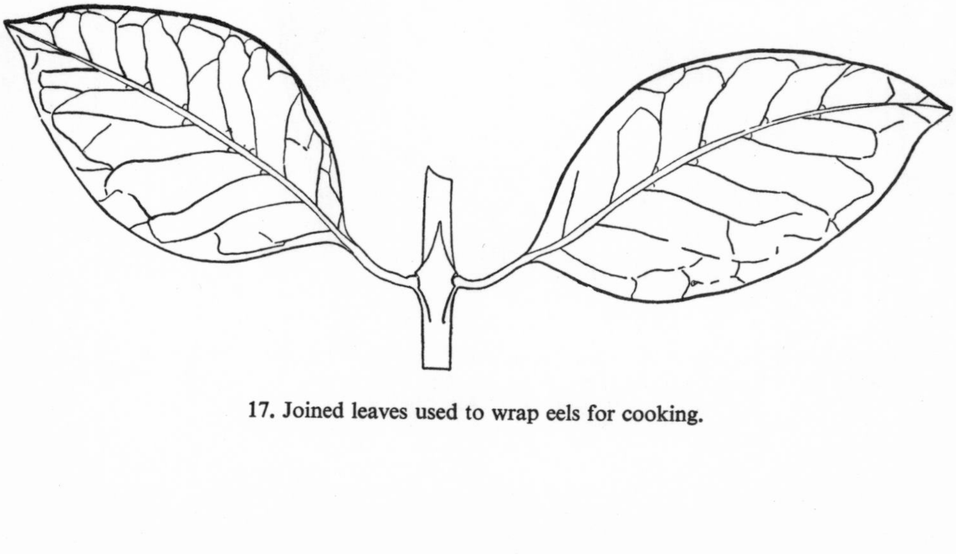

17. Joined leaves used to wrap eels for cooking.

ago. Few of these old usages have survived, but eels cooked in these leaves are said to be a great delicacy, and were much in demand by visitors to a tangi in that locality.

The patu tuna is a knife-like implement used to kill eels whether newly caught, or in the water. It is made of wood such as manuka, but sometimes of bone or stone. A unique greenstone patu tuna was found in the Wairarapa district some time ago. It was found on a farm at Pirinoa. It is the only greenstone patu tuna so far recorded, and may have been used by the tohunga for ritual purposes to open the eel-catching season. Formerly, large numbers of eels were taken annually, when low-lying Wairarapa lakes were released and eels migrated down the narrow channels. The patu is remarkable in having holes in both the butt end and towards the end of the blade. Apparently it was a device to suspend the patu tuna from the roof of a dwelling where shelves were unknown. This object measures nineteen inches in length.

Dredges

The kakahi, a dark-coloured freshwater mussel, was common in many clear rivers and lakes. In Lake Taupo in particular it was plentiful, and dredge rakes were constructed with a net attached to take the shellfish. The dredge rake was used from a canoe and the net emptied at intervals. The kakahi was not so highly regarded as mussels from the sea-shore, but was much utilised by inland tribes.

A device for taking crayfish and small fish in the thermal lakes was a thick branch of manuka twigs. Into these the small fishes and crayfish would come seeking shelter. Surprising numbers were taken by this method, but a large net had to be used to take those that dropped away as the twigs were hauled to the surface.

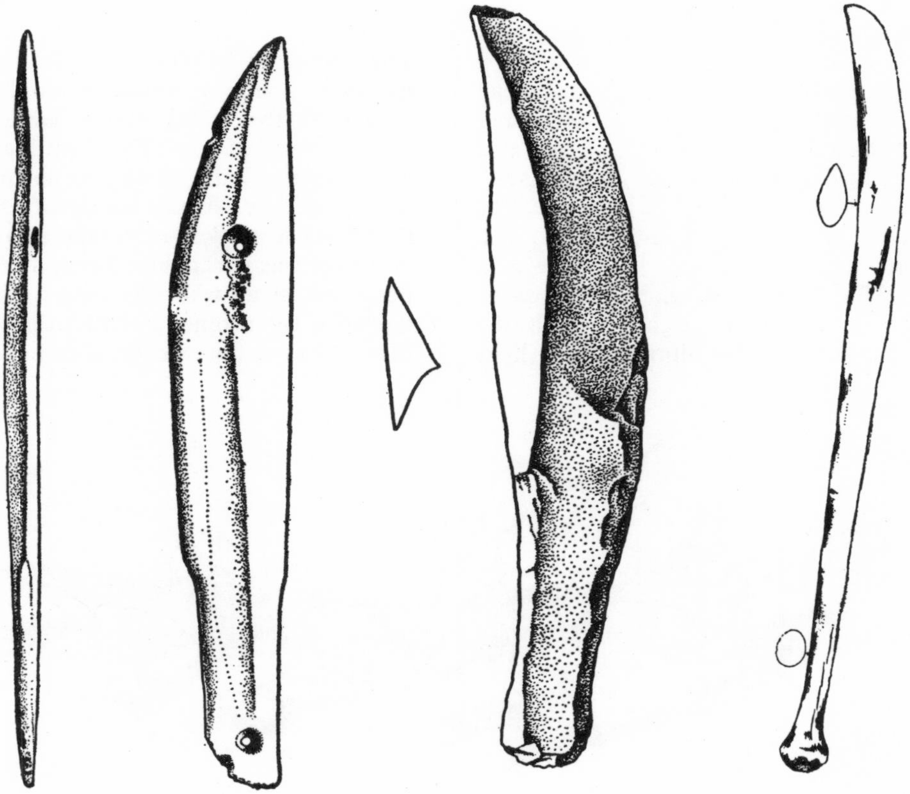

18. Patu tuna.

Floats and Sinkers

Around many of the North Island beaches pumice is common. It was sometimes utilised as floats for nets and set lines. Pieces of pumice were held be means of an irregular open fabric of lashing with strips of raw flax; but on occasion, grooves were made in the pumice to simplify the lashing process.

A large number of sinkers now in the Dominion Museum were collected on the coast in the Patea district. They were abandoned as Maoris gave up line and net fishing, or moved to new localities. These sinkers were for the most part river-worn stones, grooved around the circumference to take a line or cord. For further security, some had a second groove at right angles to the first.

About forty years ago an anchor which may have been used to hold a net or a canoe in position was found near Tauranga. It is a flattened, pear-shaped stone with a well-sunk hole above and of considerable weight below.

Another stone associated with fishing was the tapu mahe, or sinker. They may never have been used as sinkers for nets or fishing lines, but may have been mauri, or sacred stones, which held the essence of the god Tangaroa while fishing was in progress. Such a sacred stone, not a very large one, was held by Petone Maoris of last century. The late Hapi Love said that when he was a boy in 1880s it was customary for everyone to rise before the sun on the days when fishing was in progress. In the dim morning light the tohunga produced his stone mauri, and after invocations to Tangaroa, the stone was hidden until the fishers returned, when presumably the essence of the god would gradually retire from his temporary abiding place.

Drying Fish

Dried fish formerly constituted a large proportion of the food of most Maori tribes. When an abundant haul of fish was made, those that were not required immediately were hung on racks to dry in the sun. Dried dogfish of several species were highly regarded. Such dried fish might be kept in a pataka as a standby for a long period. Inland Maoris made similar use of many small freshwater fishes. In the Bay of Plenty, dried strips of snapper were greatly esteemed. They were called pawhera, and had a somewhat nutty flavour.

Whales

The discovery by Dr R. S. Duff of bone harpoon points at Wairau confirms the suggestion that some of our earliest Polynesian settlers of the Cook Strait area hunted and caught whales in the turbulent waters separating the islands. Most of the barbs found are from the South Island, only three being recorded from the North Island. It is possible that all whale hunting was done by the pre-Fleet people, and that the incoming Maoris had no knowledge of it, but evidence

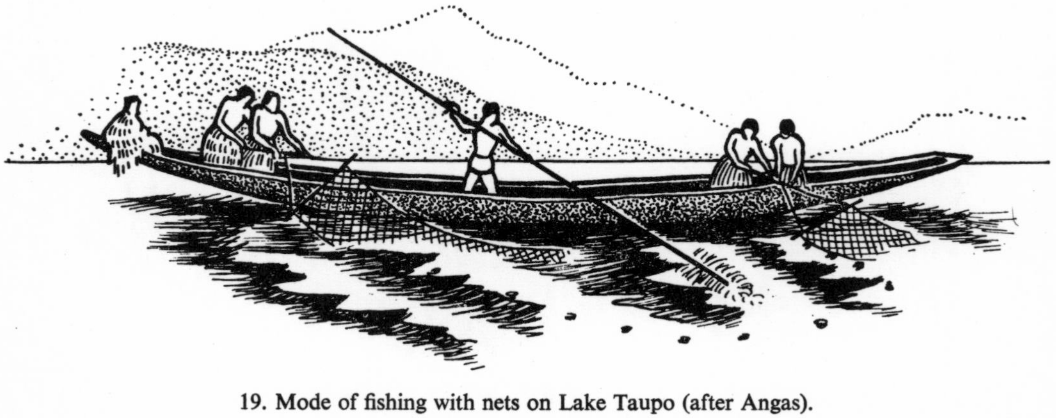

19. Mode of fishing with nets on Lake Taupo (after Angas).

so far is scanty. Outrigger or double canoes would seem to have been necessary for this work.

But little is known on the subject of how the Polynesians caught whales. We do know that whale meat has always been highly valued and stored whenever available. When Te Rauparaha and the principal chiefs of Ngati Toa were on their way to Ohau, they were feasted by the Ngati Rahira (a hapu of Ngati Awa) upon the flesh of the black fish, a large school of which had been driven ashore at low water. The Maoris ingeniously tethered them by their tails with ropes, killing them as they were wanted for food.

An ancient tale of Ruawhero eating the flesh of two species of whale and the porpoise (upoko-hue) is given in *The Ancient History of the Maori* by John White. Here we learn that eating this oily flesh caused much inconvenience and pain to Ruawhero and his younger brother Tupai who was with him. The next day they were given various foods to counteract the action of the oily flesh they had eaten.

The Maoris at Bay of Islands used a great net made of rope which they stretched from an island to the mainland near the entrance to the harbour. Many migrating whales were taken in this net. This information was supplied by Maori fishermen at Russell some fifty years ago, and local Europeans told of a wire net of Maori manufacture which for many years (after contact with whalers and traders) replaced the rope net; but of hunting with a harpoon no information was available.

The paraoa or sperm whale, the pakake or humpback whale, and the black fish (a relative of the dolphin and the common porpoise) were used as food. The sperm whale was once common in New Zealand waters. Every now and again examples were cast ashore and these provided the Maori with ivory from the large teeth and dense bone from the lower jaw. The humpback is a whale in which numerous plates of baleen or whalebone are used to strain the food. It is an ungainly animal with long flippers. The black fish is found in all seas of the world, often in large shoals. It regularly appears to commit suicide by casting itself on shore singly or in shoals, but it is also possible that it is stranded in shallow water and is thrown ashore by the waves. In former days the black fish was recognised as an important food supply whenever it appeared. This was particularly so at the Chatham Islands.

4

FOOD OF THE FOREST

Bird Snaring

The taking of birds was largely a seasonal activity. Trapping and snaring operations were carried out by experts, and called for a greater degree of specialisation than many other tasks.

The pigeon was one of the largest and most important of the forest birds. A favourite method of securing it for food was that styled waituhi, and this referred to setting snares over water to take the birds when they were thirsty. The berries of the miro are ripe in May and June, and during these months pigeons feed on them, becoming thirsty when they have eaten their fill. During the season the Maori fowler would set many snares around the edges of streams. His plan was to cover the surface of the stream with branchlets, leaving only certain clear spaces at which the birds might drink. Snares were set around these clear spaces. After drinking, the pigeon, like many other birds, raises its head slightly, ruffles its neck feathers, and shakes its head. These motions assist the fowler, for the back string of the snare catches the ruffled feathers. Sometimes a strong stick is placed across the clear opening and on this the snares are set.

The waka kereru was a wooden trough filled with water and placed in a convenient position where the bird would drink the water, putting his head through a noose to do so. The trough was placed in a conspicuous position, either in the trees, or on two posts set up by the fowler. Many waka kereru were highly prized and had special names assigned to them. Some were carved on the outside.

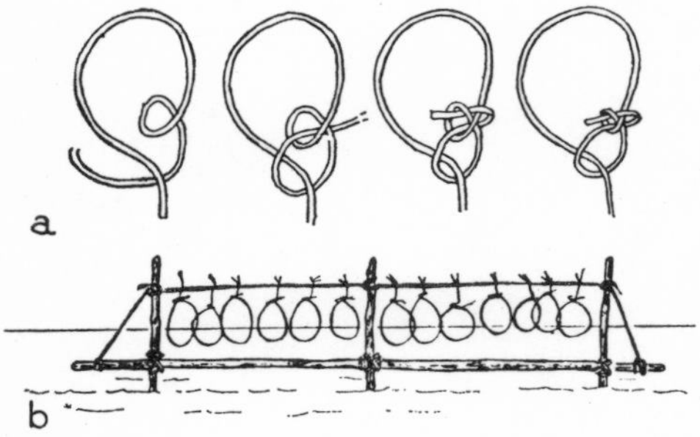

20. a. Noose snare (after Best). b. Snares above water (after Buck).

In the interior of the North Island the poroporo fruit is ripe in winter. Tui are fond of this fruit and remain in the poroporo trees overnight. They become very cold and are unable to fly on frosty mornings. Large numbers are shaken off the trees and killed. Others are caught by means of snares set in poroporo trees. Mrs Tumohe and Mrs Hetiti, the garment makers of Te Kuiti, stated that sixty years ago pigeons were so plentiful that children were accustomed to take one to school for lunch during the winter. The huia was never used as food. It was a tapu bird, for its feathers were associated with the heads of chiefs.

The first bird taken in the season was utilised as an offering to the gods. As such it might either be cast away, suspended on a tree, or be ceremonially eaten by a female of the elder branch of a leading family. The latter act would take some of the tapu off the forest and so enable women to enter it to take part in the fowling operations. Snares were examined at least once a day, and more often when the birds were numerous. Trespass on snaring places by outsiders was vigorously discouraged. Should a man chance upon such a place set with snares, he would break off a branch of a tree, leave it in a conspicuous place, and walk on.

The mutu kaka, or perch snare, was a device for supplying birds with a convenient perch on which a snare was set. The birds were caught by pulling the cord from below,

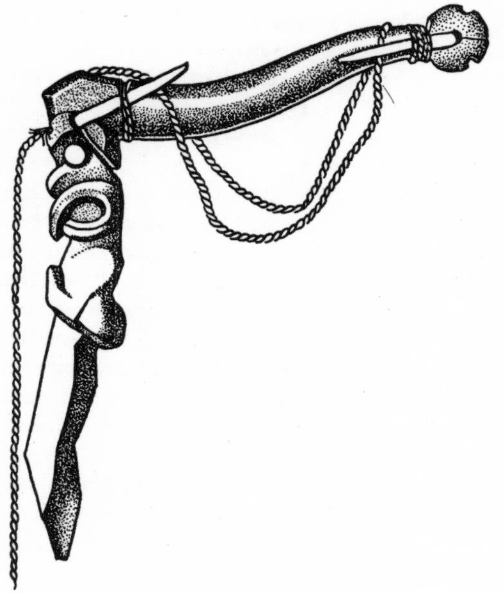

21. A mutu kaka or snaring perch used to take kaka parrot; quills hold the snare loop in position, a pull from below clamps the bird's claws to the perch.

clamping the claws tightly to the perch. There were several types of perch snares, but all were made on the same principle. Quills held the snare cord in position. An upright portion of the mutu kaka was lashed to a thin pole of considerable length, and the fowler was accommodated on a platform hidden among the branches. In one hand he held the cord leading from the perch snare, while with the other he irritated a tame decoy parrot by poking it. The noise immediately attracted other kaka parrots, who landed on the snares and were secured. Large numbers of parrots were taken by this method.

Decoys

Of the five leg-rings for tame birds in the Bollons Collection, Dominion Museum, said to be from the North Cape, two are of lead and three are of bone. Best tells us that leg rings (poria) were fashioned from human bone, whalebone, bird bones, and greenstone. In the collection mentioned, each of the five items tells its own story, the size of the hole for the insertion of the foot being small or large according to the species held captive. In museums and in general literature these objects are usually termed "poria kaka", but though often used for decoy parrots, many were obviously not used for kaka, the leg circlet being too small for the insertion of the foot of even a young bird. The smaller specimens may have been for tui and other pets.

Best* tells us that "when a Maori wished

*"Forest Lore of the Maori", *Dominion Museum Bulletin*, No. 14, 1942, p. 250.

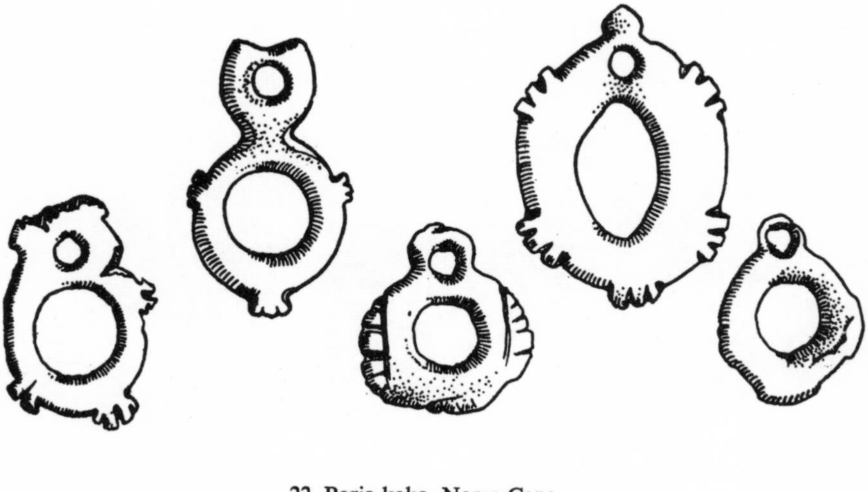

22. Poria kaka, Nortn Cape.

23. Domesticated kaka parrot used as a decoy (after Angas).

to keep a captured parrot as a mokai [pet or decoy] his first act was to prevent it from escaping; this was done by means of a cord, one end of which was secured to one of the bird's legs and the other to a rod termed a hoka . . . the cord was not secured directly to the bird's leg but to a ring of bone, stone or other material that encircled that leg; this ring was known as a poria maria, komore and takaore."

The use of lead for the two specimens mentioned above brings them to the present era, when whalers or others supplied the village needs. There are two types of poria, one in which the leg cord (maikaika) is inserted through a hole in the body of the ring, and the other in which a special projection is manufactured to take the hole for the cord. It will be noticed that ornamental projections from the outer circumference usually appear in groups of three. This may symbolise the three toes of the bird. Measurements of these objects vary from under one inch to one and three-quarter inches.

Weka Lures

When taking the woodhen, the fowler lies down to his work and waits for the weka to come to him. An original account from West Oxford, and also from Banks Peninsula in 1935, states that the fowler moved through the bushes imitating the cry of the woodhen with a little flax whistle known as "whakapi". When the bird came close enough, the snare

24. Snaring the woodhen.

25. Detail of weka lure collected by Dr R. A. Falla, Stewart Island.

was placed in front of the lure, which consisted of a weka's wing at the end of a stick. The fowler waved the wing briskly behind the snare and, ever inquisitive, the weka approached, thrust its head through the snare, and was taken. The weka wing swung freely at one end of the stick, the real fastening being some distance along the handle.

When Dr R. A. Falla recently visited Big South Cape Island, off the south-west coast of Stewart Island, he was fortunate enough to find an original weka lure with the weka wing still attached, apparently used by recently visiting muttonbirders.

From information received from Riverton and the Bluff about the snaring of weka by muttonbirders on southern islands, it seems that this method of snaring weka is called pawhera or kaha, while the stick holding the weka wing lure is purupuru and the snare pihere.

26. Barbed bird spear point.

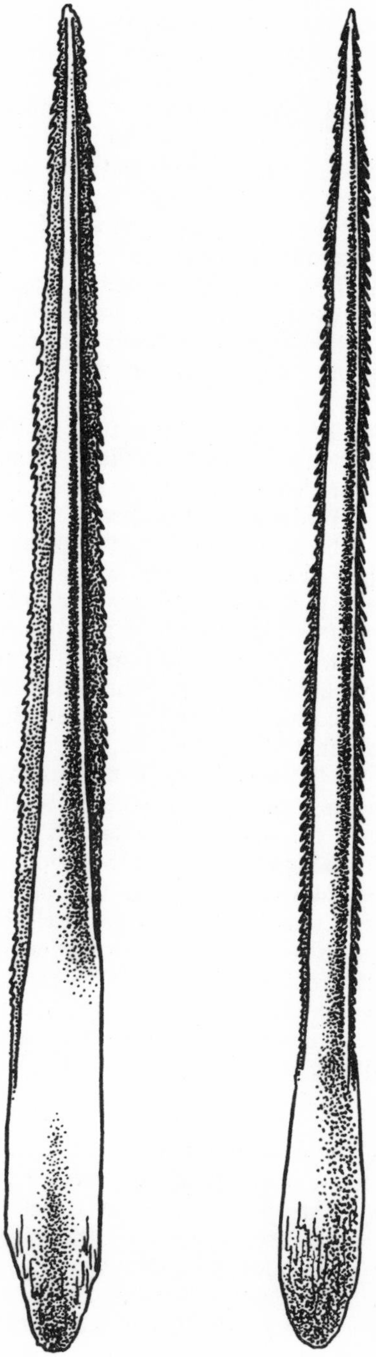

27. Tail spines from stingray used for spear barbs.

Bird Spears

An occupation vital to all communities was the manufacture of spears (tao). Long spears were used by the Maori fowler to take bush birds in high forest trees. They might be anything up to thirty feet long. They were slim poles pointed at one end and used by an operator on a platform or on the ground. To one end of the pole is attached a bone point (actually a land harpoon), usually barbed. They are about ten inches long in the Urewera; but scores of smaller barbed points which were probably attached to bird spears are found on New Zealand middens.

In localities where stingrays might be secured without much difficulty the tail spines were commonly used for makoi, or points of bird and fishing spears. One drawback to their efficiency might perhaps be that they would become worn out in a relatively short time, and so would not be as permanent as the carefully made bone spear points. Two of these tail spines, both apparently having been used for attachment to spears, measure eight inches in length. It is probable that points such as these would be bound to the spear end in a rigid manner.

Wooden hooks with a bone barb attached were used for taking the albatross at a distance from land. Sometimes these hooks were ornamented with carving. The trolling method was used, and the hook was well baited. The hooks were effective in securing not only albatross but also other sea birds, such as seagulls and mollymawks. Seagulls were at times tamed and acted as scavengers around villages.

Notornis

The takahe or Notornis was a contemporary of the moa, and once ranged freely over both islands. Like the moa, it was largely exterminated for use as food by the early pre-Maori populations. In Otago, at least, the takahe managed to survive down to the time when the Pakeha came, but its numbers must have been relatively few, and it had become a shy bird in the wild country to the west of that province.

Our knowledge of how the takahe was caught by latter day Maoris (who were probably taught by the original people of the land) is limited to a small collection of samples of the fowler's art collected by Dr R. A. Falla from a rock shelter close to the plateau where the Notornis colony lives. This locality is in the hills above Lake Te Anau. It is probable that Maoris caught the takahe by entangling their legs in one or more carefully hidden running nooses attached by a main flax strand to a short wooden bar, which would assist in securing stability and in entangling the unfortunate bird. The material of the snares is unworked flax strands as these make the best slip knots.

Dogs

Dogs were trained to take kiwi and kakapo in the forest. These birds were accustomed to hide in caves, crevices, or among the roots of trees. Both birds were highly esteemed as food by the Maori and by the early settlers. This was particularly the case on the west coast of the South Island, where Maoris taught the settlers how to catch them. It is probable that kiwi and kakapo were partly exterminated in the North Island by the first wave of Polynesian settlers, the Moa-hunters.

Penguins

Penguins were utilised as food by many southern Maoris. They were not so highly regarded as many other birds, but seem to have been eaten when other food was scarce. This was particularly the case in Stewart Island and Southland. Apparently penguins were eaten by Petone Maoris, for in the Dominion Museum there is a photograph of an old sketch of Pipitea pa showing two penguins suspended by the neck from a pole inside the gateway.

Bird-calling

Bird-calling is of very ancient origin, and appears to have been practised in most communities. The fowlers would be adept, firstly at imitating the cry of the bird, modifying this as required with mouth, tongue, and lips, and secondly in the use of mechanical aids. The more civilised man has become, the more elaborate have been the mechanical aids employed.

The Maoris were adept in imitating the various songs and cries of native birds, and in some parts of New Zealand special whistles or calls were constructed for the purpose. These were resonant artefacts with a circular chamber into which the breath was blown downwards. In shape this bird-call is more or less circular in its diameter towards the hollow, but compressed towards the suspension hole. The length is two and a quarter inches and the diameter one and a quarter inches. The second bird-call is a plain type, also manufactured from steatite or soapstone.

The Rat and the Dog

New Zealand is said to have been cut off from the rest of the world before marsupials or mammals made their appearance over the great land areas, so the only native mammals known to the Maori were the various marine species such as seals, whales, and porpoises, and two native species of bat. The bats were sometimes eaten. Two mammals were introduced from Polynesia. These were the dog and the rat. The dog became extinct last

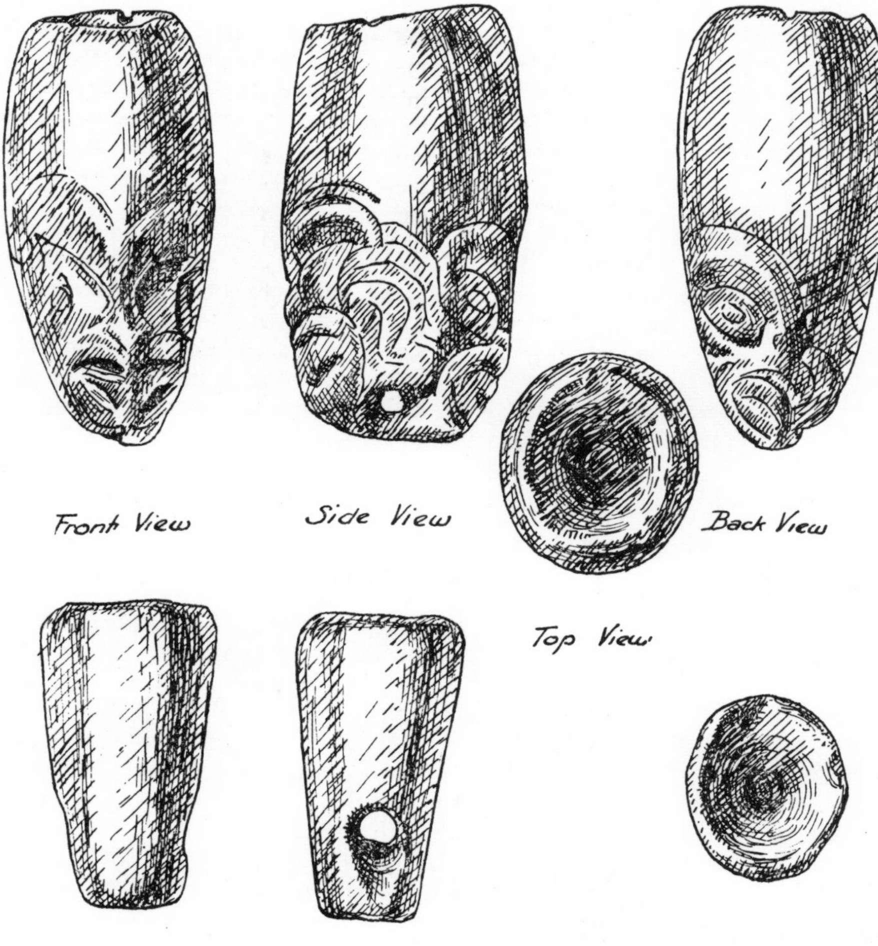

28. Bird-calls (Dominion Museum).

29. Native rat.

century, but the rat is still to be found here and there, notably on Little Barrier Island, where the European rat is unknown.

The Polynesian rat is largely a vegetarian, but it will eat young birds and birds' eggs and also enter the pataka when possible, doubtless attracted by the smell of food. It has been known to climb the vertical trunks of trees used to support the pataka. It was much more placid than the European rat, and apparently had little effect on the bird population. The Maoris had a number of methods of taking rats (kiore) for food. They were trapped on summits of ranges or spurs along which their tiny feet made well-worn tracks. They were also caught in pits. Rats were much esteemed and regarded as a delicacy. They were also preserved in fat for future use and retained in the pataka. Like the lemming of Scandinavia, native rats will at times take to the sea or to a lake in large numbers, swimming until they are drowned. A Maori told Elsdon Best that rats were frightened by the morepork; another said they swam to sea when the tawai flower was in bloom. Whatever the reason for this mass suicide, it seems that the rats were obeying some natural law to maintain the balance of the species.

In the year 1884 large numbers of rats, said to have been the native rat, invaded Picton and Blenheim districts and then turned westward to Nelson, Motueka, Collingwood, and Cape Farewell. For several months these rats were numerous in the town and suburbs of Nelson. Dead rats were found on the roads, in the fields, and in the gardens. Much damage was done to wheat, peas and other crops.

W. H. Skinner states that the Maoris

30. Tawhiti kiore, rat trap (after Best).

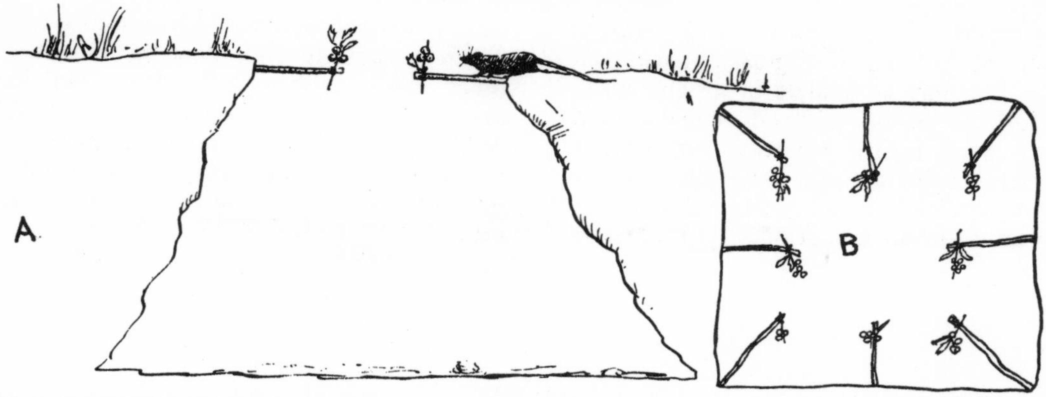

31. A. Cross section of rua torea, pit trap for rats. B. Pit trap for rats, bait on sticks stuck horizontally. (After Best.)

brought into New Zealand two types of dog: one, a small or middle-sized dog of strong build, a pure-bred Pomeranian-type with a "coat of pure white, so much so that in some places it was a sacred dog"; the other was somewhat larger with a coarse, short coat and reputed to be very strong. Neither of the dogs barked, but had a weird yapping howl. There is no doubt that the larger dog was the pariah dog found all over Asia, Eastern Europe and certain parts of Africa. This dog has a sharp muzzle, upright pointed ears, and a bushy tail generally curved over its back. It varies in colour from black, through grey, to reddish brown and white.

Probably the two breeds became mixed in later years. In general the kuri, or Maori dog, also called peropero, has been described as being a long-bodied, fox-eared, sharp-nosed, and long-haired animal. Even today it is probable that many dogs around out-back Maori settlements have in their veins the blood of this ancient stock mixed with that of introduced dogs. Here and there throughout the Pacific close relatives of the kuri are said to survive still. In fact the tame dogs of Burma

32. Maori dogs, Putiki Pa, Whanganui (from a painting by Gilfillan, 1840).

feed chiefly on a fish and vegetable diet and do not bark. The Maoris greatly valued their dogs, not only as hunters of ground birds, but also as occasional food animals. Their skins were highly regarded for making garments, being cut into strips and sewn on to a woven background of flax fibre.

Ngatoro-i-Rangi, high priest of the Arawa canoe, brought with him his favourite dogs when he came to New Zealand. Doubtless other canoes also carried dogs; but the original Moa-hunter people had introduced dogs into New Zealand long before the coming of the Fleet, and certainly would use them to hunt moa, kiwi, takahe, rail, weka, and other ground birds.

5

FOOD OF THE LAND

Agriculture

The New Zealand Maori was traditionally an agriculturalist. Voyagers carried food plants from island to island of the Pacific as new settlements were made. The coconut failed to grow in New Zealand, but the introduced kumara and taro produced good crops in suitable situations under careful treatment. Although Captain Cook saw the yam growing at Tolaga Bay, we have little information about it, but the taro was grown in many parts of the North Island. It is a root vegetable which requires an abundance of water and warmth to mature the large turnip-like root. The hue or gourd plant was also cultivated, both for its fruit in the early stages of growth, and later for the matured gourds which were scraped out and provided dishes and bowls of various kinds.

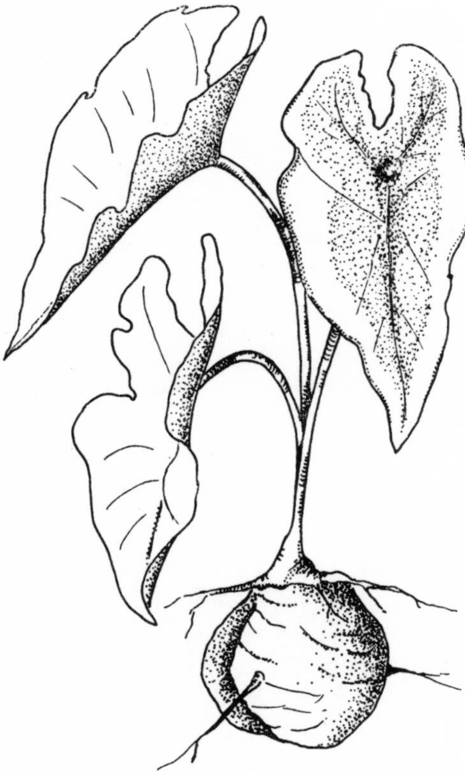

33. Common taro.

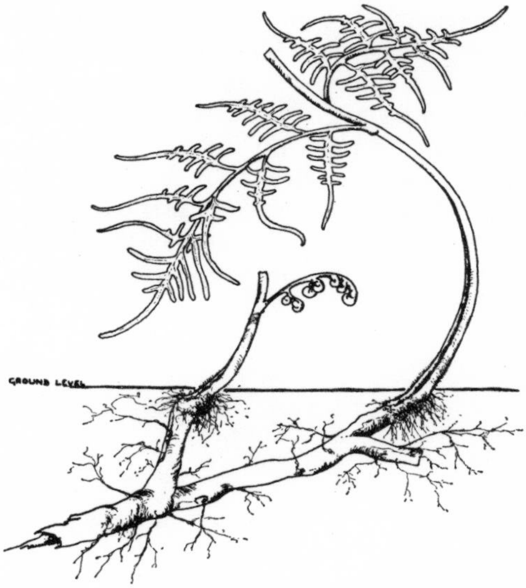

34. Bracken fern.

When the Polynesians settled in New Zealand they lost many of the food plants they had been accustomed to use in the old homeland, and reliance on wild products became necessary. Accordingly the aruhe, the rhizome, or underground stem of the bracken fern, became a principal food in many districts. Good stands of this fern were carefully conserved. Agriculture as such belonged chiefly to the Classic period of Maori culture.

Taro

As wheat is to the European races, as rice is to the teeming millions of Asia, so taro was to many Polynesians of a century or more ago.

Taro has more than once been acclaimed as more nutritious than any other food or vegetable known to ancient man in the Pacific. In Hawaii the cooked tubers were cleaned and scraped, after which they were placed in a wooden or stone trough and pounded with a rude pestle into a kind of flour, which was then kneaded into a thin paste and set aside to ferment a little, when it was known as poi, a sweet and sustaining basic food.

The Mataatua canoe is said to have brought the taro to New Zealand. Poetically it was called Tutahi-ki-runga, and was the subject of an ancient chant, but Maoris today have almost ceased to cultivate it. During a stay at Jerusalem, on the Wanganui River, about the year 1930, the writer saw a clump growing near the river, but few have been noted in Maori hamlets since that date. Some residents of Auckland city have cultivated the taro in their gardens with varying success.

The great French navigator, Dumont D'Urville, visited New Zealand in 1826–7. He made many drawings of New Zealand life and was most interested in the Maoris. One of his artists, named de Sainson, made a drawing of a scene which evidently impressed him – a row of Maori women stripped to the waist and armed with hafted adzes (toki) bent to the task as they commenced to clear and prepare a field for agricultural purposes.

Toki were used to clear the ground, and probably to loosen earth before digging, and in de Sainson's drawing there is proof of this. Roots of small shrubs and all types of small plants would have to be removed before a digging stick (ko) could function effectively. In fact the toki may have been an effective grubber, particularly when dealing with ground hardened by lack of rain. This may be why we find in museum collections a number of very blunt adzes.

35. Clearing the ground for kumara (from the drawing by de Sainson, 1827, in D'Urville's *Voyage Pittoresque*).

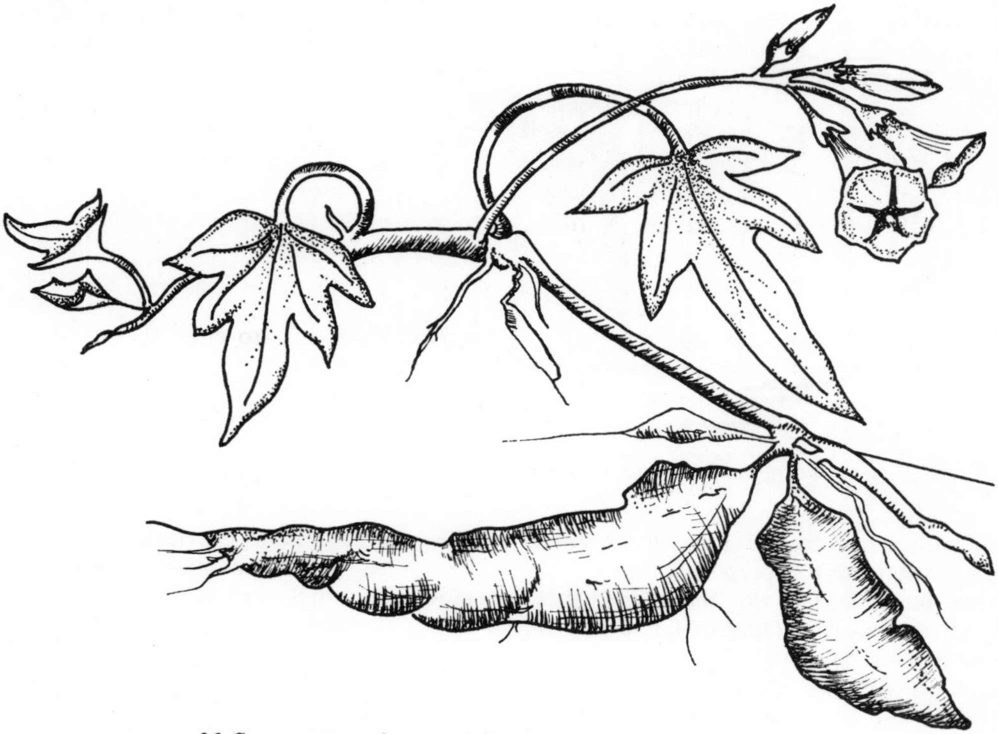

36. Sweet potato – kumara (after Cranwell, Green and Powell).

Kumara

The preparation of the ground for kumara or taro was a matter of importance. No manures were used, but it is probable that the Maori realised the importance of wood ash as an aid to growing plants, for there is much evidence of former fires on the sites of old kumara plantations. After utilising the ground for one season it was usually left to revert to a natural state for three years, when it would again be cleared and all rubbish burned off.

In response to an enquiry, Mrs Enid Tapsell writes: "In the coastal area plantations always had a northern aspect and the plants were set out diagonally from east to west with if possible a drainage slope from south to north. I particularly noticed this myself many years ago when I started asking Kouma's mother Ngatai about her cultivations, and I also noted that she placed little handfuls of sand in each hole which she watered as she planted slowly and laboriously. She said the sand was to keep the plants warm. (It also probably helped to dry out the soil in the event of exceptionally rainy weather after planting.) It was the usual custom for starter beds to be warmed by fire in much the same way as a hangi fire was prepared. On Mokoia Island kumara was grown only on the eastern aspects on the island." Recent agricultural investigations have confirmed the use of these starter beds.

At Te Kaha the people living near the coast followed the same custom as Te Arawa but further inland it was customary until quite recently to burn chips of wood and then broadcast the ash. It was not clear whether this was for warmth or for manure.

Elsdon Best has told us that at Rotorua "the kumara root was not planted until the sprout had gained some length, which caused additional care and labour". This would explain Enid Tapsell's reference to starter

37. Rua, or underground storehouse for root crops; old style, Urewera (after A. Hamilton).

beds being warmed by fire in much the same way as a hangi fire was prepared.

There have been two assertions that kumara was grown in Otago. One, a Maori informant from the Bluff, Mr Bogue West, stated that kumara could be grown in sheltered localities in Southland, provided that individual plants were covered each night with a kono (food basket) turned upside down. The other record came from Wanaka, but was less definite. Mr Bogue West was quite definite that in former times Timaru was by no means the southern limit for kumara growing. It would be interesting to put this matter to the test, but it is possible that there was a southern strain of kumara which became cold resistant to some degree.

The kumara has long been cultivated in America, the Pacific Isles and China. It was brought into New Zealand by Maori immigrants from Polynesia (though probably not pre-Maori) and furnished a continuous staple food supply. Being a plant of tender growth belonging to semi-tropical regions it had to be given much care if it was to produce a good crop. If considered necessary, brush fences were erected to give shelter from cold winds, and the maximum amount of sunlight was afforded the young plants. Planting was done only on certain nights of the moon's age, and under the direction of a tohunga, or priestly adept. When the soil was worked up fine and made perfectly clean, it was formed into little round hills called tupuke, about nine inches high and twenty to twenty-four inches in diameter, set quite close together. Here the tubers were planted.

Women were not always allowed to take part in crop digging, the time for which was denoted by the leaves turning brown. Tubers were sorted after being raised. On the East Coast all those intended to be stored in the rua (pits) were placed in large flax baskets termed tiraha, which were all made the same size. Each basket had to be quite full, and carried on the back to the semi-subterranean pit or rua. Before being used to store the kumara, the pit was cleaned and fine gravel (kirikiri) spread on the floor.

Kao

Kao were sweetmeats made in leisure hours after the kumara harvest had been gathered and stored in the rua. Some large, elongate kumara were chosen, and a specially selected stick of manuka was sharpened for use as a scraper. The point was used to scrape out the accretions of earth in the hollows on the surface of the tubers. Only an expert could use the stick properly, as the outer skin had to be removed without damaging the inner skin, which clings close to the flesh. After the kumara were washed and cleaned, they were wrapped in leaves of the karamu or puriri trees, and placed in a slow earth oven (umu or hangi) for twenty-four hours. After this the tubers were dried in the sun for as long as two weeks, and the kumara kao was then ready for eating.

At Te Kaha, kao were made from March to May, and are said to have been much used by hunters in the bush in former times. The art of making them is now mostly forgotten, and only small specimens are at present used for kao. Elsdon Best tells us of large tubers taken from under kumara plants, scraped, half-dried, and eaten raw or mashed up with a little warm water are called kao. On the authority of Sir Joseph Banks it appears that sweet potatoes were imported into England as a delicacy, long before the introduction of potatoes.

38. Kumara pit, Putiki pa, Whanganui.

Ko

Only 200 years ago our own ancestors in certain parts of Scotland still dug with a long pole to which was attached a foot-rest. When Europeans landed in New Zealand, the Maori digging implement was also a long pole of hard wood sharpened at one end, with a foot-rest attached. These poles, known as ko, were sometimes as much as twelve feet long. They were usually made from the straight hard wood of the manuka. Near the pointed end a step was attached. This foot-rest (teka) was usually made of hard wood or, very rarely, of stone. It could be raised or lowered as required by its owner. It was lashed in position by means of the tough stems of a bush climbing plant, aka. At the end of the pole there was sometimes a crescent shape, indicative of the importance of the moon in all agricultural pursuits.

Foot-rests for ko offer an interesting field for study. They seem to have varied with the individual and locality. The stone ones could offer little or no scope for ornamentation but the wooden specimens were often richly carved.

39. Ko or digging stick, ceremonial type (after Best).

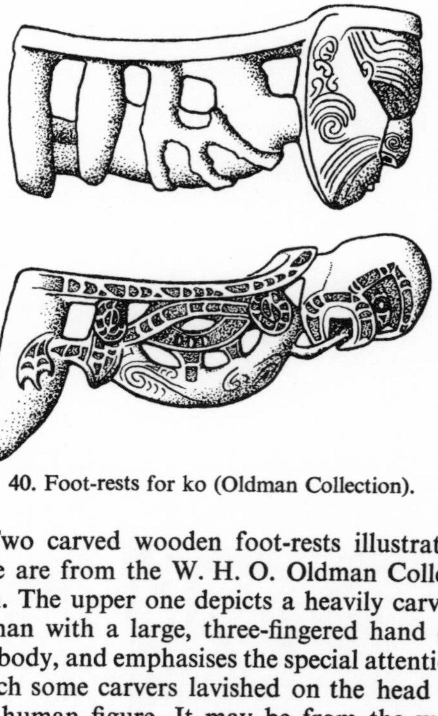

40. Foot-rests for ko (Oldman Collection).

Two carved wooden foot-rests illustrated here are from the W. H. O. Oldman Collection. The upper one depicts a heavily carved human with a large, three-fingered hand on the body, and emphasises the special attention which some carvers lavished on the head of the human figure. It may be from the west coast of the North Island. The lower specimen appears to be quite old, if the polished carved surfaces are any indication. It is in the form of a human figure with an eel-like body supported below by legs which end in the three-toed webbed feet characteristic of old carvings of Waikato and North Auckland. The crescent decoration (unaunahi) is used in adornment. These two carved wooden specimens measure seven inches and seven and a half inches respectively.

Two stone foot-rests for ko are preserved

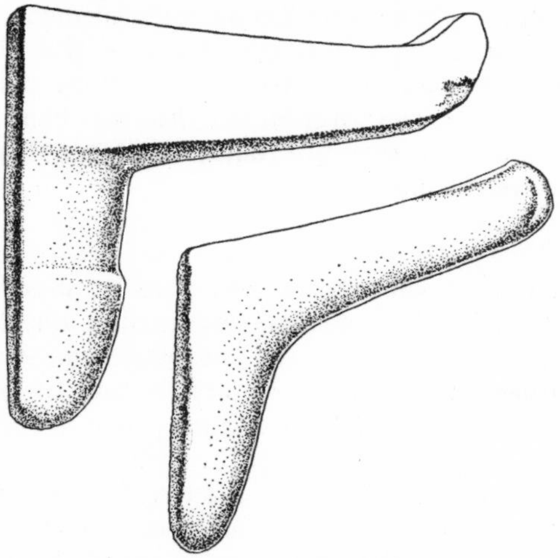

41. Stone steps for ko (Dominion Museum).

in the Dominion Museum. They are rarely met with in collections of Maori artefacts and are of much interest to students. The stone teka would impart to the ko a stability which it would not otherwise have. The extra weight of the stone might also have supplied some assistance to the digger. Of the two foot-rests above mentioned, the largest exemplifies the high quality of workmanship and finish usually associated with superior adzes.

But however good it might be, a pole could only loosen the ground. It was the army of people – men, women, slaves, and children – that came after the diggers, with grubbers, spades (kaheru), and clubs for pulverising clods, which completed the job of preparing the ground for planting. The amount of digging required depended on the nature of the soil, and implements seem to have varied accordingly.

The grubber (timo) was once largely used in grubbing and soil-loosening operations after the men had done the preliminary work with the ko. It was made from the forked branch of a tree, the blade being usually somewhat flattened and the handle rounded. Because of the short handle, this tool is generally used in a kneeling or squatting position. Similar grubbers were used in Egypt 3,000 years ago.

Also following the workers with the ko

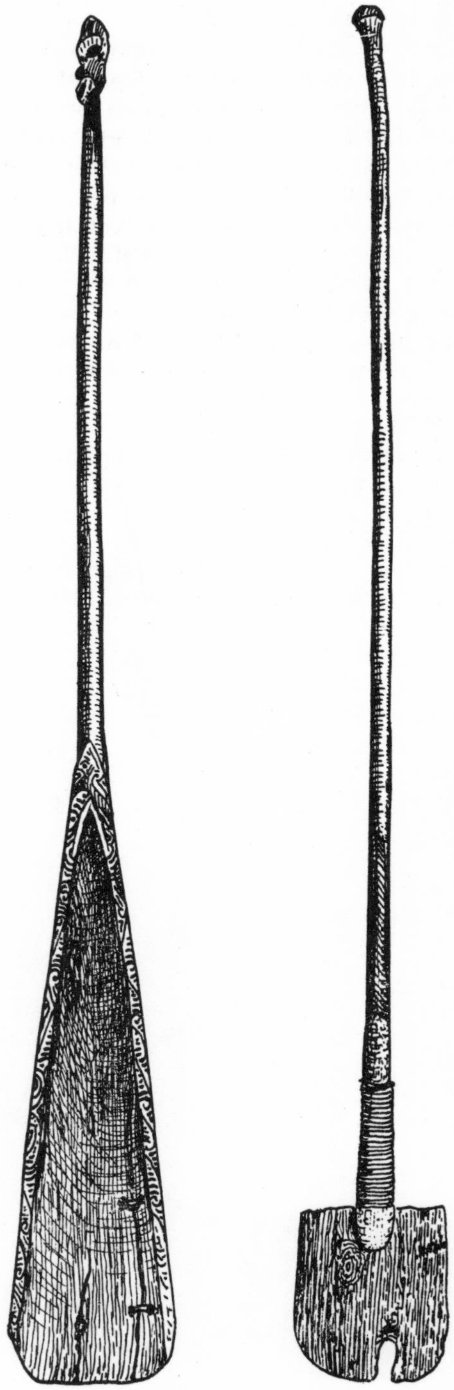

42. *Left:* A Maori kaheru (after Best). *Right:* A light form of kaheru with a detachable blade (after Best).

were a band using flat-bladed implements known as kaheru. The kaheru is a soil-working implement which, as occasion demands, can be used as a shovel for moving earth. Light forms of kaheru were used as hoes, and various pointed wooden tools were manufactured to suit various tasks. The weeding of the kumara crop was undertaken with a small pointed implement termed ketu. Sometimes a wooden spade was used as a scuffle hoe, but only a few of these have been preserved. They could be used only when the soil was friable.

Wauwau

Any pointed stick used in loosening earth, either in the excavation of a fosse or in taking up kumara crops, may be known as wauwau. Certain forms appear to have been paddle-shaped, while others are short, thick, pointed sticks. In the Wairoa District the latter type is common. The implement is fashioned from mapara, that is, from the hard resinous heart-wood of the white pine. Sometimes the wauwau has the shaft bent in a sinuous fashion or even in a crescent shape above the blade.

Shovels

A unique scoop or shovel, possibly used in ritual by the tohunga on the first day of planting (perhaps for heaping up sand around the kumara plants) is now in the Otago Museum. It was found when a drain was being cut through a swamp in the Whakatane district. In a letter Dr Skinner writes: "It is a beautiful piece, stone cut, and one of the best wooden pieces in our collection." Loaded with sand, it would have been an impossible tool, and its use would have been limited to the manipulation of small quantities of sand or earth.

6

THE PREPARATION AND PRESERVATION OF FOOD

Fernroot

A wearisome and monotonous activity in old Maori days was the apparently never-ending task of pounding fernroot. The task was assigned to women and slaves. The pounders used for the purpose were made of wood. It has been said that stone was quite unsuitable, probably because it was too heavy and not so easily controlled. The blows would have to be regulated by the size of the bundles of fernroot and the stage which the pulverising had reached. Early writers have told us that the lot of the slaves in old Maoridom was an unenviable one, and this task was certainly one of their principal occupations.

Cakes or small loaves made of pounded fernroot were termed komeke aruhe. They provided a staple article of diet. The roots of the bracken fern were first stacked and roasted, after which the hard outer skin was scraped off. Small bundles were then gathered together and pounded. The stringy part was discarded, and the remainder made into cakes. When the demands of hunger were strong, however, it was not unusual for the fernroot to be chewed and eaten without cooking.

Mr Hone McMillan of Koputaroa has said that as a boy he had often eaten the fernroot cakes, or raumeke. They were rather tasteless. His words were: "Eaten them? Of course I've eaten them. There was nothing else," he added lugubriously. Another authority stated that the cakes tasted like arrowroot.

In the Bay of Plenty, fernroot was steeped in water all night before being pounded. The bark was discarded, and the root was pounded so that the stringy parts could be removed. Much vigilance was required in cooking. The cakes were placed in the hot ashes and watched carefully so that they would not overcook for then they would become hard and difficult to masticate. A woman who was expert at timing the cooking was a great treasure. The following illustrates the value which was placed on fernroot.

In the days before organised settlement, the captain of a trading schooner running between Kapiti and Sydney fell in love with a Maori girl on the island. He gave a tin of biscuits to her parents, or guardians, and was permitted to take the girl with him to Sydney, where they were married. A child of this marriage was Hana Retter, who was born in Sydney. She was a sickly baby, and though various attempts were made to find suitable food for her, the child failed to grow as a normal infant should. Her mother sensed the trouble – the child should have a prepared dish of New Zealand fernroot. The father and mother brought the child back to Kapiti where she was fed with fernroot and all was well. Hana Retter grew into a handsome woman and in turn also married a Pakeha.

Te Manawa nui o Whete (the sustaining power of Whete) is an old proverb applied to fernroot and recorded by Elsdon Best. Whete was a valorous ancestor who, before going into battle, would consume large numbers of fernroot cakes.

Raupo Pollen

Apart from the small cakes or loaves made from fernroot, two other types are recorded. The first is the bread made from the pollen (pua) of the raupo, or common bulrush. The pollen was collected in large quantities at the proper season and made into cakes called pungapunga. When first made they were of a bright yellow colour. In some parts

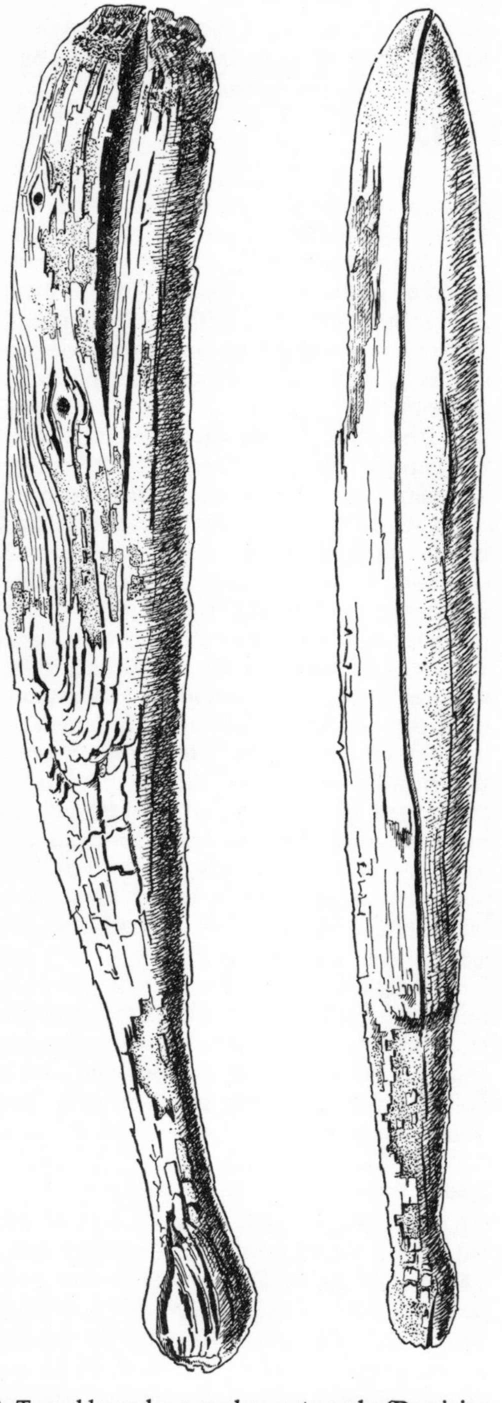

43. Two old wooden pounders, patu aruhe (Dominion Museum).

of New Zealand the pollen was produced in such large quantities that it gave a yellow dusting to the surrounding countryside. As settlement increased, the areas in which raupo grew became materially reduced. Care and patience were required to collect the pollen. The flower heads of the raupo were gathered before dawn and late in the evening and were spread on mats in a nearby shed. The mats were carried outside each day to dry in the sun, and returned to the shed in the evenings.

The next process was the construction of bag containers on a grand scale. The bark of hinau trees was stripped off in large pieces twelve or fourteen feet long, and doubled up to make bags. Large bone or wooden needles were used to sew up the sides with flax thread. A hole was left open at the end of each bag to form a mouth and the bags were then propped up with poles. Mats (tapaki) were spread on the ground beside them. The flowers of the raupo were next stripped off the stems and placed in baskets of finely split flax, which allowed only the smallest particles of pollen to escape. These baskets were shaken by the men over the mouths of the larger bark bags, while the tohunga repeated a karakia.

Sifting was done by the principal man of each family. The bark bags were opened at the bottom and the pollen, which at this stage resembled small seeds, flowed out and was caught in the small baskets. Rangiora leaves were placed on top, and the baskets were then sewn up and placed in ovens (hangi). They were covered over in the usual manner, and when steam burst out at the top the bread was cooked.

The chief divided the loaves amongst the people. Some loaves were from six to eight inches in diameter, but smaller ones were also made. The tohunga ate from the first oven, which contained only three or four baskets, and thus lifted the tapu.

Hinau Berries

The hinau, tawa, karaka, and tutu supplied berries for food. The hinau is a forest tree growing from forty to sixty feet high. The berries were collected in a creel made of split supplejack, and pounded in a wooden trough with a stone pounder. The tuki, as it was called, was used end on. The pounding separated the mealy substance from the hard inner portion, which was discarded. The mealy part of the berries was kneaded into cakes which were cooked in the hangi. They become hard as they cooled, and were then packed into the creel, or toi, which was lined with leaves. The containers were covered with bracken fern and preserved in pools where they would keep for a year or more.

Other Berries

The white variety of tawa gave an abundance berries, the kernels being steamed in the hangi. They were dried and stored, and steamed again when required for food. They were then pounded and eaten. Karaka berries were also popular, the kernels being more valued than the mealy portion. The pulp was removed by pounding. The kernels were soaked in water for some time, and then steamed before eating.

Ripe berries of the tutu were largely used, the seeds being rejected as poisonous. They were crushed and strained, and sometimes a stone pestle and mortar were used. The juice of tutu berries afforded a delicious treat, and was used as a relish to many foods. A pleasing drink was sometimes made from this juice.

A favourite vegetable was the young flower heads of the cabbage tree, i.e. the interior of the bunches of leaves. They were eaten raw when very young, but when older they were cooked in the oven.

Puwha

When Captain Cook came to New Zealand, the sow thistle with the crisped or spinous leaves was found growing here, but the sow thistle with the soft round leaves was not recorded. It is possible that this species may have been introduced later. Generally speaking, the crisp-leaved species was termed puwha and the soft-leaved species rauriki, but there is a good deal of confusion because different tribes had conflicting names for both species and their varieties. Today it is the soft-leaved sow thistle which is so eagerly collected for use as a vegetable. The importance of the sow thistle as a winter and spring vegetable food was considerable. Europeans who have tried it speak highly of its taste and quality, and such chemical analysis as has been carried out seems to indicate a high nutritive value.

Fern

Mr R. S. Beauchamp has provided information on the foods used by the Maoris living in the vicinity of Lake Waikaremoana. The most important was the fern *Polystichum richardii* which is found growing in damp localities in fairly dense bush. In many parts of the North Island the young curling fern buds – termed pikopiko by the Maoris, and locally by Europeans "pickle-pickle" – were collected in quantities in the spring and were much esteemed. At present they are usually boiled with meat. Formerly they were regarded as a delicacy when cooked in the hangi. No other small fern is utilised in this way, although the centre of the tree-fern, kouka, is still eaten on occasions.

Chewing Resins

The chewing-gum habit is as old as man himself. It is quite possible that today we do not chew nearly as much as our early forefathers did. They chewed resins of many kinds, particularly when food was scarce. The Maoris discovered chewing-gum a long time ago; in fact, it is possible that they brought the habit from their homeland. Various resins or bituminous substances often supplied the material, but one of the most popular sources of supply was the sow thistle. The leaves were plucked and the milky substance which exuded left to dry on the stalks. This was collected on a leaf and, when sufficient was available, pressed into a ball. It is at first bitter to the taste, but this soon disappears.

In the far north, the gum of the kauri tree was used, the young, soft gum being selected. At Rotorua the gum of the puka-puka or rangiora furnished the supply, while on west coast beaches various substances washed up by the tide were utilised. Resin used as chewing-gum is called kauri. Miss S. E. Traill (Mrs Natusch) told of a bituminous substance washed ashore on ocean beaches of Stewart Island, which was known as kauri and was formerly used by both Maori and European children. This resin was pleasant only after being chewed for some time. Williams's *Dictionary of the Maori Language* names this substance kauri tawhiti, and it appears to have been in common use in former times. Te Kuiti informants tell of a black gum (mimiha) which used to be chewed with relish.

CONTAINERS

Wooden Bowls

Wooden communal bowls were often used to hold cooked food of all descriptions, and in particular meat, which was usually eaten with the fingers. Some of these bowls were large, but most were of moderate size. At Patoka, Hawke's Bay, a small wooden bowl was found which, though much decayed, is of considerable interest in the study of these objects. This bowl was found in a small rock shelter, where it had fallen from a ledge on to its edge and had been nearly buried by dust that had accumulated over the years. It is finely made, oval in shape, and with a handle in the form of a human head and neck. The handle resembles a miniature tauihu of a fishing canoe prow, but the terminal outfacing features illustrate a head sketchily carved, a little broken just above the mouth and pointed below the chin.

Mr T. S. Spencer, of Bluff, an elderly man of Waitaha descent, stated that his ancestors, the Waitaha, were the aristocrats of the South Island. They lived here and there among other tribes, always maintaining their separate identity. His family were always particular in matters of etiquette. Dishes or bowls for washing were never used for food or for other purposes, and food vessels were stored in a special place.

On the muttonbird island, Ohoromai, about twenty ipu, or wooden bowls, were

44. An old wooden bowl or kumete, Hawke's Bay.

stored. Some were carved, one of them having a spout a foot or more long. Some of these were used for "tahuing" muttonbirds. This is the process by which the birds are cooked in their own fat. White-hot stones were placed in water to heat them. One of the wooden vessels in which the birds were cooked was about eight feet long. It was large enough for two small boys to use it as a boat in a pond. Such wooden vessels were later superseded by the three-legged iron pots.

Kelp Bags

In former days the southern Maoris made many journeys to outlying islands in their double canoes in search of young mutton-birds, or titi, which breed there annually. During summer, large quantities of kelp are collected for the manufacture of containers to hold the young birds. The use of kelp for the manufacture of bags was once common among all coastal Maoris from the Bay of Plenty and Waikato southwards, but it is only in Stewart Island that the custom still obtains. The poha is an important relic of the days when the seals were common. Seal meat was roasted, the oil being caught as it dripped from the spit, and meat and oil were together preserved in the vessel. The poha was then buried in the sand of the seashore. It is said that seal meat would keep indefinitely in this manner.

No large poha have been preserved in museums, yet these bags must have been of paramount importance in the daily life of a considerable proportion of New Zealand Maoris. The bags were made of the bull kelp, *Durvillea antarctica.* The distribution of the bull kelp is interesting; it is common around Wellington and on the western coast of the North Island, as well as around the South Island, but is almost absent from the eastern coastline of the North Island. Its occurrence would therefore determine the areas in which it was utilised. The growing kelp, or rimu, is cut from the rocks, either from boats, or by wading at low water. Each piece usually makes one bag.

An opening is pushed into the honey-combed part of the kelp to allow it to be

45. Constructing a poha.

inflated. This is done by making a start by hand, or by using a piece of wood, blowing air by mouth or reed into the opening, and keeping the air imprisoned. The hole is made bigger by hand pressure, adding air as required, taking care not to force the air too close to the edges of the bag, a process called koruputa.

Any natural holes in the bag are patched with a limpet and bound tightly at the conical end of the shell. This process is known as tiwha. The inflated bags are hung up on verandahs to dry, placed in a cool, dry place, and finally rolled up and placed in sacks ready to transport to the Titi Islands. Placing the birds in the bag is called whawhau. The completed bag is poha, and when the work is finally done the saying is "komutu ra".

Naturally the bags are not strong enough to stand rough handling, and as mutton-birds were used for barter long before

46. Method of suspending baskets (after Angas).

Europeans came to New Zealand, the Maoris had to devise some means of strengthening the only container available. Special flax baskets were constructed for this purpose. Each kelp bag was placed in a kete or kit which effectually protected the lower half of it, and made it easy to handle, because the kit had handles that could never be put on to a kelp bag. To protect the portion of the bag which projected from the kit, it was customary to use strips of totara bark and flax leaves, the whole being bound with flax. Some modern muttonbirders use binder-twine.

Kelp bags were used for purposes other than the preservation of food. They would hold water, and shellfish and rock oysters were boiled in them. They have been put to this use in comparatively recent years, and may even now be employed for this purpose on some parts of the coast. The water inside the bag keeps the kelp from burning. The kelp bag was a useful article, and could be regarded as the Maori substitute for refrigeration, particularly when the poha was buried in the sand close to the shore.

Baskets

Food is eaten from small flax baskets known as kono. An early voyager, Earle, tells us that in North Auckland in 1827 baskets containing left-over food were hung on props or poles, ready for the next meal. "Thus a village presents a very singular appearance as it is stuck full of sticks with various kinds of baskets hanging from them. This plan, however, is the most rational that could be adopted, as none of their eatables can be left on the ground or they would become the prey of dogs". The kono has no handle so it is probable that food would be transferred to kete proper for holding in temporary storage on props or poles.

47. Maori vessel, taha huahua.

Two types of vessel used in a Maori community were the taha huahua and the patua. The taha huahua shown here is a simple form in which delicacies such as bush birds are preserved in their own fat for future use. It is a gourd vessel encased in a basket, and often mounted on a stand. The type of feathers used to ornament the basket would be those of the species of bird preserved in the vessel. The Maori gourd is termed hue and was much in demand, both for preserving and for water-carrying vessels.

The bark basket, patua or papa totara,

48. Maori vessel, papa totara.

was made from a single piece of the bark of a large totara tree, pressed into shape, and braced above by a wooden handle. The basket is said to have been used in gathering berries of bush trees, and for general purposes. Similar baskets made by Dravidian tribes have been reported from South India. The piece of bark is carefully stripped off, and soaked for some time in water. It is then folded into the required shape and fastened with a wooden peg and a lashing of akeake. These receptacles are of all sizes from a few inches upwards. The larger ones are said to

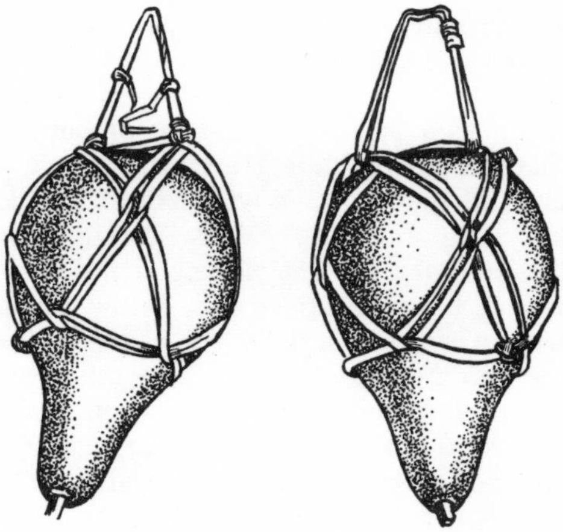

49. Gourd vessels for carrying purposes (from an old photograph).

have been used to contain partly cooked birds, packed tightly with boiling fat poured over them. By this method they could be kept for a year or two. In the Wanganui district a carved wooden cover was placed on top of the basket and called a paewae.

STORAGE AND IMPLEMENTS

Calabashes

Water was the universal beverage of the old-time Maori. It was usually collected in a gourd vessel or taha wai. Restrictions were sometimes applied to priests and tohunga. For reasons of tapu, no part of the body of a tohunga may touch a vessel or calabash, nor may he drink from a stream. The difficulty was overcome by pouring water into his hands, which were then tilted towards the mouth.

Elevated Stage

The elevated stage was found in most Maori villages. Food products such as dried fish, shellfish, pumpkin, etc. were stored on these stages away from the ravages of rats, dogs, and damp, for relatively long periods. Sometimes they were protected by a rude covering of bark or thatch to guard them from the weather. Such stages are termed komanga or kaupapa. It is probable that among many of the moving communities the elevated stage took the place of a pataka, housing all food, except kumara, for future needs. The kumara has to be stored in an underground store or rua kumara.

Knives

For cutting purposes the Maori housewife often used a chert stone with a saw-like cutting edge. One of the largest of these chert knives comes from Taranaki, probably from the midden near the sea at Otakeho, and was collected by the late L. S. Mackie. The illustration shows how it was held in the hand. It is interesting to note how such implements were designed for effective and comfortable use. It will sometimes be seen that the artisan of old who fashioned the artefact provided a hollow in which the thumb fits naturally, and so aiding the operator. The knife which has been illustrated is over nine inches in length.

The maripi is a superior type of cutting implement. A Dominion Museum specimen is unusual in that it has a well-defined handle carved with a rolling pakura design. The handle is enlarged at the lower end and has a human face at the upper end, below which appears a single spiral with a circle in the centre – an unusual feature. Two takarangi spirals occupy the body of the object, and a human head with out-thrust tongue appears at the body end. The three parallel lines suggest that the work of the carver was not fully completed and that some further rauponga adornment was intended. The cutting edge is composed of a row of teeth of the seven-gilled shark, the anterior being from the central upper jaw. The teeth have all been drilled and attached to the handle by means of binding.

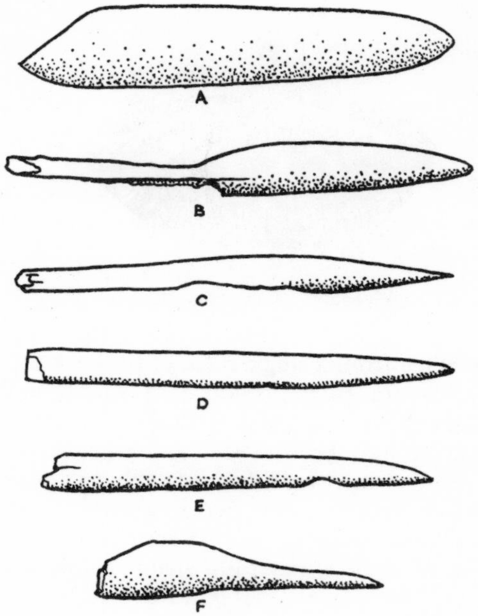

50. Bone pickers.

Forks

There appears to be little doubt but that many of the pointed pieces of bone which have been found on old Maori middens were at one time used for extracting and eating periwinkles, which had been cooked in Maori ovens. For this purpose modern Maoris use

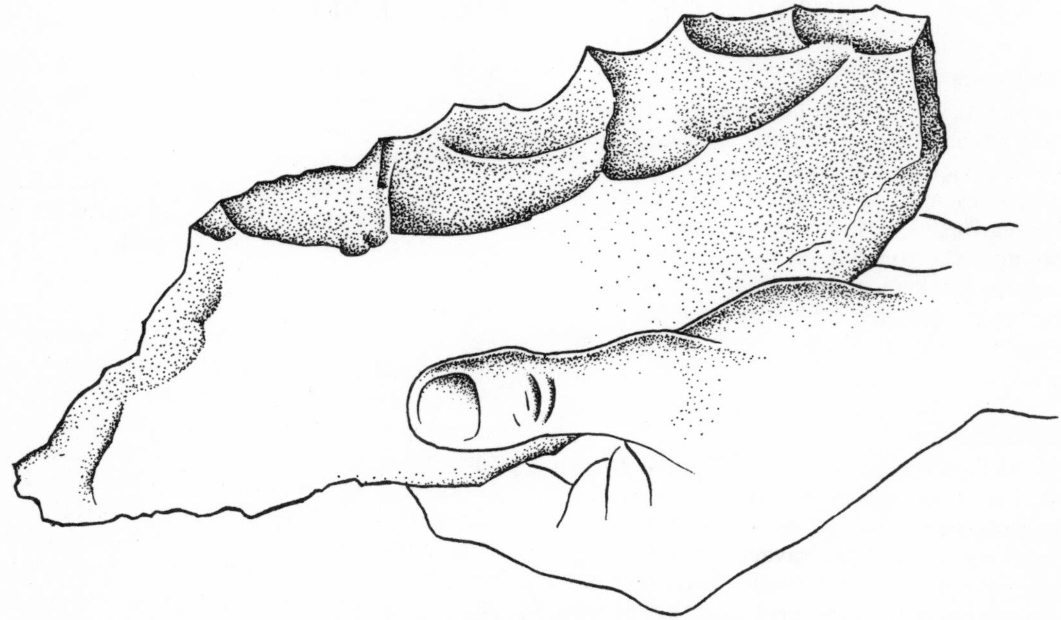

51. Flint knife, Taranaki (Mackie Collection).

darning needles and there is no doubt that great quantities of these small shellfish were eaten by Maori communities. Dr R. K. Dell says that he has seen European children extracting and eating periwinkles with a hair-pin.

It is probable that fingers were used to hold cooked food, but here and there we note the use of a fork.

A fork in the Dominion Museum has been made from bone, and would probably have been the property of a chief. Three prongs are broken, and the handle of the fork has lost a portion of its length – evidently the head of a human figure. On the lower portion of the handle is a type of rauponga in which two plain ridges form an ellipse and enclose a notched ridge.

7

KITCHENS AND EARTH OVENS

Cooking Sheds

Cooking sheds and kitchens varied with their locality. The most common were the primitive structures of a lean-to type, seemingly barely adequate to keep out the rain. Apart from these a number of different types of outbuildings were used as kitchens. The following is a classification of recognised types:

1. Primitive shelter type.
2. Kitchen with wattled walls.
3. Log-walled kitchen.
4. Tree-fern kitchen.
5. Whare umu (superior kitchen).
6. Circular or oval kitchen.

For a knowledge of this subject we must rely on published reports and on notes collected in recent years. The primitive shelter cookhouse was of the open-air type lacking any regular building arrangement. It was sometimes an earth oven with a screen to protect it from the prevailing wind, but generally the oven was covered with a roof upheld on four poles or posts, often in a lean-to style. Such a lean-to usually had a rough wall at the lower end. The Maori lived in the open air as much as possible. Less consideration was accorded to cooks and their assistants than to any other section of the community, and their cookhouses were the poorest dwellings in the pa. Of wattled kitchens only meagre records remain.

52. A simple lean-to shelter, thatched with nikau fronds, Piha (from a photo by A. P. Godber, 1916).

Under the term whare umu we could include all cooking houses in which the walls were constructed of wooden slabs set vertically or horizontally, and constructed after the manner of a dwelling. The whare umu was the superior, rectangular kitchen, usually provided with liberal outlets for smoke, and sufficiently large for the cooks to move around freely when attending to food in the earth ovens. Cooking houses of this type are described by Wakefield* who states: "In that part of the pa belonging especially to Heu-heu at Lake Taupo there is a row of cooking houses 40 feet long and 15 feet broad, and 10 feet high in the walls, which are constructed of enormous slabs, well fitted together, round windows with sliding shutters to admit the light and let out the smoke."

Wet weather could be the constant bane of cooks in old New Zealand, so it is probable that most villages had special buildings for wet weather cooking and storing firewood.

Tree-fern Kitchens

There was a distinct type of building which may be termed the tree-fern kitchen. This was a rectangular building erected in localities where tree-ferns grew abundantly. It was quickly and easily constructed from vertical or horizontal tree-fern logs. It was once the main type of kitchen in use in the South Island. Tree-fern logs lessen the danger of fire, and the logs do not easily decay. Such a kitchen would be limited in height according to the tree-fern trunks available. The building of tree-fern huts by both European and Maoris is now almost unknown in New Zealand, but sixty years ago they were not uncommon.

Cookhouses

The log-walled house, a rectangular building, was often used as a cookhouse. From an old photograph by J. Collis, a drawing has been prepared of a house of this type which once stood at Parihaka pa, Taranaki. Here the logs are short and stout and held in place by uprights which are obviously the trunks of tree-ferns. A feature of the roof construction in front is the use of a double maihi (outer rafters), one above the other and supported below by uprights (amo). Lashings of cordage or aka vine hold them in position. Four rails apparently run along the apex to hold the

**Adventure in New Zealand*, Vol. 2, 1845, p. 107.

53. Log kitchen, Parihaka pa, Taranaki (from a photo by J. Collis).

thatch in place, each being lashed at its end either to the ridge pole or to the maihi. As the doorway occupies part of the centre of the end wall of the building, it may be assumed that there is a central ridge support (pou tahu) inside the doorway. The use of tree-fern trunks is common in kitchens and in lining houses for, as already noted, they do not readily catch fire. Many sleeping houses built partly underground were lined in this manner.

54. Maori cooking house (after Angas).

In the drawing of a superior Maori cooking house (after G. F. Angas) the size of the crouched figures would seem to show that the building was about eight or nine feet high in the centre, and about three feet six inches at the sides. The view shows the tuarongo or back portion of the building. The only obvious constructional features are the upright planks for the end wall and side, each held in position by a single outside batten to which they are bound. The upright slabs (poupou) are probably sunk well into the ground. Here the pou tuarongo (post supporting the rear end of the ridge pole or tahu) is slightly carved on its outer and upper face. This is an unusual feature apparently signifying the special importance of this particular kitchen. The roof is of thatch held in position by four longitudinal rails (kaho), the uppermost of which lies over the thatch above the tahu.

Circular or oval kitchens were much in use in the South Island and in Taranaki. It seems possible that there was a tendency to relegate houses of this type, once so important in the homeland, to lesser duties, although it is true that most recorded South Island houses were oval or beehive in shape.

Earth Ovens

The purpose of the kitchen is to contain the earth oven, a more or less circular pit some three to four feet in diameter and up to eighteen inches deep. The oven is usually termed umu by the older people, but the modern generation is more accustomed to the term hangi. Quantities of wood, large and small, are placed in the pit and piled up at least to ground level. Specially selected stones termed taikowhatu or para ngahu, which will not easily crack with the heat, are piled on top of the logs. A plaited flax square is used to start and fan the fire in the oven. At Te Kuiti it is termed paroheroke As the wood burns, the stones drop to the floor of the pit. Embers are raked aside, and the stones levelled out, some being removed to place on top of the food when it is arranged in the pit.

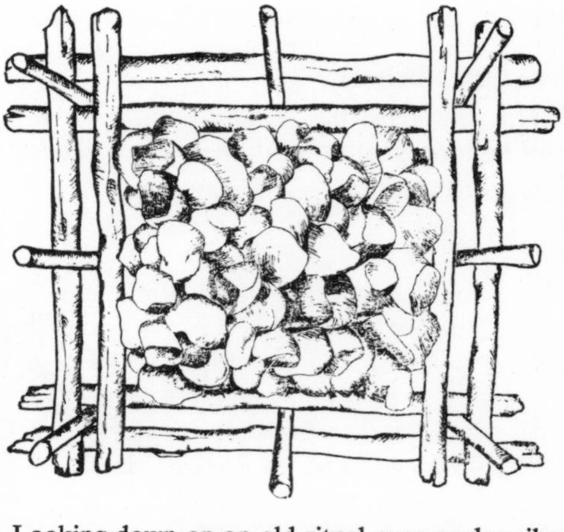

55. Looking down on an old ritual oven as described by Wiremu te Awe Awe (W. Larkins), Rangiotu.

If deemed necessary, the stones on the bottom may now be cleaned by being sprinkled liberally with water. An oven band of plaited green flax to confine the food is placed inside the oven. This is known as the paepae umu. Quantities of green stuff, such as fern fronds and sow thistle, are placed over the stones, then a layer of food such as potatoes, then more greens, and above this a layer of meat or fish, and then perhaps another layer of greens. After this should come a layer of birds, over which ruatao leaves would be placed to cover all the contents. The hot stones are placed on top and quantities of water used liberally. Then a mat covers the oven.

The steam cooking process of the earth oven preserves the quality of the food. Methods vary in details from tribe to tribe.

Food is also cooked by enveloping the object to be eaten in clay mixed with water, and placing it in a hot fire; or by enclosing the food in leaves and placing it in the ashes. These methods were probably a great deal more common than we have been led to imagine, particularly in lesser communities where little time was available for the preparation of food. The staff of life, fernroot cakes or loaves, komeke or raumeke, were also cooked in the ashes, while bush birds required for a quick meal were often wrapped in damp clay, feathers and all, and placed individually in the fire. In half an hour the feathers came off with the clay, the intestines came out in a lump, and the cooked bird remained.

Fire and the Torch

Fire represents heat, warmth, and even life to mankind. To generate fire, a fire plough is used – that is, a pointed stick (hika) is rubbed in a groove formed in a lower piece of wood (kauahi) until smoke, then a red spot, and then fire appears in the abraded dust at the lower end of the groove. Considerable speed is necessary in this operation, which is performed in two stages. In the first stage the abraded wood particles were collected at the lower end of the groove. In the second stage these were kindled. Certain persons in each tribe was in charge of the fire sticks and fire making. The wood of three trees is suitable for this purpose – the makomako, kaikomako, and the mahoe. In bush areas of the North Island it was customary to collect a dried bracket fungus (*Polyporus*) which, when dried, ignites rapidly, and it was on this that the tiny mound of glowing fire in the kauahi was usually tipped. In districts remote from bush areas, dried moss and leaves were used for this purpose. Also, when travelling, fire sticks were carried in a bundle of kiekie leaves, the ball of "dust" being swung around in the leaf until a flame appeared.

Little has been recorded of the bracket fungus and its importance in the generation of fire and in carrying fire during wet weather. Dr G. B. Cone has spoken to an old Pakeha bushman who has used it in the Thames district where it was known as "punk" to the early settlers, who learned of its use from the Maoris. Punk burns very slowly and persistently. It can be put out only when smothered. Putawai and putawa are names which have been supplied for this fungus around Gisborne; Mr Arthur Beauchamp gives the Waikaremoana name as popo tawai.

Elsdon Best tells us that the particular punk used to carry live fire was the "puku tawai found growing on beech trees; that found on tawa trees is useless for the purpose".

Punk has now been recognised as the dried flesh of *Polyporus hosularus* which may be found in many parts of the North Island. The fungus came into use again during the present century when in the depression of the early 1930s the cost of matches was out of the reach of many Maori smokers. In the Gisborne district it was an old custom to bury a quantity of punk half in and half out of the ground where it would burn for a day or more and furnish a quick light for a fire or a lamp at night.

Another slow combustion material used to carry fire was the dried stem of the flowering stalks of New Zealand flax. At night again, to quote Best, "torches used in travelling were made of bark, dried leaves of Cordyline or resinous wood such as mapara".

Several types of torch or rama were made, one of the most important being that formerly used in securing the young muttonbirds at night. A specimen was made for the Dominion Museum by Mrs K. A. Cross, of Bluff. It is of the type formerly used on muttonbird islands off Stewart Island. Muttonbirds are first taken in the burrows, and later in the rama or torching period, which commences on 20 April. It is then that the young birds leave their burrows and come out at night to exercise their wings and shed their down.

Mrs Cross was taught the art of making torches by her mother when she was about eight years old, and had already started visiting muttonbird island for seasonal work, which at eighty years she still continues. To make the torch, strips of flax about five inches apart are laid on the ground. Long pieces of totara bark, each about two feet six inches, are laid across the flax strips, and inside these the body of the torch is rolled and tied.

It was necessary to secure the bark by using a rod (kōō), cut at one end into a chisel-shaped edge, the dry totara bark being levered away from the tree from below. The bark is said to be fairly loose for a period of six weeks each year, about the end of February. The dry bark is called amoka. Inside the cigar-shaped torch, a quantity of dried grass (titaki), together with broken bark is held in position by vertical bark rods, the whole being saturated with piro or kato, the fats from inside the body of the baby muttonbird.

It was the custom for a party of mutton-birders to carry two torches, and for groups to keep close to the torch-bearers. This precaution may have assisted operations and have prevented the bunching of workers. The torch was held in the hand at the narrow end. If it tended to burn too quickly, green kelp was used to stop the rate of burning. Green kelp was also used to protect the hand from the heat of the torch. If slow to burn, the torch was whirled around the head. A single torch would burn for up to three or four hours.

In the North Island the Maori soon recognised that the heartwood of the rimu was extremely resinous, and it was therefore often made into torches for use at night. It was split into shreds and tied in bundles. The ashes had to be knocked off at regular intervals. There is also a record of the branches of totara being used for torches.

56. A Maori torch, Poutama Island.

8

GARMENTS AND GARMENT MAKING

Early Form of Dress

Tasman tells us that for clothing some of the natives wore mats, others cotton stuffs, almost all being naked from the shoulders to the waist. Tasman's sketches were rough and conventional, but he does show a Maori in a tight-fitting sleeveless tunic held up by two narrow pieces coming over the shoulders, but how it was fastened is not clear. A verification of the use of this type of clothing has been left to us in the journal of Sir Joseph Banks, who accompanied Captain Cook to New Zealand. He writes: "The first man we saw when we went ashore at Poverty Bay, and who was killed by one of our people, had his dress tied exactly in the same manner as is represented in Mr Dalrymple's account of Tasman's voyage . . . it was tied over his shoulders, across his breast, under his armpits, again across his breast, and round his loins. Of this dress, we saw, however, but one more instance during our whole stay on the coast, though it seems convenient, as it leaves the arms quite at liberty while the body is covered."

Here then is a garment which disappeared with the coming of the Pakeha, perhaps always more or less rare because of the difficulty in manufacturing it on approved Maori lines. This garment was of a type which was evolved naturally to provide warmth in cold weather, together with the essential requirement that both hands must be free. Apparently no early enquirer was supplied

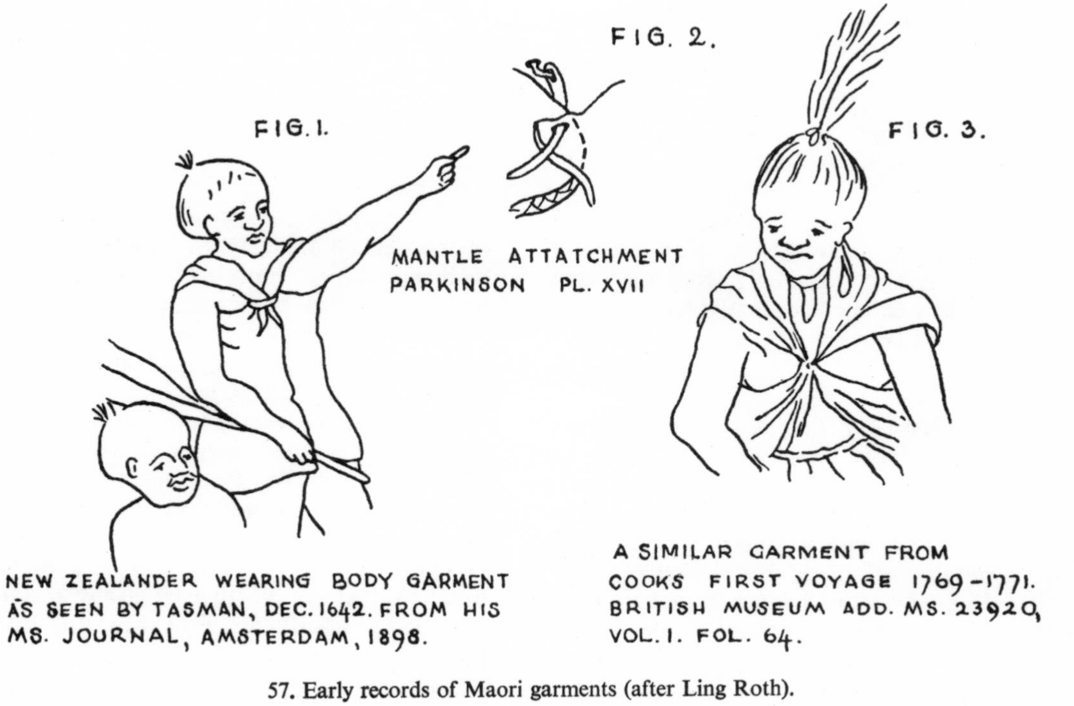
FIG. 1.
FIG. 2.
FIG. 3.
MANTLE ATTATCHMENT
PARKINSON PL. XVII
NEW ZEALANDER WEARING BODY GARMENT
AS SEEN BY TASMAN, DEC. 1642. FROM HIS
MS. JOURNAL, AMSTERDAM, 1898.
A SIMILAR GARMENT FROM
COOKS FIRST VOYAGE 1769-1771.
BRITISH MUSEUM ADD. MS. 23920,
VOL. I. FOL. 64.

57. Early records of Maori garments (after Ling Roth).

with information about it. We should not leave the matter of early clothing without mention of a long maro termed marowhara, worn by Chatham Islanders early last century.* This was a long plaited band, and the above description of a garment "tied under his armpits . . . across his breast, and round his loins" may refer to this item.

Kilts

In general, the Maori as known to the early voyagers wore two main garments: a cloak or cape which fastened on the right shoulder leaving the right arm free; and a kilt or loin cloth suspended from the waist. The kilt or rapaki was originally a thickly woven garment covered with a pad of rough curled thrums of raw flax. The thrums were termed piupiu, a term which described the rattling sound made when they were shaken. From this waist garment developed the lighter type of rapaki well known to present generations of Maoris, and now recognised as piupiu. The late Sir Apirana Ngata was most insistent on this point, which is not quite in accord with usual textbook data on Maori clothing, but seems reasonable enough as both types are in museum collections.

In dances the rhythmic click of the piupiu, which bordered the original rapaki, was much appreciated. Possibly this was one reason why the Maoris did not use the drum to accompany the dance.

The thick rough kilt was the universal article of attire. At most times both men and women were habitually bare from the waist up. In cold weather and at nights capes and cloaks would be worn.

Cloaks

The usual term for a cloak or cape is kahu. There were many types of cloak, such as kahu kekeno, a sealskin cape; kahu kiwi, a cloak covered with kiwi feathers; kahu taniko, a cloak with a taniko border; kahu toi, a rough cloak made from leaves of toi or *Cordyline indivisa*; and so on. But there were many other names for special cloaks, and a fine inner cloak is recognised. It is therefore possible that in winter Maoris in colder localities wore three garments. We know that several long cloaks, which showed off the beautiful taniko border, would be worn by chiefs on festive occasions.

"The upper margin of a cloak (kahu or kakahu) is termed ua, the sides are termed tapa and the lower border is remu. If taniko appears on the ua, it is generally conceded that the cloak is modern. It is on the remu that the taniko has been developed and additional borders (or flounces) are sometimes added to give double lines of taniko adornment. The term kahu taniko is applied to cloaks with a taniko adornment, and when double lines of taniko are attached to both remu and tapa, such kahu taniko are distinguished by the special name of huaki. Two other distinctive types of kahu taniko are known and recognised – the first is termed aronui and applies to a cloak in which there is a deep taniko border on the remu and none on the sides. This type of cloak has no thrums."†

Huruhuru or kahu huruhuru is a general term for feather cloaks. They are carefully and laboriously made, each feather being tied in separately during the weaving process. They are usually named according to the type of feather used. One, the kahu kura, is named because of the red feathers used which are collected from under the wings of kaka parrots.

Another garment which may be mentioned is the maro kopua, worn chiefly by young women and girls. Sometimes several of these would be worn simultaneously. They were made from woven flax fibres after the manner of a cloak with ornamental thrums, feathers, or even shells attached.

Among dress cloaks of the Maori, Sir Peter Buck classifies "pompom cloaks (ngore) with pompoms of dyed flax, though red worsted was much preferred after trade contact". Such cloaks appear to have been most common in the Taranaki area and on the west coast of the North Island, and to have been rarer elsewhere. They are still being made in a few localities.

*See article by R. S. Duff, *Dominion Museum Records*, Vol. 1.

†Best, note to Author, 12.2.1931.

58. Woman's apron or maro kopua with woven muka background, sometimes adorned with feathers and shells.

Sewn garments are mentioned by John White in the story of the origin of cannibalism when Rau-riki was slain. "His head was cured; the brains were first taken out and a piece of wood placed in each nostril; the skin of the neck sewn round a hoop of kare-ao (*Rhipogonum scandens*) so that it might not shrink; the lips were sewn together to prevent the teeth appearing; it was then carefully wrapped up with grass and placed on top of an umu and cured. His bones were made into needles to sew garments, then used by the people, some into hooks to catch fish and some into barbs for birds and eel-spears." Before the bone needle could penetrate the tough skin, a bone awl was used to make a hole for sewing.

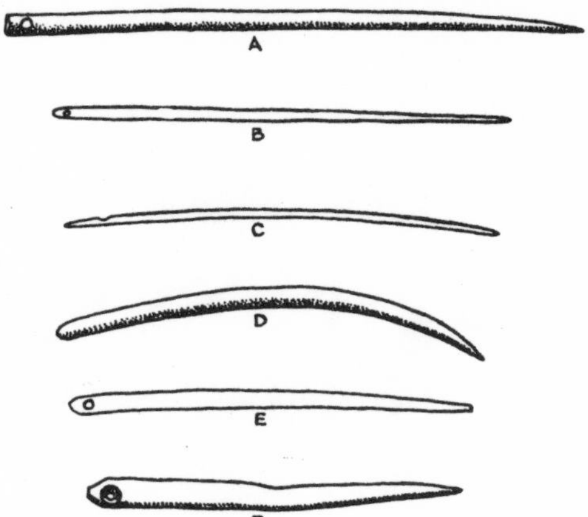

59. Needles.

Evidently some distinction was required in speaking of garments and the use of needles in preparing them, implying that earlier populations used needles in garment making, and later people did not. It seems that earlier populations used moa skins for garment making. Associated with the manufacture of garments from moa skins by the early Moa-hunter people were bone needles, sometimes packed inside bone awls for safety.

Skin Garments

Following a suggestion that southern Maoris used sealskin garments, Mr Herries Beattie stated that so far as he can remember, the old-time Maoris did not use sealskins for garments. Mr Beattie quotes the traditional story of the first fight between the earliest sealers and the Westland Maoris. The sealers employed Maoris to catch seals for them. Following their usual practice, they burnt off the skins to leave the carcases for eating. When the sealers returned and found what had been done, they flew into a violent rage and disputes led to some of the Maoris being shot and one white man being killed. This would seem to indicate that sealskins were not valued until the arrival of Europeans.

In the Dominion Museum is a piece of dogskin from a cave in Otago. This is remarkable, first because of its brownish red colour, and second because it has evidently been a prepared piece of skin for garment making, as evidenced by the holes drilled along two longitudinal edges.

Unfortunately the skin is much decayed, broken, and borer-ridden. It is approximately one foot long and something between four and five inches wide. Ridgway's *Colour Standards*, 1912, was consulted and the following colours identified in the hair which still partly covers the surface; "yellow ochre; ochraceous tawny; and black thorn brown to chestnut brown." Some portions of the surface appear to have faded more than others.

The holes round the edge are carelessly spaced, and it is possible that the object may have been discarded or never completed. It is uncertain whether this piece of skin was intended for a skin garment, or for sewing on to a muka fibre cloak; but it is worthy of record as a unique item illustrating drill holes completed, in all probability, with a bone awl.

Hamilton, in *Maori Art*, included the remarkable photograph of Rameka te Amai, chief of the Nga Puketurua, the oldest branch of the Puketapu hapu of Ngati Awa tribe. He wears what is described as a huri-kuri or cloak made entirely of whole dogskins. Quoting from Hamilton: "This mat (garment) is according to native tradition about ninety years old. The skins were prepared at Te Namu, Opunake. It now belongs to W. H. Skinner, Esq., of New Plymouth." The gar-

60. Piece of dogskin from a cave, Old Man Range, Otago (A. H. Turnbull Collection, Dominion Museum).

ment would therefore date from about the turn of the 19th century. Unless a soft flaxen cloak was worn underneath, such a dogskin garment as this would be most uncomfortable.

Flax

In the native flax, *Phormium tenax* (harakeke), the Maori people found a suitable material for use in the manufacture of garments,* floor mats, baskets, and other useful articles. It is worthy of mention here that the Maoris never wore mats. The common error of calling cloaks and kilts by the name of mats commenced with the early voyagers, and has persisted ever since.

At Te Kuiti the expert weavers grow only three varieties of flax:

1. Whenu. This variety is very suitable for use as whenu, or warp (muka) strands for a cloak.
2. Tihore. This flax is excellent for making piupiu, each of which takes 420 strands. Black tassels (hukahuka) for korowai cloaks are also made from this flax, which is a hard variety growing straight up.
3. Taeore. A soft variety of flax used for the manufacture of muka thread for the wefts or aho, horizontal elements of weaving.

Techniques of Maori weaving are now found only here and there throughout New Zealand. The following first-hand account of the work to be undertaken prior to weaving was supplied by Mesdames Hetiti and Tumohe during a visit to Te Kuiti: "The kuku or mussel shell is used to scrape the fibre or muka from the flax leaf. This process is termed haro. Before the muka is made into fine twine it must be beaten. It is roughly plaited into lengths and eight plaits are made into a roll which is dipped in water before the pounding commences. A stone pounder is used. From the time when the stone pounder strikes the roll of muka, tapu commences. Here the operator sings a karakia for good fortune. The pounding is continued until the muka is dry. Again the roll is dipped in water and pounded until dry. Now the fibre is beginning to become soft and pliable and easier to manipulate. A rubbing process now commences. This is mukumuku and each plait is rubbed separately.

"To make the fine roll plait required for the weaving process, four strands of muka are selected and placed parallel; but the flax blade is thicker at its base, so two strands are placed head to tail with the other two strands. This is regarded as a tedious work; but the work which follows this is both tedious and arduous. This is the miro process, which consists of the rolling of the four strands into fine twine on the leg, just above the knee. Legs often become very sore after 'miroing' and have to be rested some days. Some women moisten their twine with saliva. Others use ash to aid the process. When sufficient twine is ready, the weaving process commences. In weaving, takitahi is the single weave and pupara the double weave. Expert weavers could make a cracking noise as their finger moved. This noise was called pake, and signified the highest perfection of the worker.

"Dyeing the fibre for special work is best done in fine weather. The preparation of the dyeing solution consists of bruising hinau bark and placing it in an oho or other container, covering all with cold water and leaving all night. Next day the muka is placed in the prepared solution, waiwai, and there it remains for twenty-four hours, when it is removed and hung out to dry. After this the muka is trampled into black mud. After twenty-four hours it is moved gently in the mud and removed to be thoroughly rinsed at a stream. If this is not done the mud is said to rot the muka. The muka is now hung up to dry."

Weaving

The Maori weaving process is termed whatu, and is performed without loom or shuttle, the threads being manipulated by the unaided fingers. Two sticks called turuturu, about two feet six inches in height, are taken and driven into the earth. In most parts of New Zealand the right stick is particularly tapu, though in

*The paper mulberry tree introduced by the Fleet was cultivated and grown to a small extent in the far north and on the East Coast.

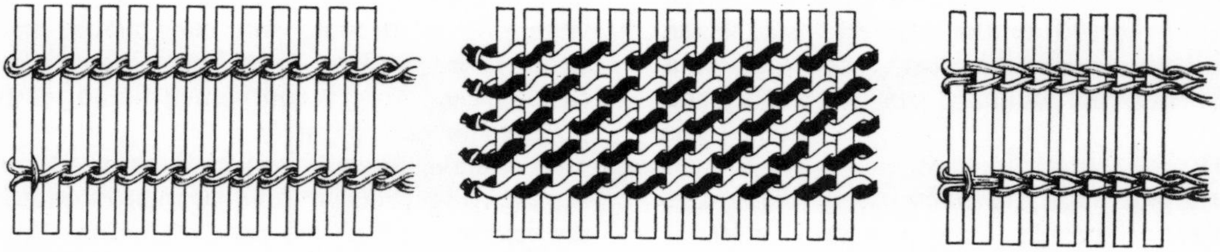

61. Diagrams of the weaving process. *Left:* Spaced single-pair twining. *Centre:* Close single-pair twining. *Right:* Spaced two-pair interlocking weft. (After Buck.)

the Wanganui district it was the left stick that was the most venerated. The turuturu sometimes are longer, and their distance apart is determined by the width of the garment to be woven. The twine consists of the fibre of the flax in the form of fine twine. Cross threads are known as aho, the first and most important being thicker and called tawhiu. From this first sacred cross thread are suspended the vertical threads called io or whenu.

The weaver works from left to right, at least two aho or horizontal threads being held in the hand and twisted around each whenu so as to enclose it. This simple method of enclosing each vertical thread by two horizontal threads and then crossing the horizontal threads before passing on to the next vertical thread actually is a form of plaiting, producing what is known as "tied cloth" by some writers.

As in all important Maori activities, some degree of tapu pertains to instruction in the art of weaving. A special house is set aside for teaching purposes, and given the name of whare pora. Sometimes men are given instruction, but usually the pupil is a woman. The instructor seems always to have been a tohunga or male expert. The pupil is required to weave a small piece of fabric under close supervision. Before beginning, the pupil is required to sit inactive as the expert recites a charm, the object of which is to force the knowledge of the art of weaving into the mind of the learner and make it permanent. As the expert finishes his recitation the pupil leans forward and bites the upper part of the right-hand turuturu, or rod, just closing her teeth on it. She then proceeds to weave the first cross thread.

Another ceremony is performed in order to remove the tapu of the proceedings from the workers. In this performance the pupil is given a small portion of sow thistle, or puwha, to eat; the ceremony itself is sometimes termed moremore puwha.

In the year 1937 James McDonald, former Assistant Director, Dominion Museum, was living at Tokaanu and supervising his own school of Maori arts and crafts. As no published account of the process of making kilted garments had, as far as we were aware, been written, we now quote Mr McDonald's instructions: "A good-sized piupiu or rapaki has in it from 200 to 250 pieces of flax. Each piece of flax is called a piupiu. Putting them in bunches of 10 facilitates counting. However, for purposes of making a simple piupiu it is not necessary to use as large a number as this; in fact, to make a rapaki you can please yourself as to how many piupiu you desire for it.

"The first step in making is to select suitable flax. The Maoris were very particular. They used only first, second, or third blades from the centre, The first, or central, blade in one of the tiny flax clumps is called the iho; the second, on either side of this central blade, is called the rito; and the third, next to the rito, is termed taumai. These were the blades usually used for making the rapaki. If the iho is long enough it can be used and gives the whitest and cleanest garment when it is dried. Rito is used mainly as it is always sufficiently long; it also dries quite light in colour. The cutting of the blades is done just where they join; and the portions used are the central parts of the blades. I suggest that anybody making a waist-garment take a single blade and watch it dry and bleach in the sun. In this way you will notice how the curling takes place, and how the green colour disappears in the sunlight.

"Before starting it is well to set out on a sheet of paper the divisions you propose to make in the blades; for these divisions will mark the pattern of the future garment. As you will remember, most Maori garments have black markings at intervals. These black markings are made by scraping the flax with the point of a knife and dipping the flax in black earth. If you lay your strip of flax on a sheet of paper and score the flax across with the point of the knife, you will make a mark which will absorb the dye; and if you take a little bit of the green substance of the flax blade away with the pocket-knife you will find that you have the white muka left. Rub this by holding it between your fingers and you will find that it readily becomes soft. A few crosses on the blades will help to make a better pattern. Maoris today usually use ink to dye their flax.

"Before you start to make this garment, decide on the width of flax which you are going to use for each blade. Then, decide on the pattern you intend to use and the portions of each blade you intend to strip to reach the fibre. The cuts that you make across the blades will go into rings when the blade dries and curls. Plait your flax at the top into as good a pattern as you can, leaving the ends to swing and then you will have a rapaki complete. Dip the blades into ink and dry in the sun. If you hang the bundles up to dry in bunches of ten, you will find that you will not have any great trouble in counting your blades to make the final garment.

"Ink has been mentioned above as a black dye, but the ancient Maori searched for a stagnant pool with a good scum of iron oxide, though he did not know it by that name. There were places where the black dye (parapara), might be obtained, but sometimes the dye was dark brown instead. Certain places in swamps often gave good results and these were kept secret to family groups or to closely knit communities. Sometimes an hour's immersion of the piupiu was enough, but usually twelve hours were required to give a good rich black colour. To fix the dye the piupiu were then immersed in a tutu or hinau bark solution. If tutu solution was used, many young branches and shoots of the plant were soaked for twenty-four hours in a wooden bowl of water or, in the case of hinau bark, the bark was bruised with a wooden beater and placed in a vessel as with the tutu. These solutions acted as a mordant for

62. Woman making a garment, *circa* 1843 (after Angas).

fixing the dye of the piupiu. It was found best to soak these for thirty-six hours and then rinse in running water." This account is a little different from that supplied by Te Kuiti weavers.

Piupiu of the korowai class, used for warmth and protection, are now becoming rare in New Zealand. It is said that, well soaked in water, they would on occasions turn a spear or a blow from a weapon. It is probable that the garment would be worn either as a kilt or rapaki, or have been used as a cape (mai). The little thrums with which the surface is covered are of raw flax which curls when dried. The raw flax is first treated by scraping and dyeing to give the effect produced.

In the early 1840s G. F. Angas drew the interior of a house at Porirua, Wellington. Towards the back of the house two women were engaged in garment making; but instead of having the garment hanging vertically between two stakes, four stakes were used and the garment lay parallel to the surface of the floor. This may have been a method of making larger cloaks which would present difficulties if made on the vertical sticks.

One of the Lindauer paintings illustrates a similar weaving method for a large cloak.

9

THE HILL FORT OR PA

Building Stockades

Forts (pa) were built on suitable hills, ridges or promontories, as well as on strategic situations with river, lake, or swamp forming a natural barrier on one or more sides. There was no standard type of pa, for they all appeared to vary somewhat with locality and terrain. One thing they had in common was the employment of topographical features as natural barriers against the approach of an enemy. For the rest it was necessary to build stockades, fosses or trenches, and ramparts. Some pa were defended by stockades alone, others by fosse, ramparts and stockade, while others again were terraced hill forts where scarps and stockades alone were used.

Apart from the erection of ramparts and the excavation of trenches, the digging of deep holes to hold main supporting posts for palisades was one of the major tasks which faced the neolithic pa builder. The single pa posts dedicated to Tiki, and even house posts, required deep holes. Digging deep holes required long poles of the ko type and some means of lifting earth or clay as the hole deepened.

The unique form of ko illustrated here may have been used for this purpose. It has three foot-rests evenly placed along its narrow bladed lower portion. The upper steps would be used as the hole deepened. This object is in the Auckland Museum and there is a replica in the Dominion Museum. The ko is cut out of the solid and would suggest that the implement would be most useful for digging post holes. It also suggests the possibility of a movable step on a plain ko being raised.

Among papers left by Elsdon Best is a page with some drawings of Maori artefacts. Of interest is a "scoop for excavating holes, the tikaro or tikoko" said to have been recently discovered The tikaro or scoop may once have had a wide usage over the country for its practical value is obvious. The kaheru could lift a certain amount of earth from post holes, but a scoop would be a very useful tool as the hole became deeper.

A superior pa might have as many as four lines of stockades with necessary fosses at

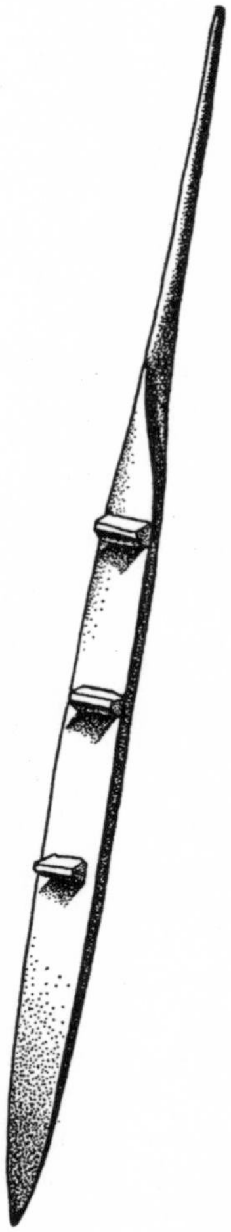

63. Unique form of ko (Auckland Museum).

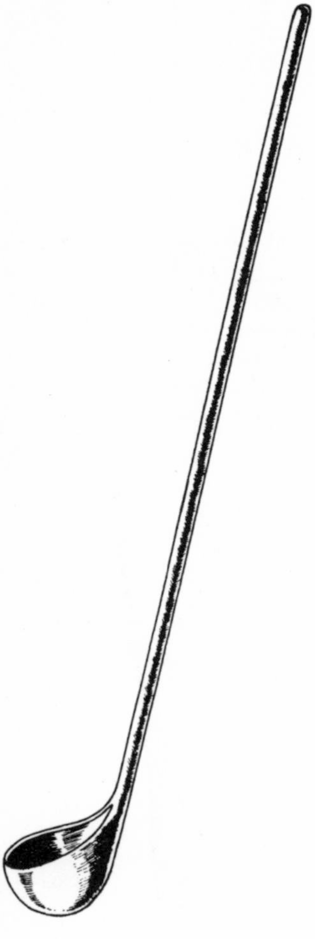

64. Tikaro or Tikoko – scoop for excavating holes.

intervals. Some of the lesser positions would be defended by stockades alone, leaving a line of retreat to the more heavily fortified areas. Much depended on the configuration of the country. Natural contours would decide on the relative amount of defence necessary. Stockades were usually six to eight feet deep. The main posts were higher, being sunk in the earth to a depth of at least six feet, and well rammed in. Whole timber trees were often used for main posts, and these have been noted as high as fifteen to twenty feet. Transverse timbers were lashed to all uprights with vines and supplejack. A favourite device was to slope one line of stockade inwards or outwards according to its position. Many outer stockades had a leaning outer screen (wita) so erected as to incline inwards at the top and serve as a support and reinforcement to the stockade. It is said that the Puke-kiore pa at Waiapa had a wide deep trench outside the wita into which the long spears of the defenders could be thrust. A drawbridge spanned this trench at the entrance and, on being raised, formed a gate or barrier in times of war or alarm.

Fighting Stages

The fighting stage within the pa was first mentioned by Captain Cook. From this darts and stones were thrown down on the attacking force. Fighting stages were generally erected over gateways to give protection against attack, and also at corners of a pa if they were vulnerable. The fighting stage was termed a pukara. Sometimes these stages were several storeys high. In times of alarm a watchman was stationed on one of the stages. He was accustomed to chant watch songs and to beat a suspended wooden gong (pahu) at regular intervals. The beating of the gong was to let the approaching enemy know that all were alert, though many pa have been taken by surprise because of inadequate watchfulness.

Fire

The inmates of a pa feared fire more than a hand-to-hand attack. Many pa were set on fire by the enemy throwing red-hot stones by means of a sling made of flax. Stockades were difficult to burn, but by using firebrands and torches the hostile force would set fire to houses within the enclosure. If this could be done, a general assault was made during the confusion. Windy nights were selected to attack the pa by means of fire. Defenders employed themselves throwing earth on the roofs of dwellings and storehouses. Sometimes rope ladders were thrown over weak places in the stockades in an endeavour to force an entrance, or a device was used to pull down or weaken a section of the stockade. The latter was a pole tied centrally at the end of a rope and thrown over the defences.

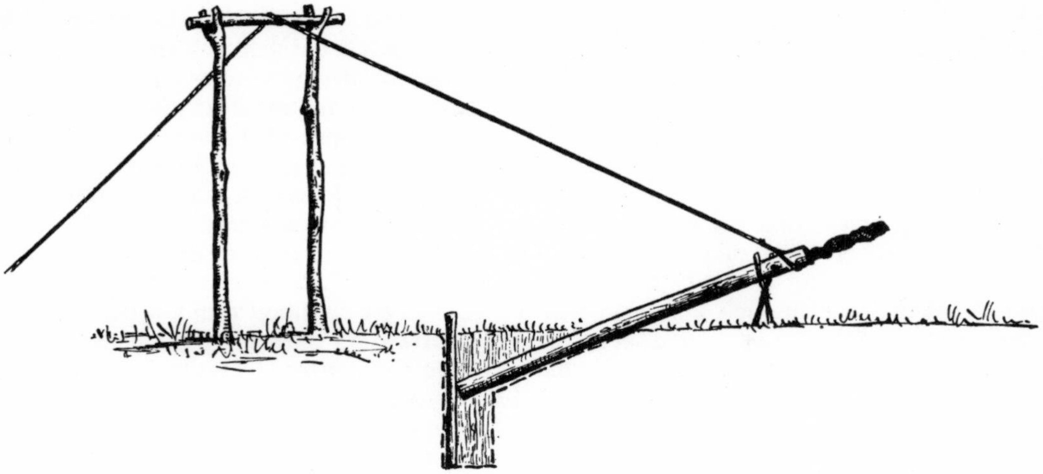

65. Method of raising a pa post (after Best).

Living in the Pa

While prolonged peace was an uncertain condition, there was seldom a long period of continuous warfare except when pa were besieged. Raids and counter-raids seem to have been an accepted condition of the pattern of Maori life.

There seems to be no reason for the belief that the whole tribe resided permanently in the fortified pa. In fact historians tell us that old pa which had been occupied at intervals for many generations had never been seriously attacked and no fights had ever been associated with them. If the summit of the hill contained a pa, it was customary to construct a village at its foot and people would reside there, going about their ordinary work and retiring to the pa only when danger threatened.

Ceremonial Practices

Every pa had its presiding or protective deity. By means of ritual performances by a priest or adept, the deity would by symbolised by a mauri which contained his essence, and which was buried under one of the main

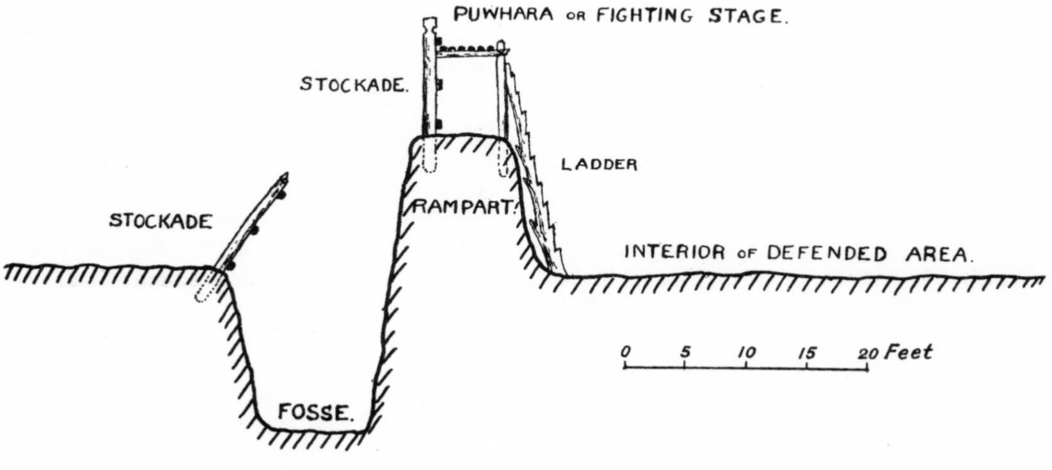

66. Section of Wharekaho pa at Mercury Bay as described by Cook and Banks.

corner posts, the first post to be placed in position. This stone preserved the mana or prestige of the pa and was the permanent resting place of the god, who might be appealed to as occasion arose.

On the opening of a new pa a woman entered first. The tohunga or adept had charge of all ceremonial performances. An unmarried girl of high rank was usually chosen. The female element was more peaceful than the male, and a woman possesses less tapu. The chosen girl first sat on the paetaku (sill) of the gateway astride the beam, facing the sun. A chant then ensued to announce that the female was present in order to ensure freedom from trouble and restriction. The tohunga entered the pa, the girl proceeding to the post beneath which the mauri was buried, where she repeated the name of the atua (god) of the pa, such as Uenuku, Rongomai, Kahukura, etc. After chanting by the priest everyone entered and greeted the girl, who later went inside the chief house and lifted the tapu by kneeling at the base of the rear post with her back to the door. After another chant the girl rose, and the ceremony was over. The ceremonial feast was then prepared. The mauri of the house was usually buried beneath this rear post. The object or person buried might be a slave, a member of the tribe, or even a valuable piece of greenstone.

Description

The best early description of an early pa is that supplied by Petit Thouars who visited Bay of Islands in 1855.* He described a pa at Kawakawa, and was most interested in the great carved figures or heads of figures which appeared at intervals along its length, to which the Maoris had given a most terrible expression, some with open mouths and tongues thrust out to an inordinate length and others which appeared to gnash their teeth. Their tongues were painted red, and sometimes whole figures were so coloured. In case of war with another tribe these figures would receive the temporary names of notable chiefs on the side of the enemy. Petit Thouars entered the pa by means of a movable post which was raised by day and replaced at night, and which provided a narrow passage into a labyrinth of palisading. He found that each house was surrounded by its own palings. Houses had only a small opening and were from three to four metres long by four to five metres in depth. The soil floor was covered with dry grass and spread with mats of *Phormium*. In the pa were better and larger dwellings with a carving above the doorway. In particular, the houses of chiefs were distinguished by the carvings with which they were ornamented.

**The Voyage of the Venus*, 1855, p. 111.

It can be stated with some certainty that the first Polynesians to occupy New Zealand had no hill forts or pa. They were strangers in a strange land, and had no natural enemies. Food was so plentiful that it made for settled living. It is probable that after other Polynesian waves reached these shores, enmities gradually arose. The descendants of members of the canoes Toi and Whatonga probably introduced a newer and more virile element into the population.

Location

One confirmation of the theory that the former population of New Zealand was numerous is to be found in the number of pa sites, which in many localities may still be traced on ridges, hill tops, and promontories. The amount of labour that must have been expended in trenching, terracing, and building stockades, all without iron tools, must have been enormous. Examination of old pa sites shows that the houses to hold the people were in many cases as close together as it was possible to build them. This is proved by the close proximity of the fireplaces, consisting of four upright stones to hold burning charcoal, one fire to each whare. However, it is unlikely that all the pa sites which we see today were occupied at the same time.

We have very little evidence of how many Maoris lived in a single pa. One record by Dr Dieffenbach who visited Waikanae in 1839 states that the pa there was very large, well fenced in, and that the houses were neatly constructed. Villages in the immediate vicinity held an estimated 700 Maoris. A plan showing sites of old pa near Urenui in Taranaki illustrates twenty-four pa all within six square miles; but in some parts of New Zealand there were very few pa indeed.

No exact count of old pa sites has yet been made; but in Taranaki alone the number of hills terraced for fortification has been estimated at over a thousand. This is based on a study made in the period 1925–35. An estimated total for the North Island would be several thousand at least. In the South Island the number would not be as great as in the North. Why did the Maori or pre-Maori people build so many hill forts? The answer may have been an abundance of suitable hills, and a corresponding abundance of timber, and that people took offence easily, and guarded their rights and privileges jealously. Fort building was not strictly a feature of old Polynesia, and we can only assume that the pa originated in New Zealand, or alternatively that some stray vessel from Fiji reached these shores long ago and that the immigrants taught the people the art.

To a Maori community the pa was the safest place they knew – a stronghold which people might confidently regard as a place of refuge when danger threatened. Here were retained many of the important pataka, the food resources so precious to Polynesians living in a temperate climate with quickly depleted winter supplies. No doubt much of the carving which embellished the gateway and the great carved posts was associated with this treasured background retreat with its food supplies, warm houses, and stout palisades. Whether the development of the pa was associated with a later emergence of cannibalism is impossible to determine, but the possibility exists. One can easily conceive the position of a people, faced by enemies and the possibility of defeat, exercising every conceivable device and the utmost ingenuity in constructing a pa that would baffle the stoutest opponent.

Water Supplies

The water supply in a pa was usually a problem. If the ground was of a clay type, water would be conserved in clay pits and if necessary filled by means of supplies carried in gourds or received by natural means. Often, sufficient rain would fall to augment the supply and so prevent alarm, but no water from the roofs of houses might be used for such purposes.* Pa were often deliberately erected either to enclose or protect a spring, or to have near access to water, and trenches to the nearest water supply have been noted extending downhill from the fort. Such trenches would have been covered and protected by stockades. Desperate sorties have been made from beleaguered pa to nearby water supplies.

*The roof was over the tapu head of man and became tapu also. Early sanitary officers found it impossible to persuade Maoris to install tanks or drink tank water from roofs.

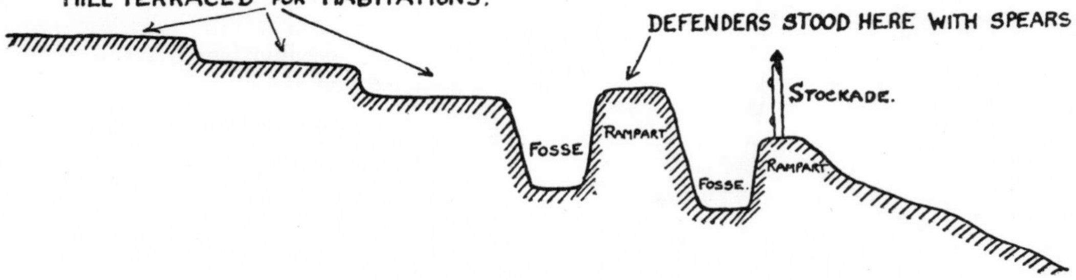

67. Diagrams illustrating method of defending a village by means of a rampart having no stockade.

10

PRIMITIVE HOUSES

Muttonbirders' Huts

The typical hut of primitive man was a structure composed of long straight saplings joined above, circular in area below, and thatched. This type of dwelling is the basis of the houses or huts once used extensively in the South Island, and persisting in the muttonbirders' huts of Stewart Island in the early years of the present century. It was also the basis of many oval dwellings used for storage and other purposes, as well as of a small beehive structure of a more or less temporary nature. A hut appearing in the sketch of a village as seen by Captain Cook on Motuara Island, Queen Charlotte Sound, is almost certainly of this type. Saplings or suitable branches were buried below or driven into the ground round the area to be covered. They were bent above and securely joined together. Preference was given to branches already bent, and these were fixed with the concavity inwards, thus giving more interior room and a better run-off for water on the outside of the thatch.

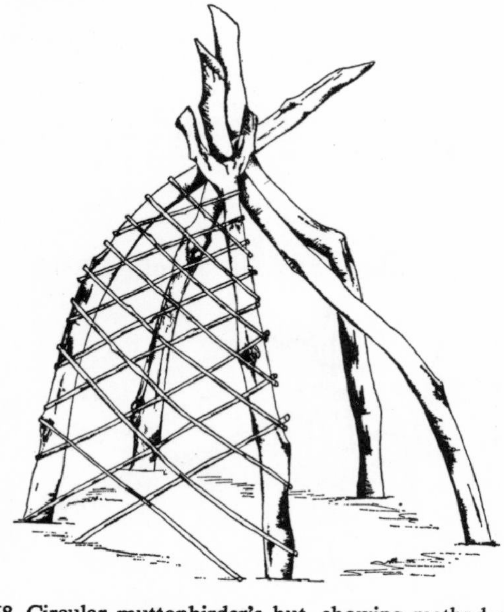

68. Circular muttonbirder's hut, showing method of construction.

Circular Houses

Many circular huts were built in a day by co-operative labour. Sometimes, a framework of supplejack was used to surround and strengthen the hut in lattice fashion, being tied at intervals to the inside of the uprights.

69. Circular hut as built by muttonbirder's, Stewart Island (a reconstruction from an old photograph).

The framework might also take the form of branches, saplings, and scrub ingeniously interwoven among the main upright supports.

Ferns were arranged, butt uppermost, and tied in bundles round the outside walls, commencing from the bottom upwards, each bundle being lashed to the structure with flax. Tussock-like grass and roots were placed over the fern in bundles from the bottom and built upwards. A large tussock is taken for the capstone of the hut, placed root uppermost, and tied below.

In the North Island there are records of huts with a circular base in at least three localities, and one at Wairau. Round holes were made in the ground in suitable localities in the Waikato district, the purpose being to obtain gravel for kumara plantations. A raised portion was often left in the centre to take the centre pole of the future circular sleeping hut. Such huts appear to have been tent-like structures with branches running from the margins of the circle to the apex of the centre pole. Circular houses of a temporary nature were also built for mutton-birders who took muttonbirds on the Paeroa ridge on the Kawhia coast.

A small circular whare was built by Wanganui Maoris at the Christchurch Exhibition in 1905. It was termed a purangi, and resembled the circular houses of the Samoans, except that it was closed at the sides. It was said by the Wanganui people that in former times their people frequently constructed cookhouses and sleeping houses in this circular pattern. Another circular house stood at Waikanae pa in 1849. This house was large in size, resembling a small haystack in appearance. It was constructed in the same manner as that built in 1905 by the Wanganui Maoris. Circular upright walls of low height were surmounted by a tent-shaped structure, well-thatched and capped at the apex. The upright circular wall presupposes the use of upright posts, securely

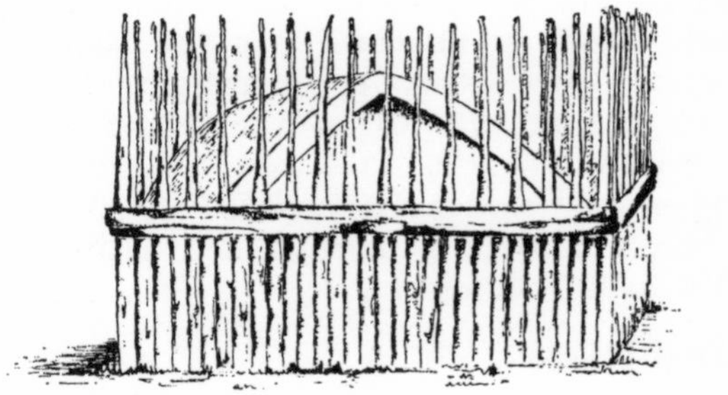

70. House on Plimmerton Beach about 1843 (after Angas). Note the stockaded enclosure to protect the dwelling and its inmates.

71. Circular house, Waikanae pa (after Swainson, 1849).

railed and lashed above, with rafters fitting into them, or attached to a rail running around the outside upper margin of the upright posts. The use of a protective outer "fence" close around the wall was necessary to provide shelter for the building, to give more security to the inmates, and to protect the walls from injury.

Oval Houses

The oval house was erected in many parts of the South Island and also in the Wellington Province. In the far south it was used for a meeting house, a store house, or a working house in times of rain. It would seem unlikely that an individual house would be used for each of these functions. Photographs confirm eye-witness accounts that such houses reached a relatively large size. They all had sunken floors to provide greater warmth. The method of construction followed the lines already laid down for the circular hut, except that large timbers were required, and some form of ridge pole was used; but on this point no information is available. In a whare whata (storehouse), on Stewart Island, a strong beam of timber formed a cover for the outside ridge. It is held in place by a curving branch, held in position on each side by the uppermost of a number of encircling bands used to hold the thatch in position.

72. Whare whata, Stewart Island.

The porch was an important feature of some of these houses. It is well portrayed in the drawing of the Stewart Island house as a lean-to enclosed at the sides with four poles which support the roof. A similar lean-to, whether a porch or not we cannot say for certain, is to be seen attached to an oval house in an old sketch of Te Aro pa, Wellington. Lean-to porches are probably original features, and were not copied from European sources, for the conception of a porch for large houses is fairly constant in houses of Maori construction.

In the south the oval building of this kind is said to be known as whare mahe, or, if used for food, a whare whata. For sleeping, the circular hut (whare moe) was preferred. Unfortunately, enquiries on this subject were fifty years too late. The old master-builders were dead, and their descendants retained only a little of what might once have been recorded.

Primitive man of long ago discovered that it was warmer to sleep below ground level than above. Polynesian Maoris not only excavated the ground to three or four feet in depth, but also heaped up earth round the walls.

Lean-to Houses

From here we turn to an even more elementary form of temporary shelter – the wharau, a simple lean-to upheld at one end by means of two or three upright poles, while the lower end rests on the ground. Such lean-to shelters were often erected against a cliff face or bank. Supporting poles were sunk in the ground and doubly secured with cross rails above. The uppermost of these horizontal rails supported the highest portion of the roof. Below, the thatch was supported by three rails or poles, across which other rails ran at intervals. A strong horizontal pole below helped to support the weight of the roof as it touched the ground. Lean-to structures such as this are said to have been used also at the Chatham Islands.

It is certain that some form of dwelling was introduced into New Zealand with the first immigrants and established here, the settlers utilising local building materials and effecting improvements as they progressed. The circular house, from which would evolve the oval house, was doubtless one of the earliest of Polynesian dwellings. From the oval to the rectangular is only a short step. It is remarkable that in the North Island the rectangular house so completely gained precedence that in many localities all other types practically disappeared.

In a manuscript note Elsdon Best once stated: "Temporary houses, such as built by persons when making a canoe, were whare porukuruku at Hawaiki and were circular."

This type of house was used not only in the homeland but also in New Zealand, as evidenced by D'Urville in 1826. Some of these houses appear to have a double door, one on each side of the central pou-tahu, or frontal ridge pole support. A later author, Polack, in his work published in 1840 also supplies evidence that this type of hut was known to him. Such a small building would be constructed on a framework of wood, consisting of ridge pole and end supports, the doorway being off-centre. Bent saplings would supply the walls. The late Mr Raureti te Huia of Waikato mentioned such a hut at Waikato and said the walls were made of bent supplejack.

73. Maori emerging from a sleeping hut (after Polack, 1840).

74. Lean-to hut, Motuara Island (after Webber). Note use of side wall boards (paepae).

Rectangular Houses

In the North Island the rectangular house became the established and recognised building for all important purposes. Doubtless the Maoris of the Fleet migration had something to do with this. Every conqueror regards the arts of the conquered as inferior to his own. So the oval house and the circular house would persist in the marginal areas of New Zealand, while a better class of building was established by the newcomers. Very large carved houses were rare, though Cook does record such a building a little inland on the East Coast (see page 83). In general the houses were small and of no great height above the ground.

The principle of construction followed in rectangular buildings is seen in the use of a central ridge pole upheld at each end by upright posts. In many houses the old Polynesian pattern of a second outside ridge pole was used to hold the thatch in position. Rafters descended obliquely from the ridge pole to fit into suitable slots in upright slabs (poupou) set at regular intervals along the side walls. All upright posts, both wall ends and ridge pole supports, were buried some distance in the ground, giving the necessary stability to the building. In superior houses young totara trees were much in demand for posts, while manuka poles of all description served for use in sheds and less important buildings. As the ridge pole had a central support inside the building and another on the inner front wall, the doorway was placed a little to the left of centre and a window on the right side. Only on the Wanganui River and in its vicinity did houses have a central doorway; but in these cases a stout central support was used in front of a narrow porch.

In the course of examination of pa sites in varied places in the North Island, we have been impressed by the relative abundance of the sites of small houses. Doubtless they were sleeping houses, but many appeared to be so small that they gave the impression of having been occupied by a single individual. Sometimes it was possible to find fire stones still intact. The house sites were often not more

15. A tree-fern whare with European-type chimney, Thames (from a photograph by A. Mundy).

than six feet six inches to eight feet long and about three feet wide. Such houses were probably occupied by important chiefs or tohunga who required a degree of isolation because of their tapu nature.

In the north the common people slept in a somewhat larger dwelling, not to be compared with the large whare runanga of today, but often large enough for several families to sleep with a minimum of discomfort. Such houses would vary in size according to family groups and location. A common size appears to be from ten to twelve feet long and six to eight feet wide. D'Urville appears to confirm this opinion. His dog-kennel huts may have been the houses of chiefs. Pa sites generally reveal one or more large house sites which may represent whare runanga. Our opinion is that many Maoris slept in the assembly house (whare runanga), which was often better known as wharepuni (warm house), for Urewera Maoris were living in such houses when Firth made his observations on houses.

Thatching

The thatching process varied with the locality and class of building to be covered. Kakaho (flowering stalks of toetoe or reed grass) were laid parallel and tied into oblong mats to line the roof interior of superior houses. Supplejack sticks were laid over these on the outside, one over each batten, to which they were tied. Raupo was laid in bundles from ridge pole to eaves, and well tied to the battens (kaho) below in some cases; in others a layer of raupo was held in position by the stick (karapi) below and raupo bundles laid over the top. Over all was placed the true thatch, consisting of more bundles of raupo, or sometimes of rushes, toetoe bundles or nikau palms laced together. Thatching with totara bark was common in many localities, the thatch being securely tied and held by means of logs or rails balanced on the roof.

11

ASSEMBLY HOUSES

Early Houses

In one of Angas's plates in *The New Zealanders*, there is an elevated store with two houses in the background. The store (whata or pataka), mounted on a single stout post, appears to have bark roof, probably of totara, which was used for a roof covering in many places. The general framework appears to be of bent saplings or supplejack with some strengthening wooden framework, constructed so that the pataka appears to be composed of two semicircular halves. For safety a wooden fence surrounds the base of the supporting pole. Poles, probably of manuka also, hold the bark roof in place on the outside.

In the backround there are two rectangular houses. The one on the left is a low-walled building with pointed frontal palings which follow the line of the roof. At first sight it appears to be a unique type; but in an old sketch of Te Aro pa in the early 1840s, W.

76. Elevated storehouse with houses in the background (after Angas).

77. Whare runanga as seen by Captain Cook, Queen Charlotte Sound.

Fox has left us a record of a similar building (or perhaps Angas figured the same dwelling). A second building is remarkable for its square shape and higher walls and roof. It is unusual in having a corner doorway, no porch, and a thatched covering (kotopihi) for the smoke escape. The latter feature has not previously been recorded; but it is probable that many houses had provision for a kotopihi in rainy seasons.

Whare Runanga

Any assumption that the large carved house of assembly (whare runanga) is a modern innovation are refuted by an early observation made on the east coast of the North Island. Such a building was falling to decay when Captain Cook re-discovered New Zealand.* The account is as follows: "When we were on shore in the district called Tolaga we saw the ruins or rather the frame of a house, for it had never been finished, much superior in size to any that we saw elsewhere; it was thirty feet in length, about fifteen in breadth and twelve feet high; the sides of it were adorned with many carved planks of a workmanship much superior to any other we had met with in the country; but for what purpose it was built or why it was deserted, we could never learn."

This seems to have been the framework for a relatively large whare runanga, the many carved planks at the sides doubtless being the poupou, or upright wooden slabs hollowed above to take the lower ends of rafters. From this we can deduce the fact that large fully-carved assembly houses were not unknown before the discovery of New Zealand. They would be much rarer than they are today. If Cook saw one such carved house on the east coast, there were doubtless others at Rotorua, in the Urewera, and at Waikato. Such a deserted house would almost certainly be tapu, this condition being the result of some unforseen calamity, such as an offence to the gods or even the death of the builder.

Symbolism of the Assembly House

To understand aright the superior assembly house of the Maori it is necessary to remember that the house is named after a revered and respected ancestor of the builders. The Maori mind does not stop here, for the house becomes a material representation of the actual man. Maori symbolism sees in the ridge pole the back-bone of the ancestor, while the frontal carved koruru is rightly his head, properly a continuous part of the tahu. The main interior pole supporting the ridge pole is the pou-tokomanawa, literally the pole of the heart. The rafters are his ribs, the window his eye, and the door

*Hawkesworth's *Account of Cook's Voyages*, Vol. 3, 1773, p. 458.

his mouth. His arms are the maihi, facing boards in front, and even his fingers are often to be seen as a termination to the raparapa or carved lower end part of the maihi.

On the East Coast this symbolism is carried even further, and the word poho (bosom) is placed before the name of the ancestor, as in the large carved house, Poho o Rawiri, at Gisborne; so all who enter the house automatically come into the bosom of the great ancestor Rawiri. Around the walls each of the large carved slabs which support the lower rafter ends is carved to represent an ancestor, distorted for reasons of tapu, or so that they may not approach too closely to the handiwork of the gods. They all remain protected in the bosom of Rawiri.

Construction

In preparing the site for a new building, the ground was first levelled by eye. At the first sign of rain visible depressions were seen and filled in. The lines for the two ends, roro (the front), and tuarongo (the back), were first laid down, and the main building was squared by measuring the diagonals. The next business was the erection of pou tahu, or supports for the future ridge pole. Originally these were either whole trunks of trees or trunks cut longitudinally in half, erected with the convex faces inwards. These may or may not be carved with ancestral figures, though carving was preferred wherever possible. The bases of the pou tahu were well buried and the earth well rammed down.

The construction of the superior house varied with locality, though in essential details all such houses exhibit tolerably uniform features, many of which have already been mentioned. The ridge pole was originally always in one piece with the koruru or parata. Behind the koruru was an indentation or neck, a feature now rarely seen. On this neck rested or fitted the outermost pair of rafters. These were often stronger than the others of the house, or even double, for they had partly to bear the weight of the maihi, which had behind it a kind of longitudinal tenon to fit into or above these rafters.

To allow for the frontal porch, the tahu (ridge pole) was generally about ten feet longer than the whare proper. In a very large house it is as much as two feet wide, being so

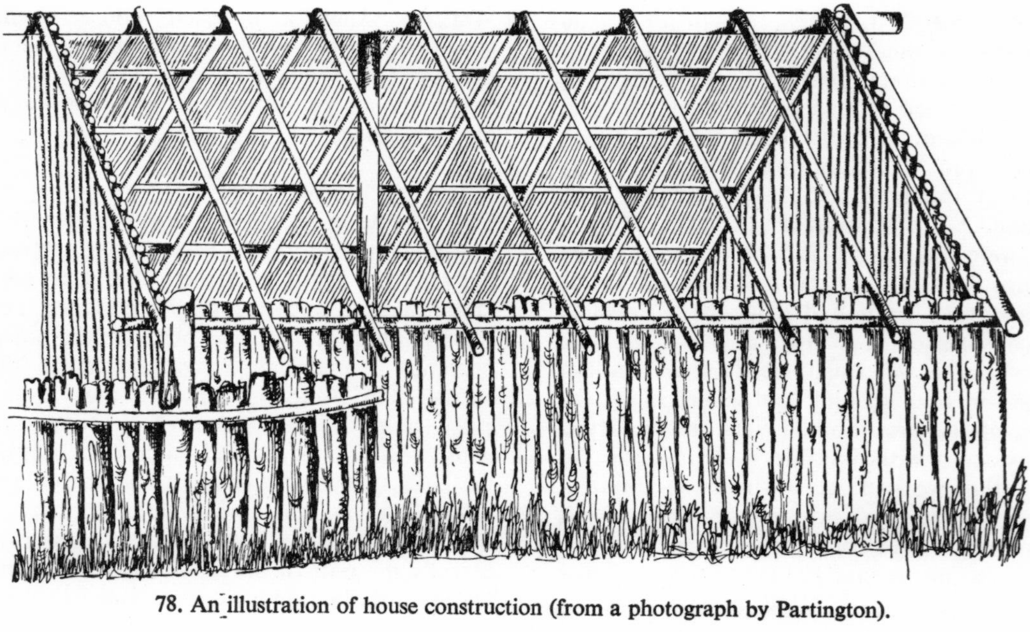

78. An illustration of house construction (from a photograph by Partington).

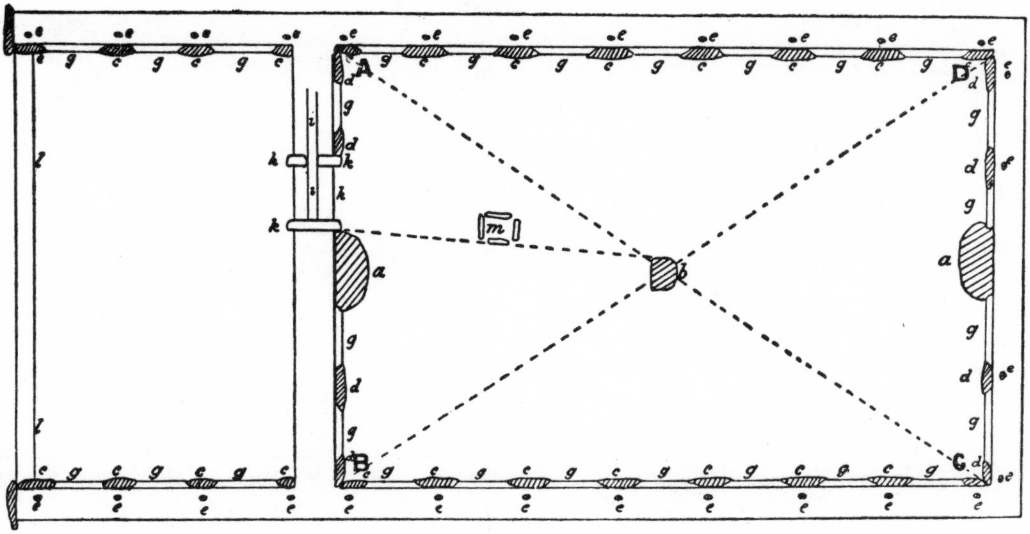

79. Superior house. Ground plan (after Williams).
AB Roro. CD Tua-rongo. AD-BC Paki-tara. AC-BD Hauroki. aa Pou tahu. b Pou-tokomanawa. ccc Poupou. ddd Epa. eee Hirinaki. ff Amo. ggg Papaka. h Paepae. ii Toanga. kk Whakawai (Whakawae). ll Paepae-kainga-awha. m Takuahi.

hewn that in section it was an obtuse-angled triangle set with the longest side below. The tahu was naturally very heavy, and was erected by stages using special scaffolding and supports. That part of the ridge pole which projects into the porch is usually carved on its lower surface with a representation of the two primal ancestors of the people, Rangi and Papa. This part of the tahu is known as the pane. The front (roro) end of a building was always slightly higher than the back end. The poupou of the walls were set opposite in pairs to support pairs of rafters. When in position these leaned slightly inwards. The four poupou at the corners of the house were tapu. Sometimes a human victim slain during the inauguration ceremonies was buried beneath a corner tahu, or at the base of the pou-tokomanawa. After a while the bones of the victim might be exhumed and placed on the altar or tuaahu, and there used as a manea (beneficial influence) for the owner of the house. Manea is described as the hau or spirit, essence of man, and also of the earth.

Curved and partly perpendicular posts are used around the outside of many important houses. These take the place of horizontal purlins, though rails are sometimes fixed between them. These posts (hirinaki) are set into the ground, and lean inwards to buttress each poupou at its upper and outer edge. This gives a rounded arching to the outer walls and wall thatch, for each hirinaki has its concave surface outermost. This procedure also keeps water dripping from the thatch away from the wall, and helps to preserve the timbers. With the use of modern roofing the hirinaki has become superfluous. Another feature used in fixing the upper ends of the poupou was a baton, or rail in the case of lesser houses, the kahopaetara, placed behind the poupou and lashed in position. The framework of the sides included a moana between the poupou, which filled in the intervening spaces.

The amo was originally a support to the lower part of the facing boards in front. In many places in New Zealand the carved house is built with a true amo (slab) fitted below the maihi with a large carved amo in front of it. Other amo had a projection which gave the

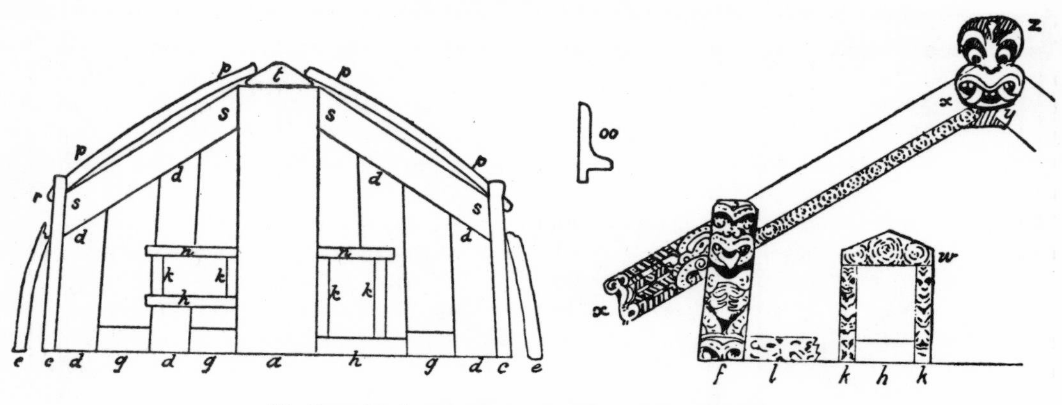

80. Superior house. Front elevation (after Williams).

a Pou tahu. c Poupou. d Epa. e Hirinaki. f Amo. g Papaka. h Paepae. k Whakawai (Whakawae). n Taupoki. oo Section of Maihi. p Heke. r Teremu. s Heke-tipi. t Tahu. w Korupe. x Maihi. y—z Koruru.

necessary support. The amo also hid the front edge of the wall, as the maihi hid the front edge of the roof. The maihi were carried beyond the amo to form an ornamental portion termed raparapa. Above, a side face figure was carved, usually termed a ngututa, and below this were the finger projections as already mentioned.

After the poupou had been well set and the ground hardened, the rafters or heke were set in place. The rafters were usually flattened above and rounded below, with the underside painted with an ornamental scroll pattern in black and red. The lower end of the rafter was often cut down into a tongue (teremu), to fit into an oval or oblong

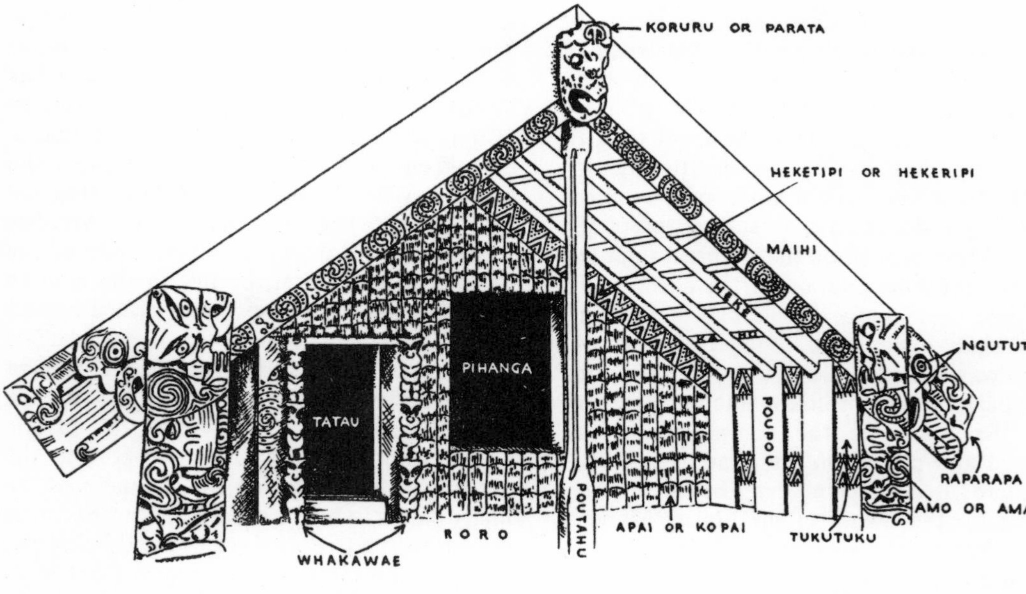

81. Sketch of a carved house, Taupo area (copied from *Auckland Weekly*, 1908).

depression in the poupou, according to the taste of the builders. In many better-class houses, rafters were curved at their lower ends in such a manner that the convex surface was outwards, giving to the poupou a downward and not an outward thrust. This curving of the rafters seems to have gone out of fashion towards the end of last century; but there is no doubt that it makes for much greater stability and a longer life to the dwelling. Many fairly old houses may be seen where straight rafters have caused an outward thrust to the walls and engendered rapid decay. Horizontal battens (kaho) cross the rafters passing over the ridge pole. It went out of fashion with the gradual use of small nails. Originally the kaho were lashed into place.

The door frame consisted of the paepae (inner threshold board) grooved to take a sliding doorway on its upper face. Upon this stood the jambs (whakawae) with their front edges adorned with human figures. Each whakawae is flanged on its outer edge to abut the outer wall behind. The left-hand whakawae stood close against the frontal pou tahu of the front porch wall or kopai. Over the whakawae lay a horizontal slab which sometimes served as a support for the carved lintel (pare or korupe), above the doorway. At other times the pare rested on the flattened tops of the whakawae. An outer wooden slab (paepae), defined the limits of the porch (raro), but this was not always a feature of superior houses.

The hearth (takuahi), was a space about a foot square, defined by four stones, and placed halfway between the pou tahu in front and the pou-tokomanawa.

Thatching

The foundation for the thatch was often formed by placing a second light ridge pole in the crotch formed by an upper continuation and crossing of the main rafters. Thatching material consisted of bundles of leaves of various plants such as toetoe, oioi, and raupo. Firstly, frames of kakaho reeds were neatly fitted on to the kaho above and firmly lashed in place. Rows of raupo covered these screens, each bundle being fixed in place. Karapi (secondary battens) covered these bundles. Over this the true thatch was placed in longitudinal layers, a thatching needle sometimes being used to secure thatch bundles to the kaho. Bundles of thatch were placed butt uppermost working from below upwards.

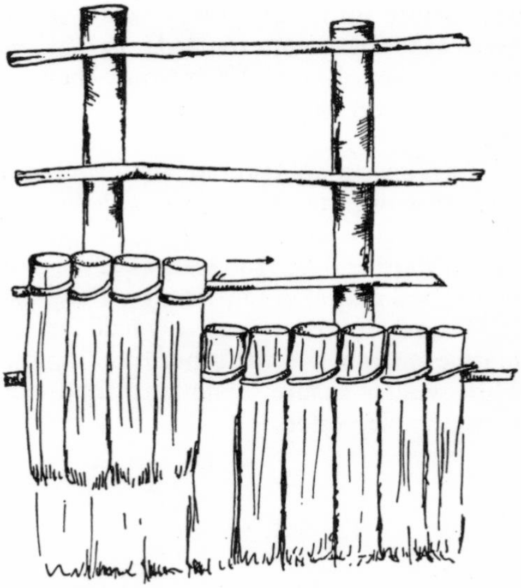

82. Method of attaching thatch bundles (after Buck).

Much variation in thatching technique exists. The thatching and lining of houses with nikau palm has never been satisfactorily worked out. Thatch material varies very considerably, the most satisfactorily thatch being totara bark in large sheets, with well-packed bundles of raupo beneath in order to ensure warmth.

12

FOOD STORE–PATAKA OR WHATA

Pataka and the Contents

The pataka (food store) was the treasure house of the people. In it was stored the food for winter consumption – dried seaweed, birds preserved in their fat, pawhera (strips of dried fish), shellfish laboriously collected and strung up to dry, dried whale meat or even seal meat, muttonbirds in the poha (seaweed vessel), etc. When empty the pataka was also used as a store for precious possessions.

The kumara was stored wholly or partly underground, but the pataka held the rest of the precious winter food. To a people living as the Maori did, the food stores of the pataka would be a matter of importance. The greatest food treasure trove was a whale or other marine mammal cast ashore or captured. This would ensure abundant food for a considerable period.

The pataka was an elevated store. It was upheld on one, two, four, or six posts. On superior pataka there was a small porch with a small doorway. The principle of construction was the same as that of a superior house, maihi and threshold boards forming a prominent feature, with amo and tekoteko also present. The main entrance to the pataka was a door below in the centre of the floor. In dry weather, it was kept open, and the front doorway also slid open. Food inside was arranged in such a manner that constant airing was made possible. A man of some standing in the community was in charge of the pataka and its contents, and he was responsible for all the airing arrangements. In particular dried fish tended to become mouldy in damp weather and required careful treatment to ensure preservation for as long a period as possible.

83. Interior of Toa pa, Petone Beach, about 1840 (from a sketch by W. Fox).

84. "Te Whata of Ahutaphanua Ko Kaihinu Pa, Atarapaua on Queen Charlotte Sound." (After Angas.)

Museum exhibits and general opinion credit the pataka with beautiful outside carving. This was certainly the case with important and well-recognised pataka in large established communities, but it now appears that the uncarved and unpretentious pataka was by far the more common. The amount of carving on the pataka would be limited by the available carvers. Presents of garments, greenstone, or other valuables would be the payment to the carvers. A few plain uncarved pataka may still be seen here and there in the North Island. Some have been adapted for use as sleeping quarters, and some for the storage of tools or other farm material.

Unlike the kumara which demands cool storage, the introduced potato would survive

85. The whole design of the pataka barge board.

quite well in the elevated store. In the drawing by W. Fox illustrating the interior of Toa pa, Petone, in or about 1840, the uncarved pataka is a central feature (see page 88). This drawing was copied in 1850 by N. Chevalier (now held by the National Art Gallery, Wellington).

Kete containing kumara (or more likely potatoes) are seen on the ground, and a man descends or climbs the log ladder (arawhata), carrying on his back another kete. The artist has left us a record of scattered groups of people, one of which includes an old man wearing an unusual type of hat.

The ladder (arawhata) from a pataka near Lake Taupo is a development of the notched pole ladder used by many primitive people. A special shape has been hollowed out at the top to fit over the threshold board, and give more stability to its sloping position.

A traditional design on the maihi of the pataka was a symbolic whale design, representing a whale or other marine mammal being drawn upwards tail first to the chief, represented by the figure at the apex. Small figures represent helpers.

Two interesting pataka carvings were excavated some twenty years ago from the bed of the Warahoe stream, and exhibit all that is best in old human carving types for pataka.

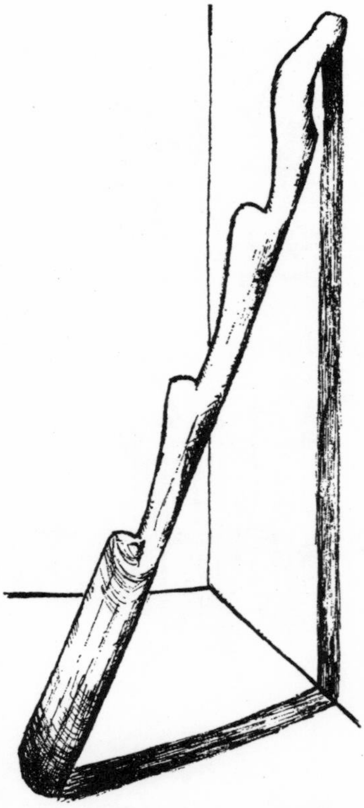

86. Pataka ladder from Lake Taupo.

Another old carving, this time an over-mantel (pare) from a swamp at Te Puke, Bay of Plenty, and now in Auckland Museum,

87. Pataka threshold board, human figures and manaia (Auckland Museum).

is shown. Here the tara tara o kai ornamentation on the human figures is well developed. The spirals are of the raised S-curve type and the central figure has an enlarged hand. Manaia-like figures at the ends have a prolonged and curling upper jaw, as seen in an old Dominion Museum maripi collected by Captain Cook.

The doorway of the pataka is usually well adorned with beautiful carving. In fact the Maori seems to have reserved some of his best carving for the pataka entrance. The actual doorway is so small that to get inside one would have to crawl on all fours, and to a large person entrance would be quite impossible.

13

ADZES

Manufacture

To the Maori the most important of all tools was the adze, which in a heavily forested country like New Zealand was indispensable. Many thousands of stone and greenstone adze heads are in New Zealand museums or in the hands of collectors. They range in time from the date when the first Polynesians arrived in this country down to Captain Cook's visit. It is only in recent years that a clear exposition of types and a classification into classic Maori and Moa-hunter adze heads has been possible. This is due to the initial researches of Dr H. D. Skinner and later work by Dr R. S. Duff.

Adzes offer a wide field for study and classification, but it would appear that until they are treated biologically, and individual type specimens established for the various sub-groups or genera, no finality will be reached. There is no complete evidence that some types of adzes originally manufactured during earliest Polynesian settlement were not being made down to comparatively recent times. However, we do know that before the Fleet arrived in New Zealand, adze making had reached a high degree of efficiency and perfection. This may have been the golden age in New Zealand history when trade in obsidian, etc. continued uninterruptedly.

Igneous and sedimentary rocks were favoured for the manufacture of adzes. Metamorphic rocks were not greatly preferred, though greenstone, the hardest known cutting substance, belonged to this class.

While an axe is ground down evenly on each side of the cutting edge, a Maori adze has a steeper bevel on one side than on the other. Some adzes are reduced or shaped above (i.e. at the opposite end to the blade). This facilitates binding to the wooden handle, and such adzes are described as tanged. The majority of adzes are untanged, and when bound to their wooden handle, rely on their slightly pyramidal ends to make the lashing fast. In use every blow makes the adze tighten in its handle. An adze is never used over the shoulder but always directly in front of the body. If used otherwise it fractures, or a rapid blunting of the stone edge is soon apparent.

Classification

The first classification of adzes was made by Elsdon Best as early as 1912.* He stated: "In cross section Maori adzes may be: 1. rectangular, as oblong or almost square; 2. ovoid; 3. triangular; 4.  shaped. Any other sectional form is abnormal, such as diamond-shaped and several others that will be alluded to." We regard 1 and 4 as quadrangular, and must recognise an additional group circular in section to be quite a small one. Best notes (page 210) that some adzes derive their ovoid cross section from the water-worn stones of which they were made.

Adzes may be classified into families based on the type of section seen about the middle of the length. There are five basic families: 1. those with an upright triangular or near-triangular section; 2. those quadrangular in section; 3. those with an inverted triangular section; 4. those with an ovoid section; and 5. those with a circular or near-circular section.

Inside the families, there are many variations in general shape and form, which would ultimately correspond to the genera and species of the biological world.

The upper extremity of an adze head is the

*_The Stone Implements of the Maori_, Dominion Museum Bulletin, No. 4, 1912, p. 204.

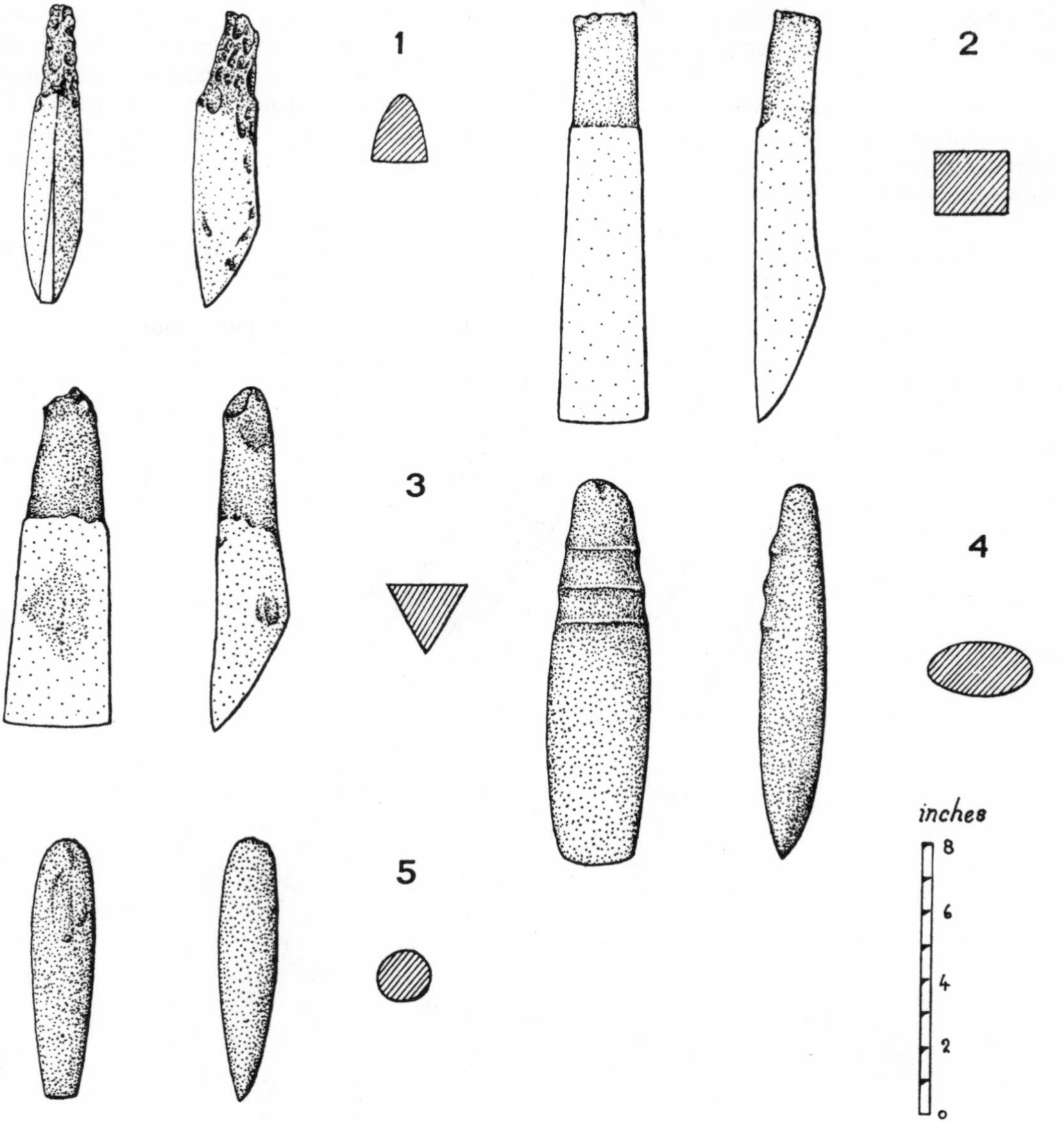

88. Adzes. Family 1, no locality. Family 2, Te Kuiti. Family 3, D'Urville Island. Family 4, Killinchy, Canterbury. Family 5, Waikato. (Mackie Collection.)

poll. That part which is lashed to the haft is the butt and the lower portion is the blade. The front and sides of the butt or perhaps the sides alone may be reduced to form a better grip for the lashing.

The triangular or near-triangular sectioned adze is often termed "hog-back" by many because of its characteristic shape. Adzes of this description have a narrow, strongly supported cutting edge. They belong in the main to the Moa-hunter period of Maori culture. The quadrangular or near-quadrangular form is perhaps the most common of all adzes. In the Pacific it is found in many places from the coasts of Formosa to as far distant as Chile, but perhaps nowhere so abundantly as in New Zealand. Adzes with an inverted triangular section are on the whole comparatively rare. It would appear probable that this adze was first made in New Zealand by immigrants from the Cook Islands, where this family is well recognised. Adzes circular in section are uncommon.

As far back as 1928 we recorded* a stone adze nearly circular in section, taken from the neighbourhood of Pahiatua. At the time we realised the importance of such a discovery. Years later, when it was possible to examine the Captain Bollons Collection of greenstone carving chisels, we found many southern specimens circular in section.

North Island chisels are often quadrangular to ovoid. South Island tools sometimes have

*_Journal of the Polynesian Society_, Vol. 37, p. 241 (W.J.P).

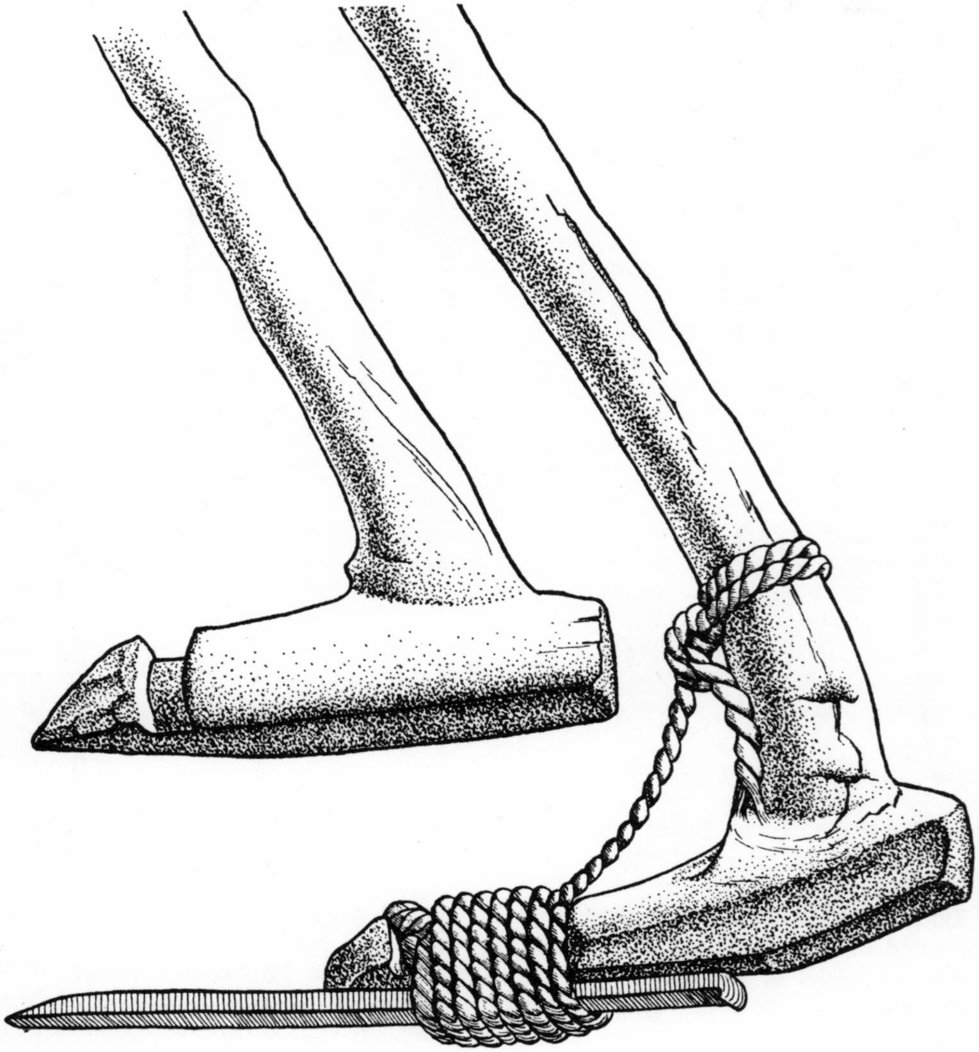

89. Toki; hafted iron blade, and a toki handle.

the blade end bevelled longitudinally. This refers in particular to greenstone carving chisels and some greenstone adzes.

Handle and Blade

The complete adze (toki) ordinarily consists of two parts, a wooden handle and a shaped stone or greenstone cutting implement. The handle or kakau was carefully chosen from the branch of a durable timber tree such as manuka. The illustration shows a section of a trunk of a tree with the branch running upwards at the correct angle, and the future "foot" of the handle already outlined on the trunk.

The ancient Maori workman, like his Pakeha brethren of today, found that his cutting tools, particularly adzes, were constantly in need of sharpening, so blocks of sandstone with a quantity of water became essential to the artisan. If the sandstone block was near a running stream, so much the better. Such stone might also be called into use for the manufacture of various bone artefacts and for smoothing down all sorts of rough surfaces.

When iron arrived with the early voyagers and traders, it was immediately utilised to replace stone and greenstone adzes. The iron blade was prepared wider below than above, being bound to the handle with the bevelled surface on its inner side after the manner of a stone adze. All adzes are so attached to the handle that they become tightly inserted in the binding after continuous use. Many carving chisels were hafted lengthwise, the handle being used in the hand and struck at intervals by a bone or wooden mallet.

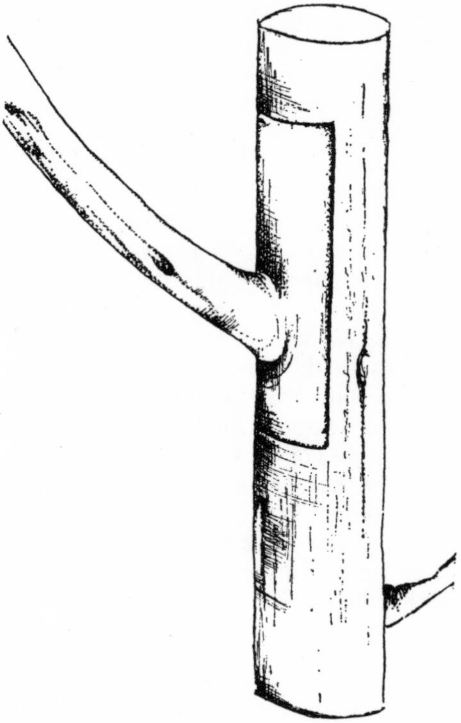

90. Section of tree trunk illustrating method of securing handles for stone toki.

When a patu was broken in a fight, the handle part was sharpened and used as an adze or perhaps as an axe. Two of these are in the Dominion Museum. Adzes were sometimes used in a longitudinal manner.

14

GREENSTONE AND THE DRILL

Greenstone

Greenstone or pounamu was the hardest as well as the most valuable and useful stone known to the Maoris. It probably came into general use something over 1,000 years ago. It appears certain that early waves of Polynesian settlers to these shores did not know of it (as in the case of the Wairau Polynesians). Legend has it that a thousand or more years ago, when Kupe and Ngahue visited New Zealand on their voyage of exploration, they discovered greenstone on the west coast of the South Island. This is probably another way of stating that they visited the west coast and were shown the Arahura River, from which greenstone boulders were taken. Legend further states that these voyagers took greenstone back to their island home, and from this, adzes and chisels were manufactured which at a later date were used in the building of the canoes Arawa and Tainui. If this was so, one incentive to the great migration may have been to visit a land where greenstone was available for their tools and ornaments. Tregear tells us: "Greenstone boulders found in the river beds were broken up and the pieces roughly bruised into shape. To insure against cracks, a deep groove was cut before breaking off, and a stone hammer, tukituki, was then used, sometimes fitted with a wooden handle, sometimes held in the hand. Thin pieces of quartzose slate were worked saw-fashion with plenty of water till a furrow was made first on one side and then on the other."

Manufacture

In a letter from James W. Stack to Dr Von Haast (dated 22 October 1882) notes on the manufacture of greenstone supplies by the chief Ato o Tu are appended. The tools used in the manufacture of greenstone were:

1. *Kuru pohatu.* Stone hammer, being nothing more than a round boulder of cross-grained greenstone, about the size of a human skull. This was for breaking off rough pieces from blocks which had been carried across the Alpine ranges on men's backs to the places of manufacture on the east coast. To ensure a straight fracture a groove was cut first.
2. *Parihi-pohatu.* A sharp-edged chip of trap, or some other hard stone. This was worked backwards and forwards to cut the groove.
3. *Hoanga.* Grindstone. Any sort of gritty sandstone for rubbing down the rough surface.
4. *Kurupaka.* A micaceous stone, plentiful on the west coast beaches, used for cutting grooves.
5. *Mata.* Obsidian for pointing the drill or pirori.

The natives in Canterbury procured the grindstones from the upper end of Lyttelton Harbour, in the immediate vicinity of Quail Island.

The manufacture of greenstone was the favourite employment of the old chiefs, who worked day and night at their monotonous task. During the day they carried the stone to their taumata or favourite seat on the top of some neighbouring hillock, where they passed the day rubbing the grindstone backwards and forwards across the surface of the greenstone block, the only relaxation being derived from watching from their look-out for the arrival of strangers. After grinding all day on the taumata, an industrious chief would carry his work back to his house, propping himself up against the wall lest he should be tempted to recline and so lose too much time in rest. When overcome by sleep he would still retain his hold of the grindstone, and starting up at intervals during the night with a peculiar grunt would renew his self-imposed task. By dint of incessant labour a mere might be completed in about twelve months, but if the stone was very hard it took much longer.

There were no religious ceremonies connected with the manufacture of greenstone, beyond those relating to its discovery in the first instance. It was the article of supreme value amongst the Maoris and became, shortly before the colonisation of the country, the principal medium of exchange.

Various records of Maori types of greenstone have appeared. These vary greatly. One list of the main kinds published in 1909 is as follows:*

Kawakawa: green of various shades, often full of small black spots and secretions, clouded and streaked or dense and opaque. . . . Almost exclusively used by the lapidary and jeweller.

Inanga: pale green and highly translucent. . . . Occurs usually in streaks and veins running through kawakawa, giving a handsome variegated appearance to the specimen. The most highly prized variety.

Auhunga: somewhat opaque, with the green colour of kawakawa.

Totoweka: a variety of kawakawa containing stains and streaks of red iron oxide.

Rau-karaka: an olive-coloured streaked or cloudy variety, often with a yellowish tinge. The essential pigment of the mineral appears to be ferrous silicate. . . . Thickly clouded and variegated specimens, exhibiting various shades of green show corresponding irregularity in the percentage of ferrous oxide.

The following list was made later this century and is of interest for comparison. Mr R. Gillespie was a man of considerable stature. For many years of his life he lived alone, always hoping and indeed knowing that gold was to be found on the Twelve-Mile Beach, Greymouth. But one day his doctor warned him that he must no more tramp West Coast beaches in search of that ever-elusive metal. So he came to Wellington and to the Dominion Museum. He said that often when gold eluded him he would search for greenstone. He had questioned many Maoris over the years and had a small,

*A. M. Findlayson, *Journal Geological Society*, London.

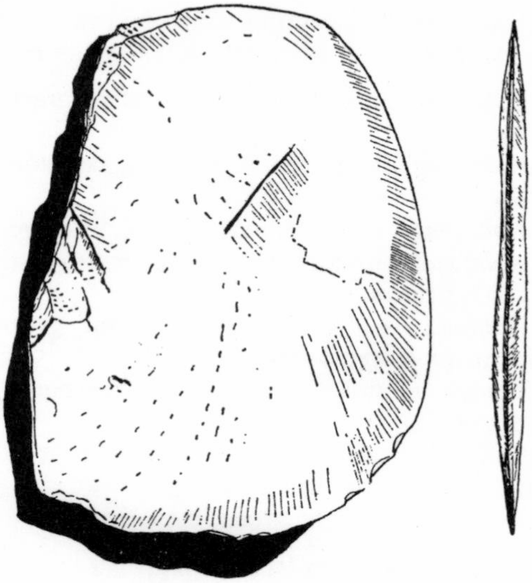

92. Face and side views of a slate cutter from the Nuggets, Otago (Bollons Collection).

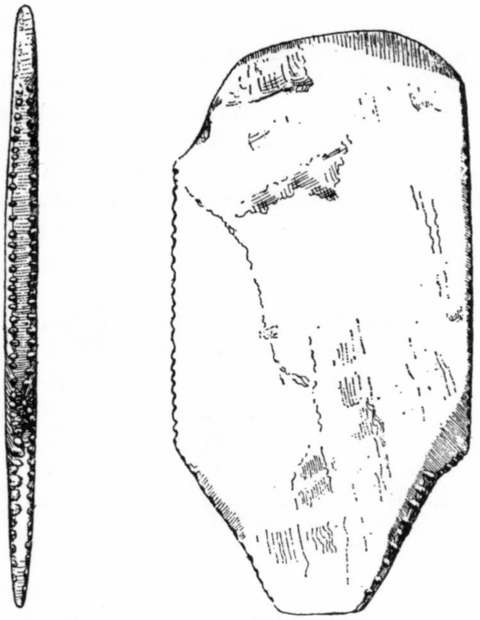

91. Greenstone cutter, front and side views.

typical, named collection which he presented to the Dominion Museum. Here is his list:

Aotea: a close-grained, dark olive greenstone.

Kahurangi: semi-transparent with a clouded effect.

Kokotangiwai: a transparent bright green.

Auhunga: close-grained, dark green, with reddish streaks.

Kahotea: semi-transparent, bright green with black irregular spots.

Inanga: light-coloured, semi-transparent and soft.

Totoweka: dark green, heavily mottled with areas of reddish and white.

Kawakawa: bright green, close-grained.

A material similar in appearance to greenstone, but known to the geologists as bowenite and to the Maori as tangiwai, is widely used in the same manner as greenstone. Some pieces are quite translucent while others show the characteristic yellow-brown colouration. Bowenite is a softer material than greenstone.

Mr G. N. T. Goldie of Wellington has made a number of experiments in the cutting and drilling of greenstone. He found that his first difficulty was to get started. In drilling with a wooden point, using sand and water, the sand became imbedded in the wood and the wooden point quickly wore out. It would be of interest to ascertain whether this would be so with hard timbers such as maire. In cutting the groove, the greatest difficulty was experienced in keeping the sand in the groove, and he ascertained that moderate pressure gave a good result and enabled the operator to control the grinding elements to the best advantage. Chapman* mentions that a great deal of cutting was done with wood and wetted sand. This was confirmed by Dr Shortland, who also supplies us with the term mania for "the thin laminae of sandstone used for cutting the pounamu". To commence the operation it is probable that a piece of perforated wood fixed over the spot would hold the drill in position as long as it was required.

Transactions of the N.Z. Institute, 24, 1892, p. 498.

Stone or greenstone cutters used in sawing are not very common in collections. This is possibly because of the abundant supplies of sandstone available. Also it is probable that most cutters would have been overlooked by collectors, for there would be little about them immediately to distinguish them from other flattened stones.

Drills

An old Urenui Maori narrated to J. F. Scott, Dannevirke, the ancient manner of cutting greenstone in his district. The block to be cut was firmly pegged down on the grass. Two pegs were put in alignment on each side of the greenstone to act as guides for the cutting process. The actual cutter was a plaited muka cord, used in conjunction with sand and water which act as an abrasive. There were several workers on each end of the muka cord and they chanted as they worked. The cord was merely the carrier of the abrasive and curiously enough was said not to wear out as quickly as might be expected. Slow motion was the rule. When iron became available, an iron cutter with sand and water was used in many parts of the North Island.

In regard to the manufacture of greenstone tiki, where a carving technique is used, Chapman states that the shell of the common pipi (cockle), was said to have been commonly employed. Examination of the perfect eye sockets of some tiki seems to indicate that some cylindrical drill such as a cut long bone or a supple-jack rod end was used with wet sand in a rotary manner. The finer points

93. Head of a drill inserted in a cup-shaped depression on the under-surface of the crossbar (after John White sketch).

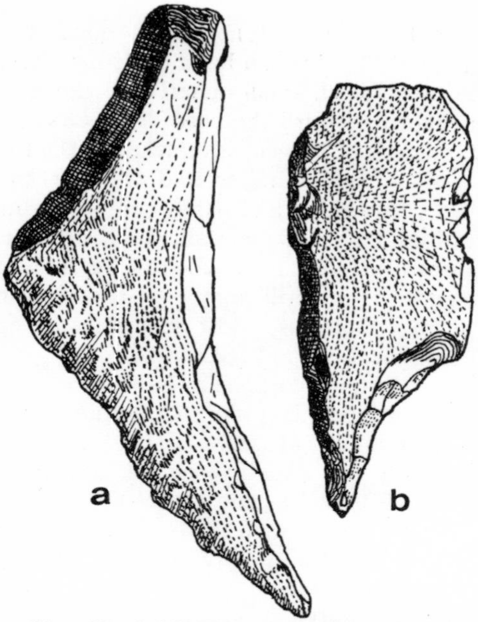

94. a. Hand drill Nelson (Lukin's Collection).
b. Hand drill, Greville Harbour (Bollons Collection).

we may never know. The possibility of the Maoris or Moa-hunter people using some sort of lathe akin to the primitive Indian lathe cannot altogether be ruled out, for some of the stone and bone reel ornaments may have been fashioned in some such manner.

We are indebted to the South Island explorer Heaphy* for his account of the cutting and drilling of greenstone. First of all a piece of greenstone of the correct shape is secured and a stock of thin pieces of a sharp "quartzose slate". The slate is used edgewise to cut the greenstone. Plenty of water is used and a groove made first on one side then on the other until the piece may be broken at a thin place. With fairly constant work, a man will get a slab into a rough triangular shape, and about an inch and a half thick in a month, and with the aid of some blocks of sharp sandy gritted limestone will work down the faces and edges of it into proper shape in six weeks more.

And now comes the difficult part of the work, to drill a hole for the thong for the handle. For this, sharp pieces of flint from

*_N.Z. Monthly Magazine_ of October and November, 1862.

95. A drill in the Auckland Museum. Length nearly 33 inches.

the Pahutani cliff, forty miles north of Taramakau, were secured and lashed to the end of a split stick. The stick measured up to eighteen inches and became the spindle of the drill. A circular bone plate (the hardened epiphysis of the centrum of a whale's vertebra), was then taken and a hole made to the correct size with the stick thrust through. Two strings are then attached to the upper end of the stick and by pulling them alternately a rapid motion is given to the drill. Once an indentation is made in the greenstone the rest is easy. As each flint becomes blunted it is replaced by another in the stick. The circular bone plate here mentioned is rarely recorded as being used in the North Island, but an interesting method of drilling was recorded in the John White MS., where the drill is supported by a frame (see page 98). This method seems very reasonable.

The cord drill was used by the Maori to drill holes in greenstone, stone, bone, and perhaps shell, although hand drills may have been used for all small materials. Known to the Maoris as tuiri, the cord drill works on the principle of two cords attached to the top of a shaft, being first wound together and pulled outwards alternately in opposite directions. Balance is maintained with practice. A stone drill point is attached to the base of the shaft. These drill points are common in museum collections, most specimens being from middens around the coasts.

Much drilling was done by hand. Two such drills from the E. H. Lukins Collection are in the Dominion Museum. They measure respectively just over five inches, and three and three-fifth inches, and are readily adapted for use by hand. Such drills would require regular re-sharpening, and constant rubbing with sandstone files dipped in water would become necessary.

15

MAORI WEAPONS

WEAPONS WERE MADE of wood, bone or stone. The Maori warrior was trained in their use from his boyhood upwards. When old enough to accompany the taua (war expedition), he chose for himself the type of weapon he preferred. Weapons may be classified into two groups, long weapons and short weapons. We deal first with the long weapons which were the taiaha, pouwhenua, spear, tewhatewha, and hoeroa. Of these the most highly prized was the taiaha, which consisted of a light wooden shaft usually about six feet long, blunted at one end and pointed at the other. The blunted end was slightly heavier, and the pointed end consisted of a carved face with a long tongue out-thrust forming the point.

Taiaha

In using the taiaha, feints and passes were employed. In discussing weapons, Elsdon Best used to mention the importance of footwork and related a tale which had been told to him by an old Maori. It was to the effect that in man-to-man combat the neophyte was so trained that one eye must always watch his opponent's big toe on the right foot. For a fraction of a second before he delivered a fatal blow, the opponent would tend to grip the ground with this toe. It was then that movement out from under the stroke became essential.

The most attractive feature of the taiaha was the protuding tongue figure carved at one end. The protruding tongue showed defiance. A favourite feint with the taiaha was to poke an enemy somewhere about the middle of his body with the pointed tongue and then, while he winced, bring the other end in overhand fashion on the top of his skull.

Pouwhenua

The pouwhenua resembled the taiaha in the rau or blade portion, but the carved face was

96. The tewhatewha in a posture of the war dance or tutu ngarahu, Tauranga, 1865 (after Robley).

replaced by a plain, blunt point. Most pouwhenua have a carved band or ridge around the shaft. Like the taiaha, the pouwhenua was used in both hands and in much the same manner. Both taiaha and pouwhenua were highly polished or slightly greased so that they would slip easily through the hands.

Tao

The ordinary and most widely used spear was a slim form termed tao, which was usually from seven to nine feet long. The spear or tao was pointed at one end only. If pointed at both ends it was termed koikoi, but names varied with locality. Sometimes spears were used as striking weapons. A very long spear

97. Taiaha carved ends (Bollons Collection).

was known as huata, and was used in defending villages, fortified or not. Sometimes important spears were highly notched at the pointed end and even ornamented with a carved figure.

Tewhatewha

The tewhatewha was said usually to have been fashioned from the root of a maire tree the wood of which was found to be very hard. One end was pointed, and at the other was a blade. Suspended from the blade was a bunch of split hawk feathers. A favourite trick of the fighter was to flick the bunch of feathers in an opponent's eyes, and while he recoiled to poke him with the sharpened end; by reversing arms, to use the back of the blade to advantage on the opponent's head.

Hoeroa

The hoeroa was a long thin curved weapon made from the lower jaw of a sperm whale. Hoeroa means, literally, a long paddle; but if manufactured for this purpose it would have had some sort of hand grip. Synonymous names are tatu paraoa, huri taniwha, and paroa roa. Sir Peter Buck has told us that this weapon was used mainly in pursuit, and thrown with an underhand movement after the fleeing enemy. A long cord held the weapon attached to the left wrist of the pursuer, who could run on with undiminished speed. One of Cook's companions remarked on a wooden specimen of hoeroa, but none of these have been preserved.

Patu

We deal now with the short weapons which were made from the hard and tough woods of the forest, bones of marine mammals, and closely grained stones found in river beds and other places, including the much valued pounamu (greenstone). Strength of arm, wrist, and hand was required to wield these short weapons, most of which were nicely balanced with a well-formed handle and an enlarged though flattened body. The term patu is used in a general sense to apply to all types. The most valuable of all weapons was the patu pounamu or mere-

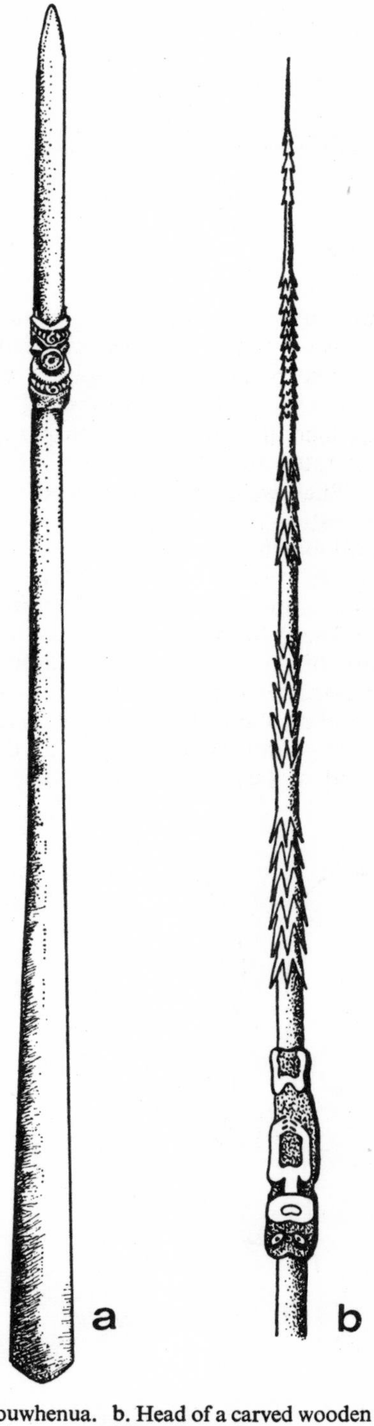

98. a. Pouwhenua. b. Head of a carved wooden spear. (After Angas.)

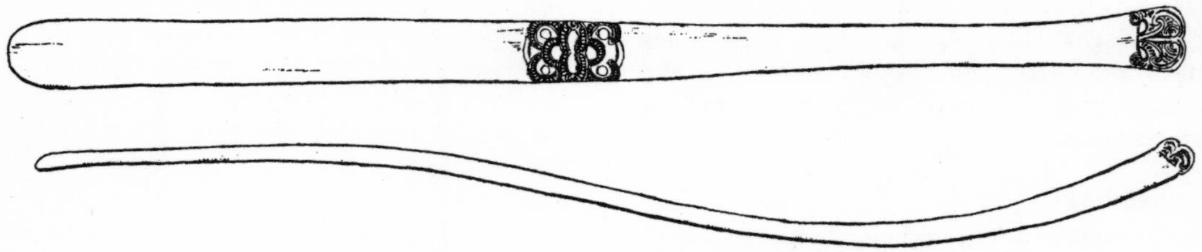

99. Hoeroa or tutu paraoa – weapon made from whalebone.

mere used by chiefs, not only in combat but also to give emphasis to a speech of importance. (These remarks may apply in varying degree to most Maori weapons.) Many valuable meremere were given proper names, and venerated by all members of the community. Such weapons were passed on from one generation to another.

Shaped like the meremere was another form made from argylite or greywacke, the patu onewa, a common weapon of which numbers may be found in museums. It was said that the blade of this weapon could readily make a downward or edgewise thrust, as well as being used as a shield. Like the meremere, a hole in the butt held a thong of dogskin (tau) used to suspend the weapon from the wrist of the user, and enabled the fighter to hold the weapon in combat.

Elsdon Best once related an account of the last mass-manufacture of patu onewa. A certain Maori chieftainess of high lineage who lived in Hawke's Bay in the 1890s became financially embarrassed and called together some of the wise men of the tribe. Two men who were expert artificers were first summoned, and it was agreed that with the help of a grindstone and other tools, a large number of patu onewa would be made and sold to unsuspecting Pakeha collectors. Helpers were assembled and all was carried out according to plan. The patu onewa are said to have been exact replicas of samples from the pre-Pakeha days. For a while the

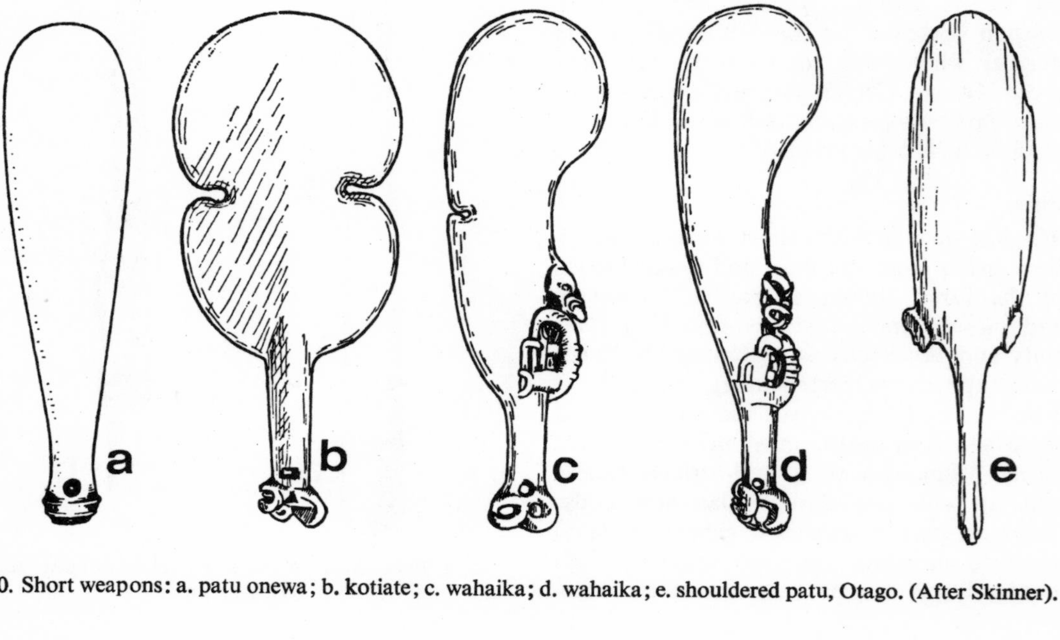

100. Short weapons: a. patu onewa; b. kotiate; c. wahaika; d. wahaika; e. shouldered patu, Otago. (After Skinner).

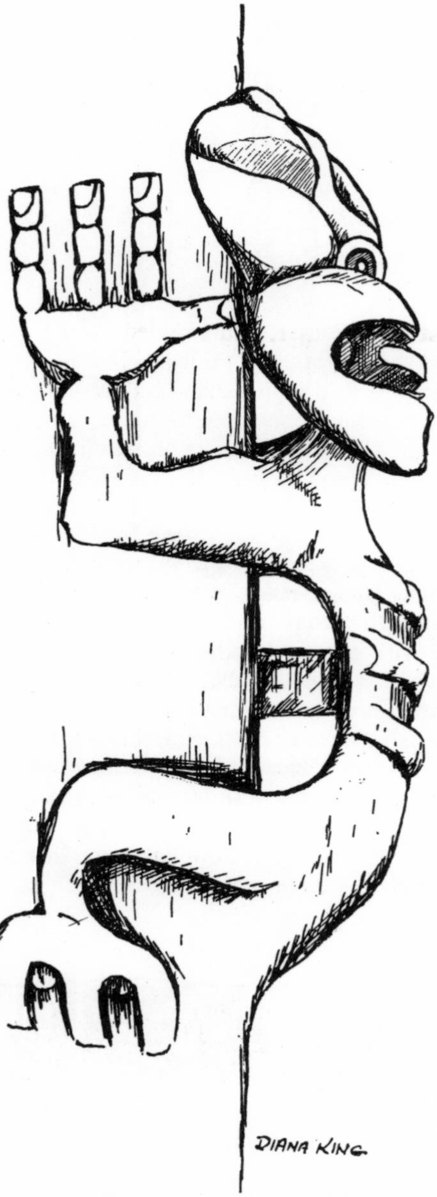

101. Figure carved in bone on a wahaika (Dominion Museum).

tribe and their chieftainess grew rich; but all good things come to an end, and the market was soon saturated. How many of these spurious patu onewa have found their way into museums we cannot now say.

The bone form of meremere was termed patu paraoa and was made from a bone of the sperm whale. Another two types of bone patu are the kotiate, of a peculiar lobate shape, and the wahaika, probably derived from the kotiate being lobed one side with a carved figure on the other. Both these weapons are light types which would be much used in ceremony and speech making. Wooden forms were partly ceremonial, being copies of bone and stone types. Some were made from a hard wood termed ake rautangi.

A rare weapon of which only a small number have been preserved is the toki pou tangata which is an adze or toki, often beautifully carved. A long greenstone blade is fitted in place of the usual stone blade. Prisoners captured in battle, knowing their inevitable end, might make a request that they be despatched with one of these weapons, which was used in exactly the same manner as any other toki.

Bow and Arrow

Most students have found so little evidence of the bow and arrow in New Zealand that few incline to believe it was ever used here. However, Herries Beattie* has something to say in support of the use of the bow and arrow in the south. If the bow and arrow was used by early populations of New Zealand, it is perhaps in the extreme south that we would expect to find evidence. Beattie tells us that in Riverton, Maoris used their paketehoroeka (lancewood bows) in play in the clear space in the bush and scrub at the mouth of the Aparima River. His informant was Kurupohatu, who stated that the use of small bows was a practice of Maori children right up to the time when the Pakeha came. It was a kind of play and they shot at birds in sport, but there was a time very long ago when men used bows in archery contests.

Though meagre, the evidence seems to indicate that the bow and arrow may have been known to our early Moa-hunter people and later rejected by the Fleet immigrants. Incidentally, we may here mention that it has now been shown that the bow dug up at Mangapai, Northland, and now in the

*_The Morioris of the South Island_, 1941, p. 47.

Dominion Museum, is not made of any native New Zealand wood. A small sample was submitted to Mr J. S. Reid, Forestry Department, for detailed study and the reply was that it was not of titoki as suggested, nor any other known timber.

Tete

In northern parts of New Zealand a wooden dagger, termed tete in Waikato and oka further north, was used in warfare, but this usage was not very common elsewhere, though a stone dagger, now in Otago Museum comes from Central Otago. Gudgeon mentions an old chief known as Nga Tokowaru who carried a bone dagger. When captured in warfare, in a desperate struggle, he drew the dagger and stabbed Te Putu, chief of his captors. Then he quickly smeared the blood of Te Putu over his head and body, thus making his body tapu and saving it from the degradation of the oven.

102. Stone dagger from the Nevis, Central Otago (after Philip George). Now in Otago Museum.

Modern Weapons

With the European traders in flax came new weapons of war: trade axes and flint-lock guns, and the old triangular bayonets used later as spear points. Trade axes had no handles, so the Maoris made their own handles and fitted on the iron heads. Thus were established two new types of weapon, one with a long handle, the kakauroa, and one with a short handle, the tomahawk called patiti. These were much sought after.

Small spears or darts were thrown over-arm into pa, or when a body of men were assembled with war-like intentions, the throwing spear being termed kotaha. We are unable to state just how common this form of warfare was in past days.

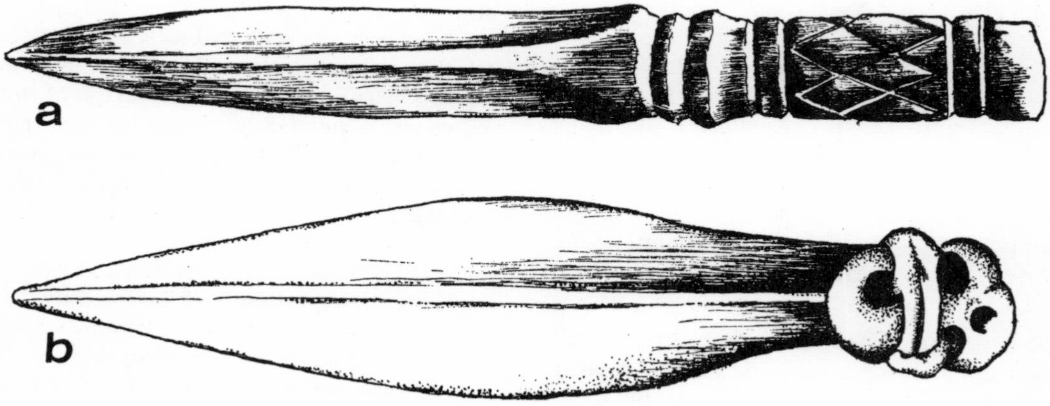

103. Two wooden daggers, tete, or oka: a. Waikato district; b. Tuhua near Taumarunui. (After Best and Angas.)

16

CANOES AND CANOE TRAVELLING

BEFORE THE COMING of the Pakeha there were well-known bush tracks, often crossing mountain ranges. Sometimes there were trails over lonely waste land, lines being defined only by the natural features of the landscape. There were the well-defined tracks around coastal areas and rocky headlands, usually including long stretches of sandy beach. But because New Zealand was a land of many rivers, there was always the problem of river crossings. They were often made by a party using a long log or branch from a nearby tree, with several holding on to the log with their hands and walking across. If one member of the group came to deep water he would be helped by the others. But if rivers were swollen by rains, or a large river had to be crossed, it was necessary to utilise rafts or canoes.

Rafts

Two main types of raft were used, these being quickly and readily made. In the first instance a number of logs were laid parallel, and firmly lashed together by means of short cross logs underneath. Longer logs were lashed above extending outwards and, at some little distance from the original raft, lashed to a much smaller log bundle. The main raft was termed mokihi, and the smaller balancing raft became the ama-tiatia or outrigger. This raft was recorded on the east coast of the North Island. Another type of craft was made from raupo lashed into bundles and tied together, sometimes in the form of a boat. The raupo raft seems to have been the most simple and common type of raft formerly used in New Zealand and has been recorded from both islands.

Building Canoes

The work entailed in the production of a superior Maori canoe demanded considerable effort on the part of many people. Women would attend to everyday affairs while the men were absent engaged in one or another of the various tasks involved. First the tohunga lifted the ban of tapu on the forest, and Tane was propitiated with appropriate ritual, for to the Maori all objects around him were endowed with life. The selected tree was struck with a leaf, held in position in a flax flower-stalk, while the tohunga ceaselessly intoned the correct karakia. Later, chips were cut off and burnt in a sacred fire. During the day no food was eaten and workers remained under the ban of tapu.

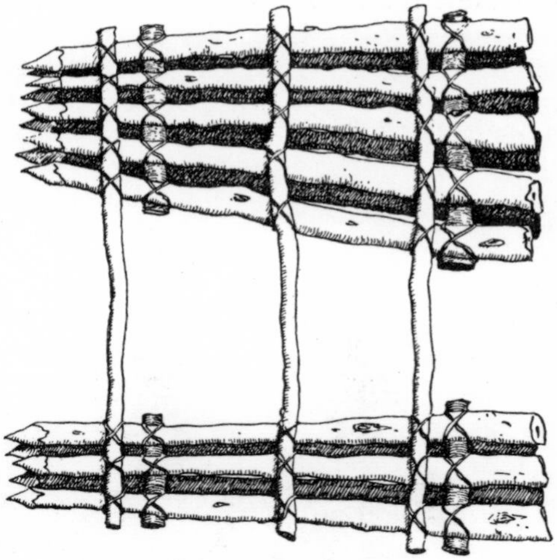

104. Log raft, East Coast (after Best).

Totara was the tree usually chosen for canoes. Sometimes trees were selected long before the actual felling commenced. The bark with a portion of the trunk of the east side was mitilated to cause decay and to facilitate future work, including the hollowing-out process. Sometimes fire assisted the

105. Raupo raft or mokihi (after Best).

workers in the work of felling, but most depended on the men with their stone adzes, who gradually made a V-shaped incision into the base of the tree. Relays of workers were employed. In this way all the daylight hours could be utilised. After the tree was felled came the lopping off of side branches and the hollowing process. Again, fire was used to make the work easier. Women were not allowed near the tree until the hollowing-out had been completed.

Double Canoes

The double canoe appears to have been used

106. Double canoes in Otago Harbour (after D'Urville).

in the South Island up until the time of the whalers and organised settlement. A double canoe would give stability to a vessel in rough seas. It would allow the use of a raised platform, and demand less finish on either of the attached canoes. It is of interest to note that the prows of the canoes in the illustration appear somewhat to resemble the heads of birds. A rauawa or top-side gives greater depth.

A remarkable canoe was dug out of swampy ground at Strath Taieri, Otago, in 1891, and is now in the Otago Museum. Near by was another and apparently similar canoe, seeming to indicate that this canoe, which was a well-hollowed log, was one of a pair and lashed to another similarly hollowed log. The most curious feature of the canoe in the Otago Museum is the manner in which the sides curve over to cover the central portion. The canoe is about twenty-three feet long. Holes on the top-sides may indicate points of attachment to its neighbour.

The vessels that came hither from Eastern Polynesia were by no means of huge size; in fact they were not so large as many that have been made and used on these shores. The outrigger that has been quite abandoned since Cook was here was essentially the salvation of the deep-sea vessels of the Maori.* Best speaks of the narrow proa-shaped vessel as being the one in common use in Cook's time.† Proa is a Malay term for a narrow vessel found as far away as the Caroline Islands. The large war canoes used in New Zealand when the first settlers came here were of a class evolved in this country and Cook remarks that some of these large canoes would carry sixty, eighty, or a hundred people. So the canoe from Otago may have been one of the early proa types – perhaps resembling some of the narrow outrigger canoes of Melanesia, in which the hold is so narrow that an occupant has to place one foot in front of the other.

The double outrigger was possibly used in New Zealand, for Best tells us that reference

*Best, *Canterbury Times*, 22.7.14.
†See also *Dominion Museum Records* in Ethnology, Vol. 1, fig. 61 (W.J.P.).

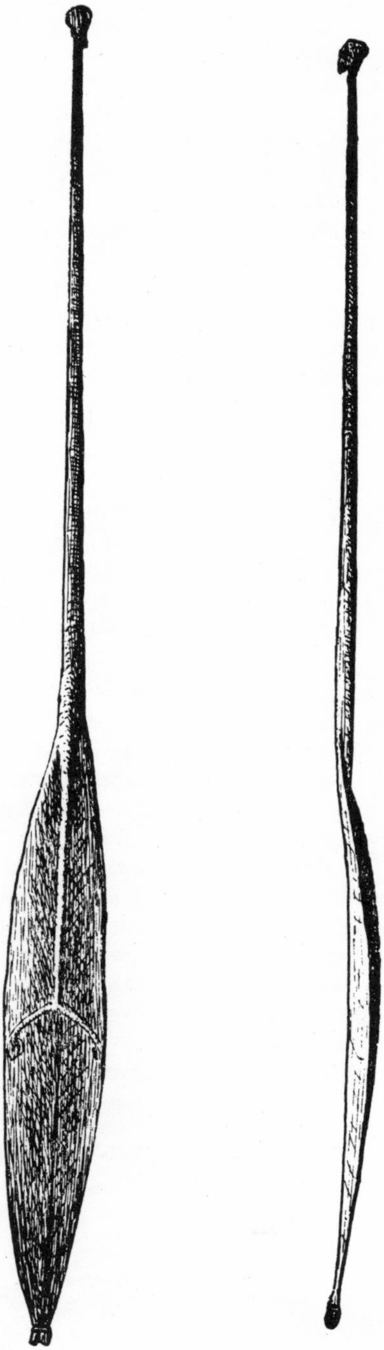

107. Taranaki paddle, said to have been from Aotea canoe (after Best).

to the double outrigger, one on each side of the vessel, is noted in the traditional account of the Takitimu canoe. The Canterbury Museum is fortunate in possessing an old outrigger. This came from Monck's Cave, Sumner. Recently another outrigger has been found near Wellington and is in the Dominion Museum.

Parkinson, writing on Cook's first voyage, states that when passing Te Mahia some canoes with outriggers were seen, and remarks: "Several of the canoes had outriggers and one of them had a very curious piece of ornamental carving at the head of it."

Paddles

Paddles were known to the Maori as hoe. They were manufactured chiefly from manuka, though some were of matai or maire. They were light and slim, yet able to withstand the strain of constant use in the water. A noticeable feature of most Maori paddles was a thickening near the lower tip. This prevented breakage and splitting of the blade. The paddles were neatly made, and rather slender in outline. In large canoes the paddlers would sit on the thwarts, but in the smaller canoes, which far outnumbered the large ones, they knelt on the floor. Paddles were usually some four or five feet long. Those used for steering were longer, about twice the length of the ordinary ones. The steering paddle often required two men to manipulate its movements. The canoe was never sailed directly into the wind and waves, but was kept always obliquely forward for fear of being swamped.

We supply a study of carved paddle heads which may be of interest. Nos. 1 and 2 are Taranaki types of unusual character, in that 1 is lugged and 2 is pointed above in Taranaki style. Nos. 3, 4 and 5 are Wanganui types, while the locality of No. 6 is uncertain, though it appears to be an East Coast type from north of Hawke's Bay. Nos. 7, 8 and 9 are all East Coast types carved in manaia style in taratara o kai adornment. In general, No. 1 appears most closely to approximate the old Polynesian rendering of the human face. Nos. 2 and 4 are elongate and related in the type of upper lip and tongue. No. 3 is a stereotyped carved head with the use of S-curve spirals, while No. 5 is much more realistic than one would expect to find and may be modern. No. 6 is highly conventional with a tongue and no sign of chin, and is ornamented with three-sided notches in the ridges.

Sails

In some Maori canoes a lateen sail of triangular shape was used. It was held in position by means of ropes tied to the thwarts, and manipulated according to changes in the wind. An old sail, presumably collected by Captain Cook, is in the British Museum. It is made of raw flax strips slightly scraped. Attached to the sail are a number of strong loops and also an appendage known as matai-rangi which flies out like a streamer or flag as the canoe moves. The loops are for attachment to side poles.

Bailers

In large canoes fitted with a deck or floor of manuka rods, one or two openings termed

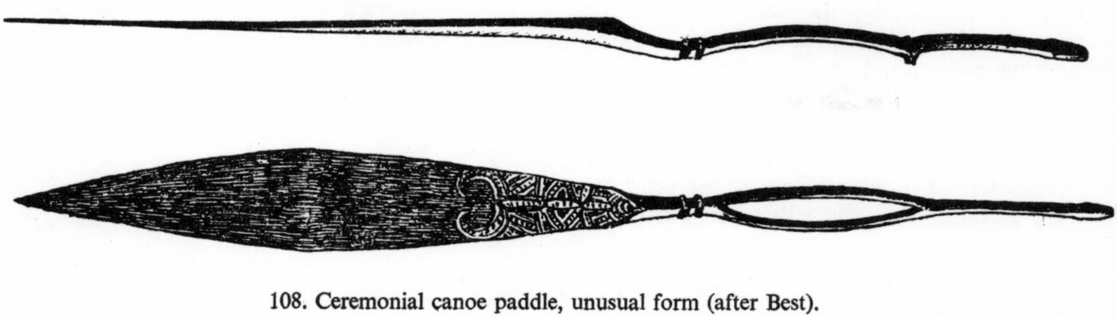

108. Ceremonial canoe paddle, unusual form (after Best).

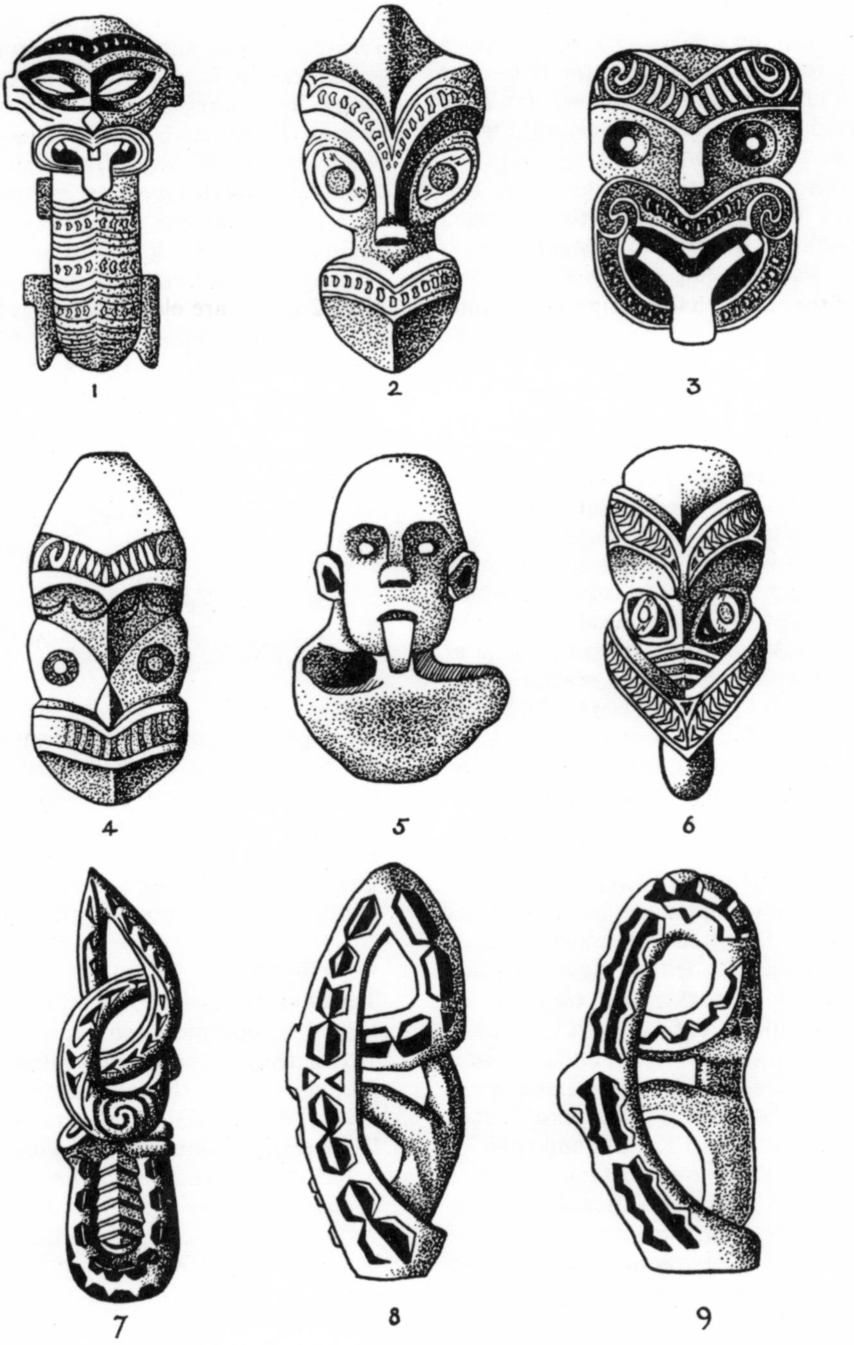

109. Carved paddle heads (Dominion Museum).

puna wai were left so that bailing operations might be carried out. The Maori bailer was of a flattened spoon shape with a handle above projecting forwards in the centre line. This prevented undue strain on the wrist during long periods of continuous bailing when rough seas were encountered. Each puna wai had its own attendant, and sometimes two men would be employed alternately. During the work charms were constantly repeated to cause fine weather and ensure a successful voyage.

Anchors

Mooring stones or mooring trees on the seashore have always been highly regarded and generally given proper names. Te Punga o Matahorua is a land anchor or mooring stone of a large canoe from the beach at Paremata, at the entrance to Porirua Harbour. Tradition has it that this great anchor stone once belonged to the Matahorua canoe in which Kupe journeyed to New Zealand. When soldiers under Major Long were stationed at Paremata, one of them broke several pieces off the anchor and greatly annoyed the Maori inhabitants. Shortly afterwards some of the soldiers were drowned in the harbour by the capsizing of a boat. This was naturally regarded by the Maoris as the direct result of tampering with a tapu object.

As further damage was being done to the stone, the Maoris later consented to its removal to the Dominion Museum where it may still be seen, but neither Ngati Toa nor Ngati Raukawa have ever laid claim to Te Punga o Matahorua, even though it is theirs by right of conquest. As explained by Mrs Te Ua Kotua of Nelson, descended from Werawera, the father of Te Rauparaha, it is still "the mana of Ngati Kahungunu tribe".

The mooring stone was so tapu that it is said to have left behind it a sacred influence which haunts Porirua Harbour. No Pakeha can see it, but Mrs Kotua said that by floating in one spot on the harbour, the wraith of Kupe's mooring stone foretells the death of one who is aged, whereas if the stone glides along the shore or on the surface, someone younger is due to pass from mortal ken.

War Canoes

The Maori war canoe, as seen by early visitors to our shores, was a vessel of grace and beauty. In size it was about sixty feet long and carried about eighty men, all, except a few high chiefs, armed with long paddles which were rhythmically dipped according to the chant of a fugleman. When not in use the war canoe was carefully dismantled and the hull and its several parts stored in a beach shed. Side boards (rauawa) were specially carved and were re-lashed as required, the most common lashing being the aerial roots of keikie. To tighten the lashing, a two-pronged implement termed tanekaha was used to give the necessary

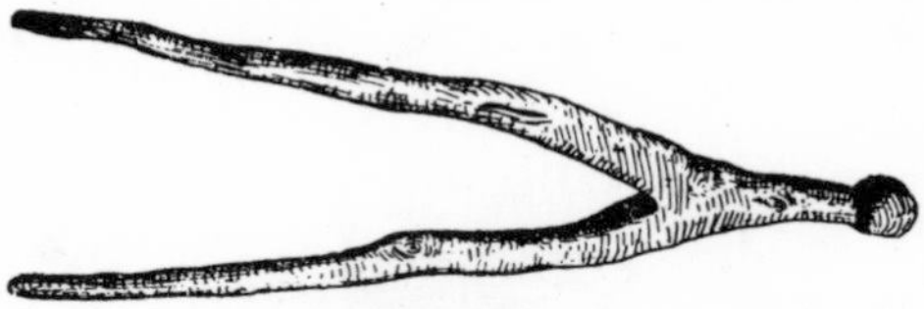

110. The tanekaha used to tighten lashings of the topstrake, rauawa, of a canoe (after Best).

leverage. The prow had always seemed to me to symbolise the desire for speed, while the taurapa was the embodiment of beauty. These were often adorned with hawk feathers, hawks being the predators of the land, while under the lashings on the side were albatross feathers, again symbolising speed.

Figureheads

The figurehead of a Maori war canoe, usually carved in one piece, embodied much of the artistic skill of the Maori craftsmen, and has become one of the outstanding features in collections of Maori art and workmanship. Generally, the tauihu (figurehead) was composed of a grotesque human figure in front, connected with a square rear end by a vertical, highly-carved portion, the whole being supported by a strong base carved on top and sides. It was secured to both the topstrakes of the canoe and to the two sides of the hull underneath by the usual method of lashing.

A second type of prow was also used in

some northern parts of New Zealand. Hari Wahanui of Waikato gave Mr Best the name tuere for this prow. From another unverified source we have torere for the prow or the central part of it while Mr Hare Hongi (H. Stowell) states that in the north of New Zealand the tauihu is called whakatei among Nga Puhi.

The tuere (which means we prefer) is remarkable as being almost identical with certain New Guinea types of today. It seems to have been disappearing just about the time that New Zealand was settled. It is even possible that this would be the type of prow used by certain of New Zealand's earliest Polynesian immigrants and adopted by later arrivals. Probably the better carved and more elaborate prows of this class are the result of the application of a higher type of decorative art to an already old and well-established structure. Below the upright centreboard in front of the tuere is a carved head known as parata or toiere.

Sternpieces

The sternpiece of a canoe known as rapa or taurapa was elaborately carved on the war canoe but plain on other canoes. The carved specimens were highly prized and all consisted of a series of scroll patterns with a strengthening rib running most of the length. Generally this strengthening midrib is the elongate body of a bird-like figure often seen in Maori carving, the manaia. "The taurapa is attached to the hull and to the ends of the topstrakes; and in war canoes a feather

111. Centreboard of northern form of canoe prow, tuere (after Best).

ornament termed the puhi ariki or puhi kai ariki is attached to the inner edge and top. From the top of the taurapa two long streamers or trails of feathers were attached. These are the puhi moana ariki and float in the air after the manner of a flag as the canoe moves. The puhi kai ariki pertain to the gods of the winds and the puhi moana ariki to the sea-gods who are the guardians of the vessel. Formerly the taurapa was anything up to twelve feet high; but such large examples are not now seen." (Best)

Ihi-ihi are the two long wands projecting forwards from the figurehead of a canoe and used as an adornment to the tauihu. The rods or wands are usually of manuka or tanekaha, and have small bunches of feathers tied to them at intervals. One account says that the patungaro, or ornamental design at the terminus of each wand, and the eyes of the canoe and are endowed with magical power.

Model Canoe

About the year 1928 an addition to the Dominion Museum of more than ordinary interest was a model of a Maori war canoe. It was no modern model of the old style of craft, but an old miniature canoe, complete in all its detail, and large enough to hold two men if required. The history of the canoe, why it was made, or for whom, does not seem to be known. Sometime in the 1840s it was acquired by a visiting warship and taken to England. After it had reposed in the Royal Naval Museum at Greenwich amongst the collection of model craft, the Admiralty offered it to the New Zealand Court at the Wembley Exhibition, and from there it came back to its native land. This model is twelve feet in length and eighteen inches broad in its widest part. It was made from a kauri log, and the topstrakes were carved with a very old snake-like Maori pattern of the rare unaunahi type. All the inside lashings are done in the approved Maori fashion. The carved prow (tauihu) is remarkable in the possession of wings rather than thrown back arms, perhaps symbolic of speed in the water. The high sternpiece (taurapa) is well made with typical scroll work. There is one feature of the construction of the canoe which shows that the old Maori had little to learn from the modern builders of speedboats. The under surface of the bow end of the canoe has been roughened into grooves, providing an air cushion which increased the speed of the craft through the water.

Plain Canoes

The plain, armless figurehead usually attached to a fishing canoe was called tete. Best tells use that these figureheads were permanently attached to the hull, not being removed when the vessel was laid up, as was the case with the waka taua or war canoe. The grotesque

112. Tauihu with projecting wands, ihi-ihi (after Best).

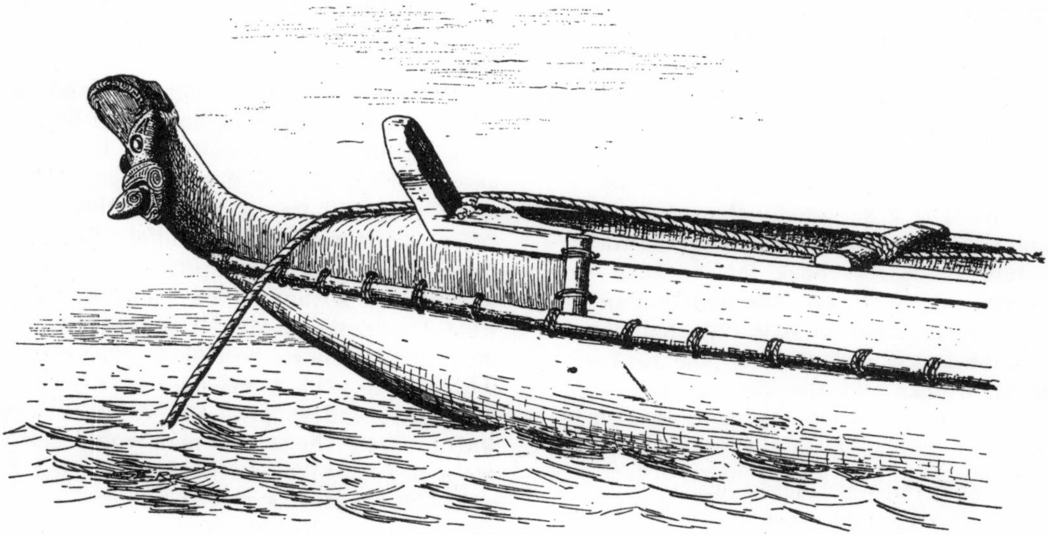

113. Fishing canoe prow, illustrating method of anchoring (after Best).

head with tongue out-thrust widens into a body, above which is a splash-board, while the sides approximate in height and are lashed at the back of the rauawa. Canoes used for everyday purposes, such as carriage of goods, trading, and fishing, were also usually adorned with a plain type of figure-head, such canoes being referred to as waka tete. The anchor was a large river stone well shaped and grooved around its circumference or alternatively with a hole drilled through a shaped upper portion.

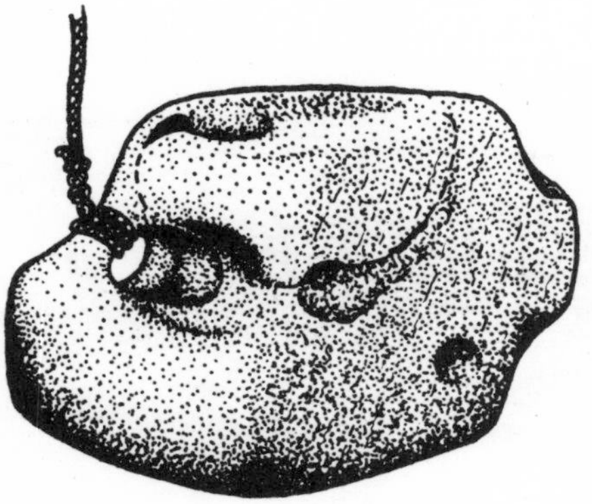

114. Mooring stone, Paremata (Dominion Museum).

A small canoe from the Waikato River, now in the Dominion Museum, illustrates the need for a light transport canoe, easily handled by one or two men. A remarkable feature of this canoe is that it has had the upper portion of what is probably the prow end removed as far back as halfway along its length. This would probably increase manoeuvreability in small streams, lightening the prow, and enabling loads to be piled in the stern portion. Two holes for lashing top-strakes (rauawa) remain near the upper margin of the stern half. The floor of the canoe is thicker forward, decreasing in strength towards the stern. The total length is twenty-two and a half feet and the depth is thirteen inches.

Poling Canoes

About the year 1930 the writer made enquiries at Hiruharama and Koriniti which tallied, and was thus enabled to get an account of the poling process on the Wanganui River then gradually becoming a thing of the past.

Originally poling was carried out under the direction of a chief whose place was in the stern. As a general rule there were only three men engaged in poling each canoe, but latterly as many as twelve participated. The polers were: bow man (Ko to te ihu); middle man (Ko to waenganui); stern man (Ko to te kei).

The pole was called toko. The crew came under the headman of one of the above divisions. The bow individual or party was required to keep a general lookout, to watch for sunken logs or rocks, and to keep the bow pointing upstream. The middle man or party was required to bale out should the canoe be leaky, and also to pole forward. The stern man did the steering and sang the poling song of encouragement which was in part:

> No wai waka nooku waka
> No nga mahaanga a Tute
> Kohirangi hia akiakina
> Te waaru e hoe waaka

Latterly this chant has been seldom used and present-day Maoris substitute "Akina kia rite" repeated over and over again. Holes in the bank and holes in the rock in the river were called rua toko and the following terms were used in the poling process: kia tika – straight ahead; tuteia – outward from bank; takapau – inward under the canoe; poua – to hold pole down whilst others prepare.

The banks are of papa formation, and only a few seams of shell-rock occur, but holes in the solid rock are seldom defined, the roughness of the rock giving enough grip. Holes rise for several feet in most localities, and different sets were used for different levels of the river. All the way upstream the eddies were taken advantage of, so that canoes were constantly passing from one bank to the other. Whenever possible a space allowed the poler to walk a few steps back with his push grip, and so push the vessel forward with his feet. The second man would always get a new grip before the first released his pole. The pole was placed as close to the canoe side as possible, and often under it, so as to maintain a straight direction. The pole usually bent with this push. A push any other way, naturally, would drive the canoe off its track.

The most valued poles were made from one of the tall straight species of ramarama. This wool is exceedingly tough, light, and quite durable, and will float if lost. Poles are also made from the kopua (white manuka),

115. Canoes on a raiding expedition (early Missionary publication).

but these poles tend to sink if lost. All poles were selected with care and usually cut green. A large fire was made, and bark and sharp points from smaller branches burnt off. This is a strengthening process. Burning off all the bark at once was called tahu, and burning a piece at a time was called tahutahu.

The big or root end was selected and sharpended. This was called the mata. If any irregularities existed in the poles, they were straightened by placing one end in a forked tree during the burning process and while the poles were still steaming bent into line. Poles were then taken to a cool place and left for a little over a week to allow the sap to dry out. It was essential that this locality be dry as well as cool, as dampness caused bends later. For this short account we are indebted to Messrs A. V. Waitford, T. W. Downes, and others.

Decrease in Numbers

Several factors have been responsible for the great recent decrease in the numbers of canoes on most North Island rivers. The clearing of the bush for settlement has often been responsible for sudden floods in waterways not previously subject to such conditions. On one river alone – the Wairoa in Hawke's Bay – an observer at the end of last century noted an amazing profusion of canoes large and small. Now nearly all have disappeared following disastrous floods. This may in part be due to neglect to safeguard canoes from such unusual conditions.

Another important aspect of the reduction in the numbers of canoes has been the replacement factor. As canoes became cracked, worn out or unusable, it was customary to build others, and the numbers were maintained. Wars, economic stress, and the sale of forest lands where suitable trees were available, have all played a part in the lack of replacement. The gradual availability of other transport facilities, such as the ownership of horses, has doubtless also played a large part in the discarding of canoes. Maori owners have fitted a few of their canoes with inboard engines as these became available from old motor cars. Even the fine old canoe in Wanganui Museum has at one time been so equipped. But this was a passing phase. We must mention one bright aspect of the subject, and that is the fact that Maori canoe racing on the Waikato river at Ngaruawahia has become an annual event.

17

MAORI CARVING

THE MAORI has a strong instinct for beauty, but that beauty is not necessarily in accordance with our conception. The art of the Maori is the expression of a people who never learned to write. It is the outpouring of an inner urge along definite lines. The Maori artisan does not copy, but exercises his originality inside definite limits – limits which he dare not pass if he would gain the respect and approval of his compeers. His carving art is essentially curvilinear, and in this differs from the art of the remainder of Polynesia. The majestic scenes of bush, lake, and mountain had no artistic appeal to the extent of reproducing them in painted design, but following in the conservative path laid down by his forbears, he limited his art to a number of features such as the human figure, a side-face figure (manaia), a peculiar being called marakihau, and a lizard, together with decorative designs consisting of a variety of patterns.

Ancestral Figures

Above everything else the Maori preferred to carve the human figure, naming figures after his own loved forbears. This preference was engendered by a deep ancestral reverence and a filial piety which seems to have been part of his Polynesian makeup. It was a deep sentimental regard of which we can have little understanding, for it included an awareness of the dead which is quite foreign to our own outlook. It is true that from his ancestors the Maori derived his name, his rights to land, forest and fishing, and all that made life worth while, and even modern carvers retain this old tradition.

For nearly 200 years, the Maori carver has had available to him tools of iron or steel with which to execute his work. The result of this has been that many larger and more profusely adorned pieces of carving have been produced, some for personal use on houses, food stores, canoes, etc., and others to sell to Europeans. Traditionally, carvers inherited their art in a direct line from their ancestors, and famous carving families were known and recognised in most large tribes. Such a family group was established at Lake Okataina during the last century and their productions became known as belonging to the Okataina school. One of the greatest of these was Anaha te Rahui who carved a series of established types, drawn by Sir Peter Buck from Dominion Museum photographs.*

The Maori carver displayed much ingenuity in his presentation of the human form. There was distortion of some sort and very often this distortion took an extreme measure of exhibitionalism, startling in its departure from the accepted standards of human sculpture, yet with a beauty and symmetry that demanded admiration. It was in the frenzy of the finale of the haka that the Maori warrior became a distorted though living being. The tongue was out-thrust to its limit, the eyes opened wide and rolled in their sockets and every muscle became taut with emotion. Probably it was from this that the early carvers derived their inspiration, for in what higher earthly state could they imagine their ancestors than in the tense agitation which came to all after the haka on the eve of battle.

However, there were other reasons why ancestral figures should be distorted. There were reasons of tapu, fear of the gods who made men perfect, conservatism, and a custom of distortion inside the established code. In distortion we notice the shortened limbs with hips and shoulders masked by spiral carving while the head was enlarged,

*Described in *Maori Carving*, 1941 (W.J.P.).

often with an open mouth and a tongue which reached down on to the body. Distortion arouses the emotions and the observer needs must take heed. Whether the carving portrays simply crude defiance or contempt, or whether traditional figures in curious posture assailed or protected by manaia claim our attention, there is strength and virility about all distortion; it is art calling for recognition by its own peculiar merit and demerit.*

Elsdon Best refused to theorise, but he did point out that on the northern burial chests, the arm of the man resembled a bird's wing to the Maori, while the fingers were skeletal fingers or claws (haohao). This may be the local answer to the three-fingered hand – it was a bird's claw and the ancestor after whom the carving was named had after death the power of entering the consciousness of a bird in the carving. The three-fingered hand is a world-wide feature of carvings in many lands of the old world and the new. It was found in ancient Greece, Egypt, India, China and South America. Some of the Maori explanations for the three-fingered hand are already recorded but as these vary greatly we mention only one. Tiki, believed by some tribes to have been the first man, traditionally had three fingers and so all carved fingers from the dawn of time had three fingers also.

Origin of Maori Carving

Where did Maori carving in its present form originate? One thing appears to be certain – in its earliest presentation all carving was much less elaborate. Simple forms in which the human ancestral figures was predominant would give rise to the many variations which gradually developed. We are indebted to Sir Gilbert Archey for his pioneer researches in this direction.† Certain elementary carving conceptions would be introduced by the successive waves of immigrants, and the general conservatism of the tohunga class would retain these and permit development inside given limits; but as the years passed this simplicity of the earlier productions would give place to the more complex. It is possible that a wide distribution of greenstone, as well as efficient carving tools, had gradually built up among the North Island tribes to reach a climax in the eighteenth century, paving the way for the over-elaboration of the iron and steel era.

The Development of Carving

Some carvings that have survived the passage of time seem, from their archaic and un-Maori appearance, to belong to the Moa-hunter era. One of these is the well-known Kaitaia lintel with its central human figure, with well-developed chevrons on each side and out-facing toothed manaia at the ends. The theme was later modified and elaborated in the pare (door lintel). The toothed manaia became a beaked side face and the central human figure became enlarged with shoulder and hip spirals, though the concept of distortion remained. Then there is the canoe prow from Doubtless Bay, first described by Sir Archey.‡ Here we notice the close connection with the Kaitaia lintel in the use of large triangular teeth and triangular notching around the head and neck, this adornment doubtless being an early form of the tara tara o kai. Certain small bone chests from a northern cave also exhibit triangular teeth typical of these early carvings. These are peg-shaped below. All these specimens are now in the Auckland Museum.

It is remarkable that the next specimen which we regard as archaic and of Moa-hunter origin should come from a swamp near Temuka in the South Island, seeming to indicate an early carving school extending over both Islands and characterised by the use of a triangular and tooth-like decoration. This is a crescent-shaped object with a hollow square below, perhaps indicative of its once having been mounted on a post. Such an object may have to do with moon veneration in relation to crop growing, or may itself have been a mauri for such purposes. This specimen was found in 1947 and presented to the Canterbury Museum.

*See *Maori Carving*.
†Archey, *South Sea Folk*, 1937.
‡*Auckland Institute and Museum Records*, Vol. 1, 1933, p.213. pl.39.

It is from a study of the older carvings rescued from swamps, etc., that some idea of the background of the more modern carvings may be established. It is a difficult matter to determine whether or not a carving has been executed with greenstone carving tools. In fact Mr J. M. McEwen, who made important experiments, decided that it would be practically impossible to say whether crude iron or stone tools were used.

Manaia

The manaia is a side-faced figure used in Maori carving, sometimes resembling a bird or even a human side face, sometimes like nothing but itself, essential features being a beak with nose and eye above, with or without a shoulder and a hand or hands and body. It is probable that in the past manaia types were known by distinctive names such as the manaia called ngututa on the lower barge-board of a carved house. This is distinguished by having a tongue running upwards under the upper lip. Manaia are often associated with ancestral figures.

The line drawings by J. M. McEwen illustrate some of the varieties found in house carving. They may be said to have the manaia signature, eye, nose, mouth and tongue, one having a humanised body. Following these are drawings of manaia of unusual type, one from a Bay of Plenty pataka, another from the maru pataka in the Museum of Ethnology, Berlin, and yet another (page 122) from the Beetham pataka which formerly stood in Wellington.

Marakihau

In the Bay of Plenty district the legends of deep-sea taniwha and ocean gods became crystallised in a figure known as marakihau. There will always be a suspicion that this

116. Two manaia types used on the Kauwhata carved house, Feilding, and a related type of closed-mouth manaia used on the carved house, Uawhaki, Levin.

117. A manaia on a Bay of Plenty pataka (Dominion Museum).

119. Marakihau, probably the earliest recorded, *circa* 1840 (from an old photograph).

figure arose from an attempt to depict our own legends of mermaids passed on by whalers and early European contacts at the beginning of last century. Whether this is so or not matters little. Marakihau have become an established feature of a number of Maori houses originating from the Bay of Plenty and now found throughout New Zealand, and even male and female figures are recognised. A feature of some of these marakihau is the crown on top of the head – an enlargement of the tara tara o kai (the side cut notch) – but which here may be derived from Pakeha contact.

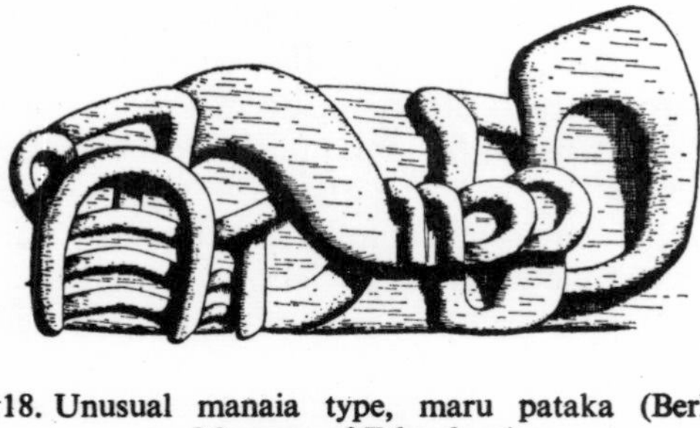

118. Unusual manaia type, maru pataka (Berlin Museum of Ethnology).

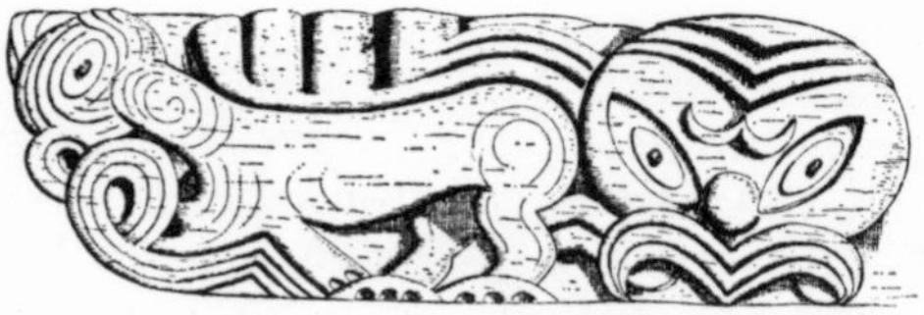

120. Manaia type, Beetham pataka, Wellington.

It seems certain that marakihau as a mythical sea monster entered into Bay of Plenty legends before the time of European contact. Marakihau were said to have a human form and in addition a long tubular tongue (ngongo). Through these long tongues they could draw down and swallow canoes and men on the surface. Elsdon Best tells us that "several stories are on record in which the Maori claims that certain ancestors of his were, after death, transformed into marakihau". Two marakihau carved in traditional style dating from 1875 appear on the porch of the carved house at Te Kuiti.

The Lizard in Carving

We must here include the lizard, seen occasionally in Maori carving. The large tuatara lizard had disappeared from most of the mainland by the time the first European settlers arrived. It is now confined to a few coastal islands. The tuatara was eaten by early inhabitants as is indicated by jaws found on southern coastal middens, but it was in general much feared by Maori populations. This fear of lizards was gradually concentrated on the green tree lizard, the sighting of which throws a whole tribe into confusion. Even today the sight of one of these lizards in an area of the Urewera being milled for timber is usually a prelude to the cessation of work for that day, and, in some cases, even longer. Perhaps the memory of the crocodile in a far distant tropical homeland and the dread which it inspired was transferred to the smaller lizards. The personified form of the common green lizard is Rakaiora, who is viewed as an atua (spirit god). The lizard is not distorted in carving.

Spirals

The study of Maori spirals is a fascinating subject. Most spirals are double, that is two volutes swing around in parallel fashion to meet or coalesce in the centre. Sometimes the number of volutes is increased, the carver's object doubtless being to bewilder the beholder and increase the beauty of his production. The most simple spiral element is the koru, a curving stalk with a bulb at one end of it. This is seen to profusion in most of the rafter patterns of large houses. From the koru we derive the primitive Maori spiral illustrated in a slate breast ornament from Shag Point, Otago, as also from an old boundary stone, Opunake, Taranaki. An old stone figure in the Auckland Museum is a Janus grooved for suspension and adorned with spirals of this simple type. For the rest this small object is adorned with curving grooves reminiscent of the Banks Peninsula canoe bailer in the Canterbury Museum.

Double spiral types are illustrated: one, quite unusual, illustrates a double koru, while the other is the basic S-curve spiral. These are taken from a ceremonial stone sinker from Nelson. It will be noted that the central S-curve is to be seen in many spirals in carvings from the Rotorua – Bay of Plenty area, while more common on old Whakatane – East Coast carving is the interlocking type of spiral where the two volutes completely interlock in the centre. This spiral is commonly seen on the sternpost of a war canoe, where it is perforated and termed takarangi. The notched ridge or pakati is here bunched into groups supported by the plain ridges. The usual type of interlocking spiral has the plain ridges interlocking with parallel notched ridges (pakati).

Worthy of mention is the spiral common in many of the older carvings such as the burial chests where the two central volutes approach each other but do not quite interlock leaving an S-curve hollow in the centre, seeming to indicate that the spiral with partially interlocking arms may be older than the complete interlock. The partially interlocking hollow is also common and may here be seen in the background of the S-curve ridge of our illustration. Remarkable and unusual spiral types sometimes appear as on a bone in Napier Museum where a swastika spiral makes its appearance, our first note of this type being in the old carved house at Te Ore Ore, since burnt down.

Carved Heads

A group of carved heads, koruru, illustrating a variety of presentation, is given overleaf. The first is from a locality near the town of Wanganui, but is apparently the work of an imported Arawa carver (note the S-curve interrupted spiral and the double tongue). These features seen together usually denote a carving of Arawa origin, always remembering that the Arawa confederation of tribes includes many Bay of Plenty Maoris, as well as those of Maketu and Rotoiti.

No. 2 is typical oblong form carved from a prepared slab. Like No. 1 it is highly conventionalised.

121. Maori decorative patterns.

122. Koruru, various types.

No. 3 approaches nearer the realistic but the features are still largely distorted, most striking being the well-set circular eyes and large mouth.

No. 4 is from a tekoteko in the British Museum and illustrates an old feature of a blind eye. The large mouth with the protruding tongue gives character to the whole. There is little doubt that the protruding tongue denotes defiance, for, as noted already, it is an important feature of the finish of the haka when men, flushed with contempt for their enemies, rush on to do battle.

No. 5 is a good example of pierced work. It is practically a mask. The locality is almost certainly the west coast of the North Island. This is evidenced by the deep-rooted tongue, divided above. Here, as in several other heads, a central feature of the forehead is a spiral, parallelled in Indian carving by a chakra or spiritual centre in this region.

No. 6 resembles No. 3, save that there is a different treatment of the forehead, and the lower jaw is missing. This example appears to be from the East Coast.

In several areas of the North Island exclusive types of carving gradually emerged. In Taranaki highly convoluted human and manaia figures appeared. The human figures often had pointed heads wide above with ridged convoluted bodies, while on the Wanganui River with its timbered surroundings, larger, heavier and more striking figures were the rule. These had deep-rooted and out-thrust tongues, the side-faced figure being termed kaeaea by the late T. W. Downes.* A high development of carving technique appeared on the East Coast, where the carved house Te Hau ki Turanga exemplified all that was best in this traditional art. In North Auckland human figures were produced with pointed heads and wide mouths.

South Island Forms

South Island carving is rare and inclines to resemble some of the carving of Wellington to the Wanganui area. Human faces have an almost sketchy appearance without detracting from the presentation of the general picture. A box in the Canterbury Museum portrays a type of human face where the artist has given the impression of one head on the left, half hidden by the main head on the right. Secondary adornment consists of a pakura design in which crescents may become straight lines. Notched ridges are absent.

*This regional carving was noted in fuller detail in *Maori Carved Houses*, 1955, p. 73 (W.J.P.).

18

RAFTER, TANIKO, AND TUKUTUKU DESIGN

MOST MAORIS have a good sense of form and symmetry. It is therefore not remarkable that painted drawings of the human form were used on poupou when carvers were not easily available, or where the full carving of interiors was too costly a burden for the builders of large houses.

Colours

Three colours, black, white, and red, were used to adorn the rafters of Maori carved houses. The red was to Maori eyes easily the most beautiful and was obtained by mixing kokowai or red clay with hot shark liver oil. But there were many grades of kokowai, and not all were easily powdered. In all cases pounding was necessary before the kokowai was sufficiently fine for mixing. In the Dominion Museum are a number of old pounders and pounding-stones with the kokowai still clinging to the stones. It is said that this old-time paint was noted for its strong smell, and when used on rafters was almost overpowering, so that the houses became more or less tapu for some days.

Kokowai was an important article of trade and barter between tribes, for good material was not to be found in all districts. In some instances at least, the white colour of the rafter patterns was obtained from pipeclay; but here again good material was not always available, so the natural colour of the wood was often utilised as a substitute for white. Black was obtained from soot, or black earth from the raupo swamps or peaty bogs. Archdeacon Williams stated that the Ngati Porou tribe in the Waiapu District sometimes added a blue-grey, produced by a slimy clay known as tutaewhetu. Colours were arranged in a definite sequence according to the taste of the painter, but certain rules appear to have been observed in all patterns, an alternating sequence of reds and blacks bounded by lines of the main design giving a rhythmic effect to patterns and enhancing their beauty in a way that nothing else could have done.

Designs

Both the S-curve and interlocking designs of the double spiral were present in Maori rafter patterns. Another design used to make up the rafter patterns in common use was a crescentic pattern, but the crescents were incomplete, as rows of circular niches were made around the outer edge, evidently koru bulbs without their stalks. All designs have names, though many of these are lost. They relate designs to similar objects in the surroundings. One represents the waves of the sea, another the hammerhead shark, and another the sand flounder (patiki).

123. Section of rafter, original Ruatahuna house of Te Kooti.

124. Maori rafter patterns (after Rev. H. W. Williams).

125. More Maori rafter patterns (after Williams).

The Maori decorator did not copy. As far as he could, he carried the designs in his head, and used his mind as a picture gallery from which he could cull at will the patterns he required. This method of producing a pattern does not at all accord with our modern notions. We notice that the ancient artist refused to cramp his designs. Patterns were often too large for the slab or panel, and instead of suiting the pattern to the material the artist would draw what he could and leave the rest to the imagination. Patterns consist of curves of one kind or another. Most of the straight lines seen in rafter patterns of present-day houses were absent in former times.

Williams supplied some twenty-nine rafter patterns in black, white, and red which are reproduced here.* Williams commenced his notes with a regret that any scientific discussion of the decorations is rendered extremely difficult, if not impossible, by the fact that none of the old school of painters were then living and that little, if any, of their work had survived them.

*A. Hamilton, *Maori Art*, 1897.

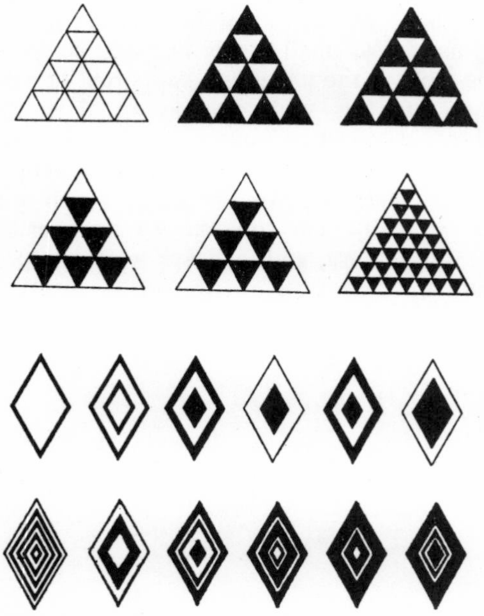

126. *Top:* Triangular units. *Bottom:* Diamond units.

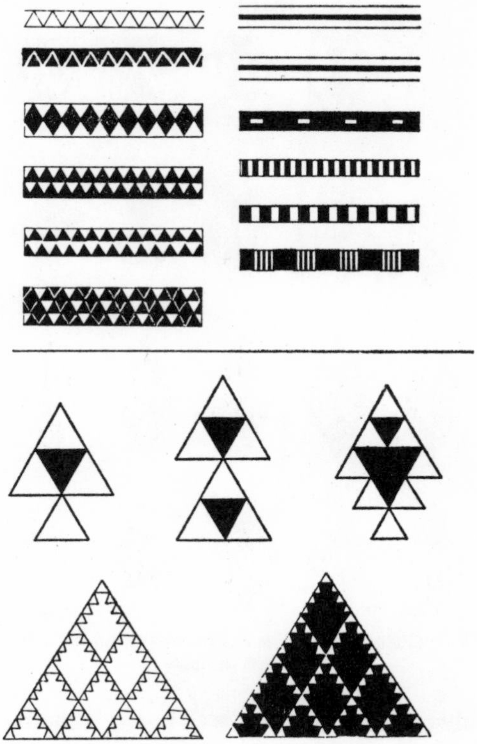

127. *Top:* Triangular, diamond and oblong units. *Bottom:* Triangular units.

Taniko Design

Taniko is mainly the application of a given series of designs to a woven fabric, and so it needs must be rectilinear, as are the tukutuku designs, to which certain taniko work has a close affinity. In a booklet of *Maori Designs* published by H. H. Tombs Ltd in 1943, taniko designs are analysed for the first time and individual units figured in natural colour. By arrangement, the publisher has kindly consented to us copying three of the plates for inclusion here. These illustrate triangular, diamond and oblong units of taniko as well as large triangular units, together with a page illustrating the hourglass design and its variations. Yellow appears only rarely in taniko designs. This is said to be a dye derived from the bark of the tanekaha tree. Colours are usually alternating red, white, and black.

Taniko is used in a superior carved house

128. Elements of taniko design: diamond with hour-glass units.

only on the heke tipi, a wall board high up on the back of the porch and sometimes on a false wall board inserted above the poupou. For the designs as submitted a careful examination of the large collections of taniko cloaks in both the Dominion and the Auckland Museums was made.

Tukutuku

In the Cook Islands the Polynesians were accustomed to construct screens from thin white stakes secured from the purau tree.* They were termed kaka'o. When the Polynesian immigrants arrived in New Zealand they seized on the white flower stalks of the toetoe and called them kakaho, using them vertically as screens for the panels of the walls of houses and as a lining for the roof in superior houses. To these screens horizontal rods of fern stalks were added by tying. These were called kakaka. This tying by means of flax or kiekie gave rise to patterns which gradually evolved into a recognised series. Later, horizontal wooden rods or laths became recognised as more durable for superior houses. They were adzed from totara or rimu. These rods were set so that they covered the kakaho, leaving just enough room to pass the flexible material through to form the tie and so the pattern. Laths were painted black or red. These superior type laths were termed kahotara by Te Arawa, and kahotarai on the East Coast.

On the East Coast a special vertical rod passed down the middle of the panel to be fixed to the face by a special stitch. Apparently this was unknown elsewhere. The rod was termed tumatakahuki. Scorching of panels or groups of panel elements to make a design was a common practice in the Urewera.

The stakes and rods were stitched together by hand. For small panels an expert could do the work if the panel was supported at each end, and this was probably usual in old Maori days when houses and paneis were small. Large panels called for two people, one on each side of the panel which was set vertically. The tohunga was responsible for the pattern, and mistakes were not permitted.

*See Sir Peter Buck, *Transactions of the N.Z. Institute*, Vol. 53, 1921, p. 452.

19

ADORNING THE HEAD

The Topknot

As among other Polynesians, chiefs and men of standing wore their hair reasonably long, drawn well back from the face and done up into a topknot (tikitiki) on the crown of the head. This work is usually done by the man's wife, who must become proficient in the art of oiling, combing, and dressing the hair. In the topknot, feathers of such birds as the huia, the long-tailed cuckoo, the heron, etc., were worn.

129. Topknot from a tattoed chief (*Cook's Voyages*).

The topknot enters into tradition as the wrap used by Maui's mother for her baby soon after his birth. As has been noted elsewhere, the tapu of the head remains with us even today, lingering among the people as a daily reminder in all their domestic undertakings. It is indeed strange that, with this tapu so deeply engrained on the mental outlook, the dressing of the hair and the use of the topknot so quickly became less evident in the years following Cook's visit. Whaling operations and the sight of Europeans with short clipped hair, together with the demands of a new mode of living, would perhaps be a reason for this. The old way of life was passing as a new one slowly made its appearance.

Combs

In addition to these, ornamental combs were added, some of bone and others of wood. The bone combs were made from a piece of flattened whalebone, and were termed heru tuki, or heru iwi, a small human or manaia head being carved in one of the upper corners. Such combs were handed down as family

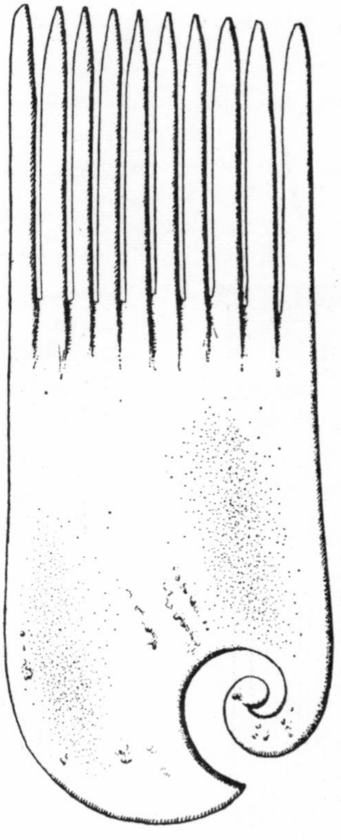

130. Bone ornamental comb from Poretua, East Coast (Bollons Collection).

heirlooms and much value was attached to them.

Wooden combs were known as heru mapara, and were used as hair ornaments as well as in dressing the hair for special occasions. Some wooden combs in the Dominion Museum are beautifully made, the workmanship in the binding of fine twine being equal to some of the finest Polynesian techniques. Separate wooden teeth are lashed in position. Certain of these combs have a safety-string for tying the object into the hair.

Closely associated with the head are small scratchers made from bone or steatite. These are very rare objects and may even have gone out of use at a relatively early date. Miller* has given us a list of insects which attacked the Maori in pre-Pakeha days and they were much the same as those that attack all primitive societies.

The koukou method of doing the hair up

Journal of the Polynesian Society, 61, 1952, p. 21.

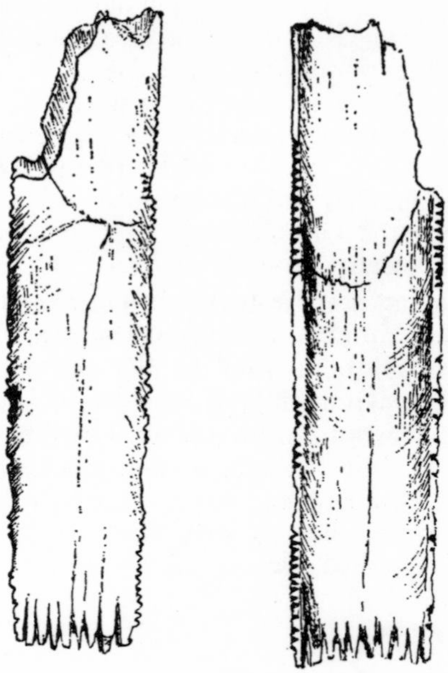

132. Bone ketu or scratcher, Waikuku (Bollons Collection).

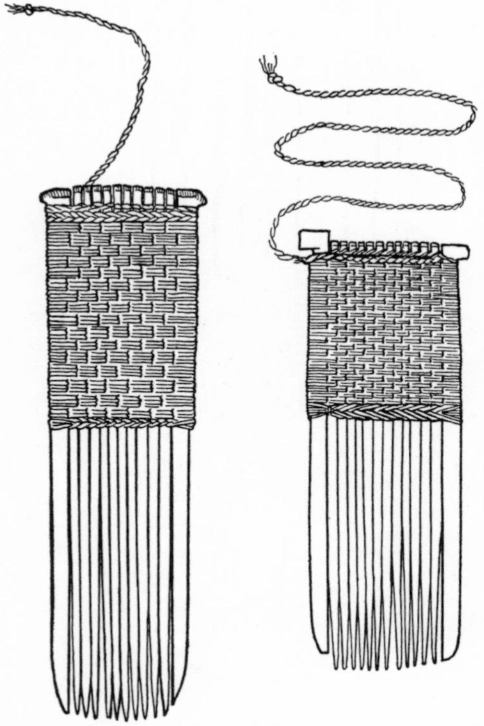

131. Small wooden combs (Dominion Museum).

to the crown sometimes required two ties, one around the forehead, and the other on the crown. The plaited band used was the kawe, described elsewhere in this work and also known as tauhere. But there were many variations in this method. Parkinson mentions a Maori who had his hair on the crown in two bunches. Others perhaps whole families, permitted their hair to run freely beyond the crown.

Feathers

Feather clusters worn in the hair are in Taranaki termed raukura, where the feathers are usually those of the albatross. As these feathers are from a sea-bird they do not become spoilt when worn in the rain. In Pakeha times, feathers of white geese have been used. The midribs of the feathers are carefully split from the tips to the quills then tied together with muka fibre. In the Vienna Museum there is a waka huia or carved treasure box which was collected by the Austrian naturalist Andreas Reischek while he was in New Zealand. It is labelled papa raukura – a repository for feather clusters.

The puhipuhi or bunch of split hawks' feathers which hang from the blade of a tewhatewha are made in much the same way.

Huia feathers, black with a white tip, were the most highly esteemed of all feathers worn in the hair. They were the prerogative of chiefly families and much valued everywhere. When in the King Country, Andreas Reischek had presented to him two sets of the tail feathers of the huia, which are now in the Vienna Museum. One set, called hua by the Maoris, was regarded as the signature of chieftainship. The total number of feathers in a huia tail is twelve but this number is rarely found in museum specimens except in young birds. It is remarkable that no hua is to be seen in a New Zealand museum.

Caps

Caps were apparently not uncommon in old Maori days, and some of these seem to have been ornamental. Captain Cook speaks of having seen a form of feather head-dress worn by natives of Queen Charlotte Sound in 1770. He writes: "The women in these canoes and some of the men, had a head-dress which we had not before seen. It consisted of a bunch of black feathers, made

133. Two Hauraki boys illustrating forms of head decoration (after John White).

up in a round form, and tied upon the top of the head, which is entirely covered, and made it twice as high in appearance as it was in reality."

Cook also mentions caps made from bird's feathers, which were far from unbecoming. Parkinson, in his short vocabulary of Maori words, gives *potai* (potae) as the name of "the feather ornament on their head". He also gives *heebeeke* (he piki, plumes) as denoting "a bunch of scarlet feathers which they stick in their hair". In Cook's account of his second voyage he speaks of the Maori folk at Dusky Bay decorating themselves to meet the Europeans "with their hair combed and oiled, tied upon the crowns of their heads, and stuck with white feathers. Some wore a fillet of feathers round their heads, and all of them had bunches of white feathers stuck in their ears."

134. Widow's cap or potae taua.

A widow's cap is termed potae taua and consists of a well-woven base of muka fibre into which are inserted numerous seaweed tags covering its outer surface. It is worn as a mark of honour when the husband is slain on a war expedition. Among some tribes the widow may not remove this cap until it wears away.

20

TATTOO

Legendary Origin

According to legend, Maori tattoo commenced with a quarrel between a husband and a wife in the ancient homeland of Hawaiki. The two people concerned were a man, Mataora, and a woman, Niwareka. Niwareka was descended from the ancient gods of Polynesia and her father Ue-tonga dwelt in Te Po-nui, the world of spirits. Niwareka, went there and was admitted by Kuwatawata, the keeper of the entrance. Mataora followed, well dressed and penitent. He was forgiven and united to Niwareka, but Ue-tonga criticised his son-in-law's tattoo, which could be rubbed off with the hand; so Mataora consented to be properly tattooed from head to foot. Only then would Ue-tonga consent to Niwareka's return to the world of man. The tapu of the tattoo was removed by Ue-tonga and the couple started on their homeward journey. At the gateway they overlooked or neglected to make the customary gift to the janitor, Kuwatawata, who reported this mistake to Ue-tonga. Also they are said to have concealed the prototype of woven cloaks. Thereupon Ue-tonga placed the penalty of unrelenting death on humanity. But the designs of the tattoo remained to be copied by all.

The Operation

Maori tattooing was no light operation. It was carried out with a small bone chisel (uhi) hafted to a handle which was tapped with a light piece of wood or a fern stalk. A bluish pigment was rubbed into the wound. When the face healed the deep lines of the tattoo furrowed the whole countenance. It was a long and painful process, during which both operator and patient were under a state of tapu. All work was done in the open air, and the tattooing artist was paid for his work with presents such as finely woven garments and ornaments.

The conclusion of the ordeal was a day of rejoicing, when a feast was prepared and all congratulated the novice warrior and admired the lines of his tattoo. Neighbouring tribes were invited, and speechmaking, songs and games were the order of the day. When a high-born girl had her lips and chin tattooed a similar feast was held at the conclusion of the ordeal. At this time she would be adorned with the finest garments, necklaces would be placed round her neck, and her tattoo would also be admired.

Designs

Some types of triple spiral are usually seen in face tattoo. The triple spiral is used only rarely in carving but may be found here and there on museum pieces. Other designs are more or less identical with the kowhaiwhai (rafter pattern designs) of the Maori carved

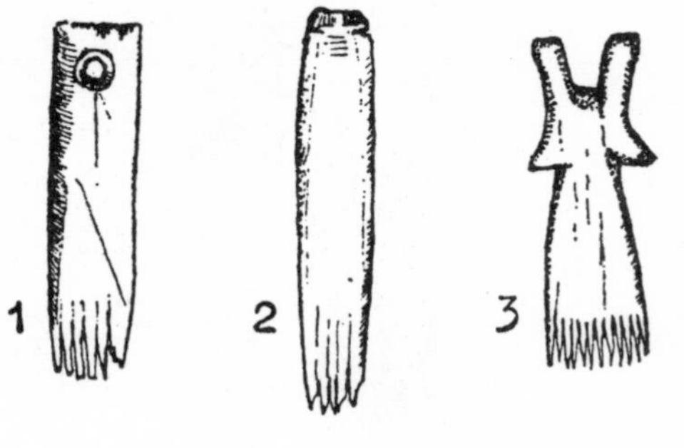

135. Types of tattooing chisels. 1. Amulet form from Opito, Thames. 2. Elongate form, notched above, North Cape. 3. Anthropomorphic form from Moeraki, Otago.

house. On the side of the face balanced koru types of umbrella or mushroom shapes often appear.

A large number of names have been recorded for the various designs which appear in tattoo. Some of these are synonyms, for not all tribes would use exactly the same term for the same design. The lines of tattooing at the side of the mouth are termed pakiwaha or pawaha. These lines encircle the mouth at the sides. Tattoo cheek spirals are known as kawe, as are hip spirals on men. Paepae is also applied to cheek spirals, and koropetau is used for all spiral lines. The umbrella or mushroom pattern is termed kokoti. This is to be seen on the forehead and at the sides of the face. Pongoiangia or poniania are the tattoo marks on the sides of the nose.

A rare type of tattoo seen by Captain Cook consists of ladder-like rows of short lines defined by narrow vertical spaces. Over all runs another blank space pattern which is derived from, or allied to, Maori rafter patterns. Here we may see the rafter pattern forming an S-curve, one of the basic spiral forms in many wood carving scrolls.

The Rev. Richard Taylor makes mention of the use of small strokes of tattoo when he states: "The ladies had their lips and

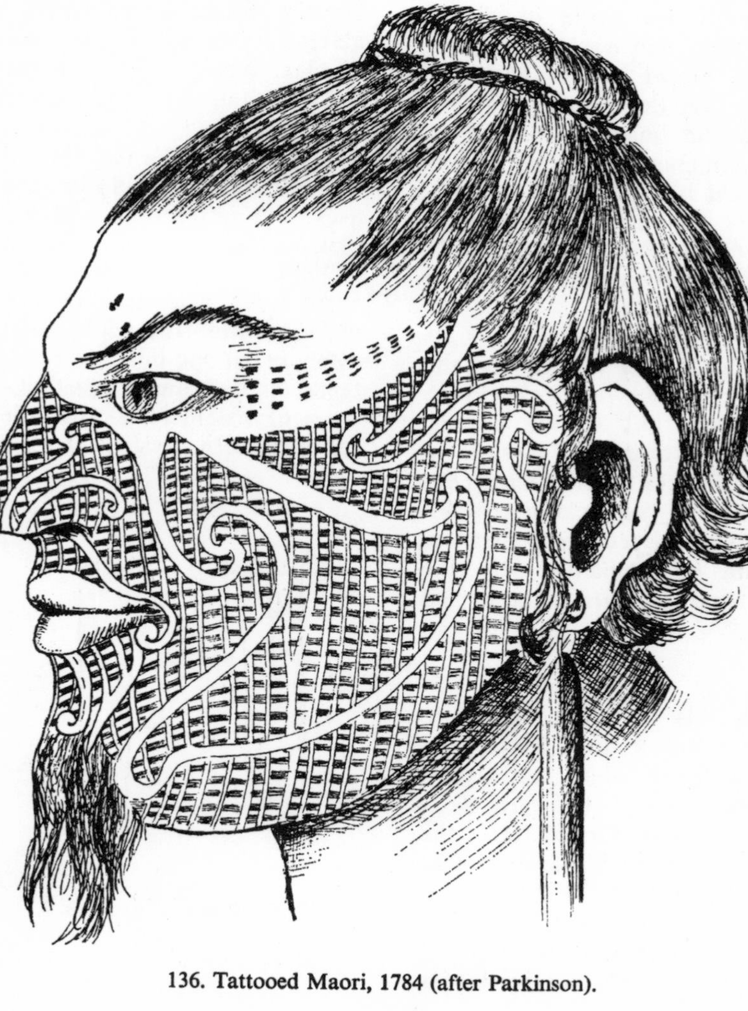

136. Tattooed Maori, 1784 (after Parkinson).

chins operated on, with a little curl at the corner of the eye; frequently their persons also were covered with small strokes of tattooings." Here is evidence of the use of small strokes of tattoo.

Pigment

Certain vessels were reserved for holding the pigment for tattooing. This pigment was usually made from soot obtained from the burning of resinous wood or gum of the kauri pine. The soot would be mixed with water or the juice of berries of the mahoe tree.

137. Tattooing patterns; a. full pattern; b. chin; c. forehead; d. cheek; e. woman's chin.

Tattooed Heads

Tattooed heads of deceased elders were held for many years by their relatives. On a great occasion these heads would be taken out and placed in a prominent place, mounted on sticks with side supports. A cloak was

138. An unusual type of short-line tattoo (after Tregear).

thrown over each so that from a distance visitors might think a party of chiefs squatted there to give them welcome. In 1863 such a group occupied a hill top in Northland. A visitor (Judge Maning) approached as a breeze of wind came sighing along the hill top. The heads nodded a welcome but a cloak blew to one side. The horrified Pakeha approached to find that the heads had no bodies under them.

21

MAORI ORNAMENTATION

Red Ochre

The most universal means of personal ornamentation was a red colouring for the body or parts of the face, so in any consideration of bodily ornamentation we must commence with red ochre or kokowai. It was the colour of rank and opulence, the colour of the gods – a rich warm red said to be something of the colour of a well-burnt brick with a matt surface. Great chiefs painted their whole bodies, lesser individuals heightened the colour of their cheeks. Bidwill, who travelled to New Zealand in 1839, found that coming into contact with Maoris was impossible without being soiled with kokowai. Sometimes all garments would be saturated with this substance, and chiefs would even carry around a small quantity to re-colour their bodies as required.

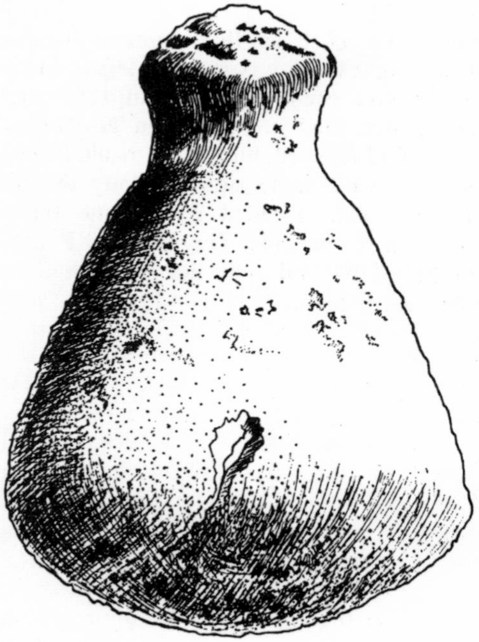

139. Kuru or pounder, Matata.

Kokowai was first roasted in a hot oven and afterwards ground to fine powder with either a flat stone or a kuru, a short pounder used endwise. When required for personal use, it was often mixed with vegetable oils expressed from the seeds of the titoki, kohia, or miro, all of which were more or less pleasant to smell. Captain Cook noted the prevalence of the use of kokowai. However, it appeared to have had an excellent utilitarian usage in protecting the body from the changes of temperature and from the annoyance of sandflies, mosquitoes, and other pests.

The raw material, red ochre or oxide of iron, is found in deposits in many parts of New Zealand. Many varieties were recognised, especially in North Auckland. Kokowai was found in liquid form at Pukupuku on the Wanganui River. Taranaki Maoris often used swamp oil skimmed off as required to make the necessary mixture. All over New Zealand the kokowai mines of old were important spots, sometimes kept secret to a particular tribe or family.

Greenstone Tiki

Maori ornaments for personal use were many and varied. Few objects of ancient times were more highly prized than the greenstone tiki, particularly if it had been handed down through a number of generations. There is no feature of which we are aware in the manner of carving of the tiki which cannot also be found in wood carving, including the inward bending of the legs. Those who see in the tiki any remarkable features which would place it in a class of its own would do well to study wood carving in relation to the human form. Thus we may assume that before tiki were carved in greenstone there was a wooden prototype already in existence. Just as painted designs would precede wood carving, so would wood carving precede carving in stone, provided that no outside contacts altered the general cycle of events.

Remarkable in the study of the evolution of the greenstone tiki was the discovery in the neighbourhood of Whangarei of a little tiki composed of coarse quartz sandstone. The colour is dark brown. This tiki is now a treasured possession of Mr J. T. Scott, Dannevirke. The pointed head is typical of the north; but the feature that makes this tiki of special interest is that one eye is enlarged and the other partly obliterated, a feature which we believe to belong to an early period in the portrayal of the human form. This feature even extends to the South Island, and is found only on objects which appear to be of considerable age. In its side view the little object appears to be the miniature of a large Easter Island ancestral figure.

A careful study of the various opinions on the tiki expressed by leading authorities has been made. The general consensus of opinion is that the tiki has some fertility association, and hence was worn by women rather than by men, though some men certainly wore famous tiki as symbols of good fortune, or as the revered possession of a line of famous ancestors. The late Hari Hongi* believed that in the tiki is enshrined the "story of the first human pair, namely Tiki and Hine-ahu-one. . . . As woman is the bearer of man, it is proper that woman only should wear the tiki. . . . The tiki is sometimes, and quite improperly, termed a hei-tiki. This hei is merely the cord or necklet worn around the neck from which the tiki itself depends."

In certain tiki there is sometimes a divided tongue running outwards from the side of the mouth, and even on to the breast. This is evidently a remote traditional memory of the snake. Most tiki have the hands on the hips and the head on the right shoulder. Some have the head on their left shoulders. Tiki with upright heads are very rare and not necessarily older than others. Those with one hand on the body and the other on the hip usually have a remnant of a beard and some indication of ears. Tiki from western parts of the North Island have a pointed head, and this feature is to be found even among Nga Puhi. As nothing approaching a tiki has been recorded among pre-Maori material we may assume that it is a comparatively modern innovation, probably belonging to later migrations.

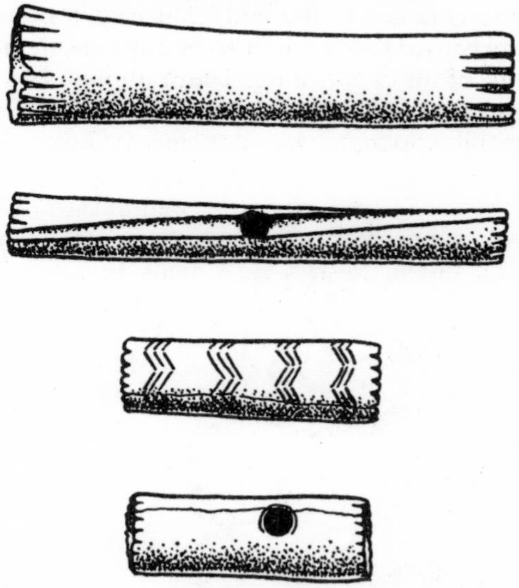

140. Toggles.

In wearing the tiki, Waikato people tell us that it was worn suspended sideways in that district, and the cord slung through one of the arms of the figure. This is probably correct, for a Dominion Museum painting of King Tawhiao shows him wearing a tiki suspended sideways. Such a usage would of course obviate the long and laborious drilling for the hole at the top, but there is no evidence that any group of tiki were without the hole above. It is obvious therefore, that this was a local custom. The tiki was often suspended by a plaited cord looped at one free end and attached to a bone toggle at the other. The toggle was thrust through the loop and pulled tight.

Six tiki in the Dominion Museum which are illustrated here exhibit types of variation to be found among most collections. Several

*Hari Hongi claimed to be a graduate of the last Ngapahi school of learning

illustrate in greater or lesser degree the tendency to produce tiki with a divided tongue. Nos. 2, 3, and 5 are from the Wanganui-Taranaki area, where a pointed ridge above the head is the rule. No. 3 further illustrates a vestigial tongue running downwards between the shoulders to divide into two below. No. 4 is one of a less common class originating from the northern and eastern districts of New Zealand. Here one hand is raised to the body and in this case a finger enters the mouth, and we note the indications of ears and a beard though No. 2 has also a beard. In the South Island a special topknot was present to hold the suspension hole. This is exemplified in No. 6.

An unusual type of amulet on which is portrayed a human figure remotely resembling a tiki is made from part of a human skull. This is in the British Museum and appears to have been used as an amulet. The head is remarkable in that its shape has been modified to fit two large circular eyes, each with four concentric rims, the inner space being filled with paua. Detailed ornamentation covers shoulders, arms and legs. The right arm becomes the body of a bird, the beak being attached to the lower left leg. The left arm may symbolise the tail (or wing) of the bird.

141. Tiki, various attitudes.

142. Small carved stone figure said to be from D'Urville Island (Andresen Collection).

The spiral scroll on the shoulders is a type rarely seen in Maori artistry unless it be the balanced koru of the rafter designs, but here the koru bulbs are missing as well as the stalk. In short, the design consists of two joined spirals in which a relatively wide notched ridge interlocks with three plain parallel ridges which join to a point at the centre. Two partially interlocking ridges with an S-curve hollow make up the hip spirals. The legs each end in three toes. It is probable that we have here a representation of a bird man for there is some general resemblance to figures on a cave wall at Albury in the South Island, so this is probably an ancestor who has passed on to become a bird guardian.

A carved figurine made from a hard and gritty type of soapstone and said to be from D'Urville Island is to be seen in the accompanying illustration. It has been drilled above for suspension as a pendant and came to our notice during an examination of the collection gathered together some years ago by Mr H. M. Andresen. It is of interest as an unfinished object embodying two well-recognised conceptions in the presentation of the human form. One is seen in the head, wide above and narrowing below, an old Taranaki feature; while the other is to be seen in the position of the arms, one upraised to the head and the other reaching downwards to the hip, a feature of certain old Te Arawa carvings, but also seen elsewhere.

This carved stone object was probably intended for use as a tiki. Its length is three inches. The central thickness is a quarter of an inch, though this is much reduced on the head and greatly so around the suspension hole. There is no sign of hands but a U-shaped hollowing where the arm meets the head could indicate the beginnings of a manaia beak. The form of the body is modified and somewhat out of alignment because of the position of the arms, and the need to maintain a uniform and harmonious presentation – a feature of certain other carvings of this kind. A little scratching on the face may indicate an intention to carve features. This may or may not be modern. Four short fan-shape lines appear on one shoulder.

A small group of anthropomorphic pendants are shaped to represent the human figure, at least to some degree. Similar pendants are not uncommon on old Maori middens of Otago. The central pendant with cord attached is remarkable in that a group of five human incisor teeth are attached to the upper end. The first of the three pendants appears to be unusually large, and is notched after the manner of many old objects of Moa-hunter times. A knotted cord simulates the head of the figure, a unique feature. The central figure is shaped above to indicate shoulders or arms. Below all figures have a hollow to indicate hips.

143. Matau, found at Waikawa, 1928.

Pendants

A form of matau* pendant is shown (page 141). This object was found in the sandhills at Waikawa, Wellington, about high-water mark. This matau is, as far as we know, still held privately. It is made of greenstone and is a little flattened. The head of the matau well exemplifies that feature so common in many pendants – the suspension hole becomes the eyes and its surrounding form takes on a head shape.

In the Bollons Collections are three pendants made from soft bone, a little "greasy" to touch, and at first sight somewhat puzzling. Apparently they were originally outgrowths on the supraoccipital bone of a groper (hapuku) or some other similar fish. These pendants are already formed, the size being up to two and a half inches, requiring only a hole to be drilled at one end.

The rei-puta is a large ivory pendant made from a tooth of the sperm whale and said to have been common in the days of the earlier voyagers. However, it is probable that by the few records we have of specimens existing today, it was a comparatively rare pendant worn only by chiefs of importance and so claiming the attention of visitors. Teeth are cut or ground longitudinally in their upper portion and a semblance of a human head carved near the point. This represents an example from Ohaeawai, North Auckland. It is quite possible that most known North Island specimens would originally come from Northland. A South Island specimen is of interest. It comes from Lake Ellesmere and has on it a human bird man figure with wings in place of arms. Similar figures may be seen in cave drawings.

A paua shell pendant from North Cape is figured. It typifies a common type of ornament, particularly in that locality. It belongs to a class in which several suspension holes are drilled above. In this case one hole has broken out, probably in process of manufac-

*As with the tiki, the term "hei" is used when the object is suspended.

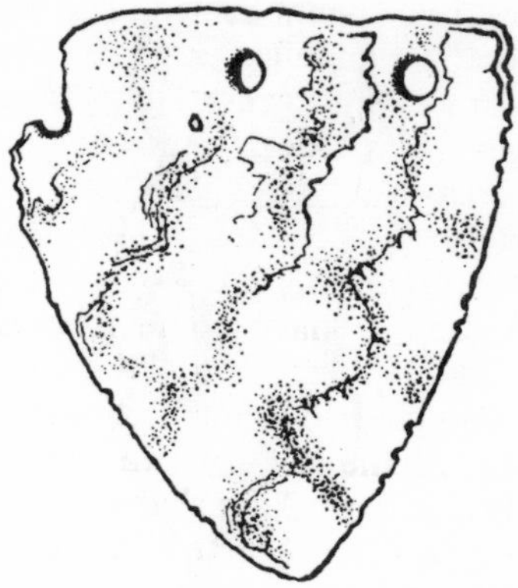

145. Pendant, North Cape.

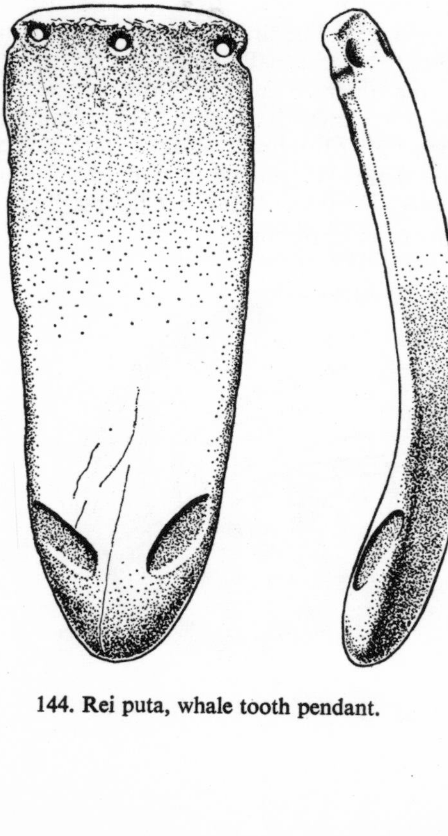

144. Rei puta, whale tooth pendant.

146. Greenstone pendant bearing some resemblance to a fish. Said to come from D'Urville Island (Andresen Collection).

ture, and two others drilled. The pendant is, in general, triangular in shape and shows indications of groups of notches ornamenting the edges. Such objects may have been made by children.

A greenstone pendant is illustrated bearing some resemblance to a fish or a porpoise. This is said to have come from D'Urville Island. The pendant is ninety-two mm. long and is flattened to a maximum thickness of five mm. in the centre with reduced width towards the edges. A fin shape appears above, and a protuberance below, which may also represent a fin, is notched in two places. The "eye" or suspension hole is drilled in a much reduced frontal area and is somewhat splayed-out as might be expected. An object such as this may have been the work of children or learners who were handed an irregular piece of greenstone and instructed to approach the fish shape if possible. In general appearance there is some lack of finish on the surfaces, due in part perhaps to the manner in which the greenstone flake had been prepared.

As an ear pendant the bill of the female huia was a much prized possession said to have been worn only by a chief. Birds were skinned, leaving mandibles and wattles attached, but wings and legs were discarded as useless. Sometimes whole birds would be worn as ear pendants, but usually only the head and part of the skin of the neck was so utilised, the tail feathers being reserved for head ornaments of chiefs. These tail feathers were black with a white tip. To the Maoris the huia was a tapu bird which was never eaten for food and killed only when its tail feathers were in demand.

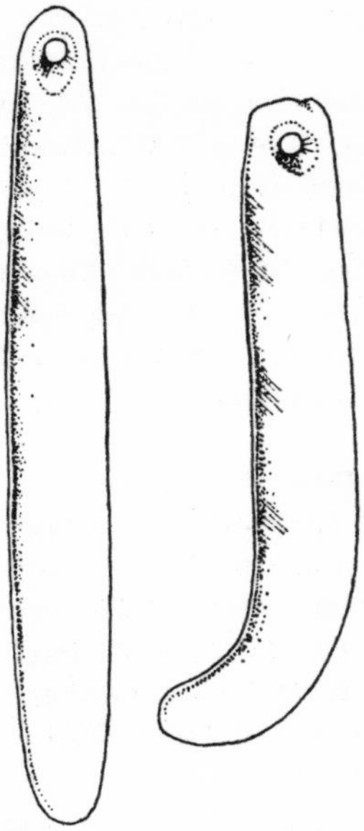

147. Greenstone pendants. *Left:* Straight type, kurukuru. *Right:* Curved below, kapeu.

James Cowan has recorded* a photograph of a painting of Tukukino, an old fighting chief who was shown wearing in his ear the dried skin and head of a huia bird. Our illustration portrays a female huia beak, wattles attached, mounted in gold and made into a brooch some time before 1865, when it was acquired by a Wanganui resident. When

**Pictures of old New Zealand.*

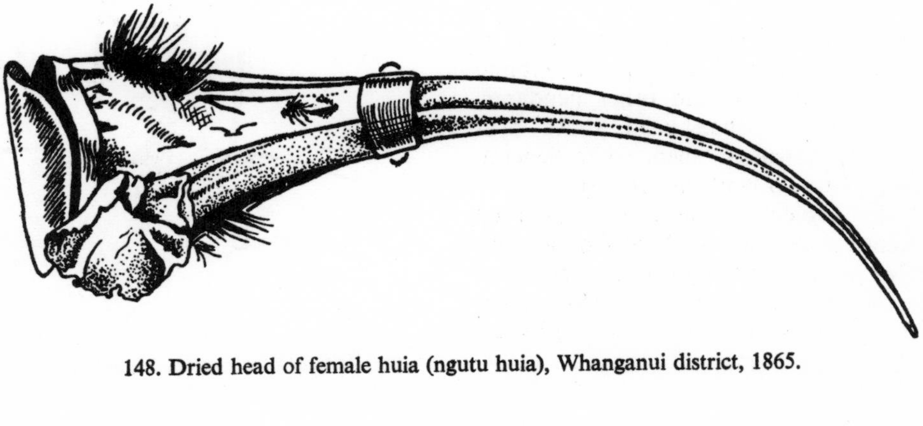

148. Dried head of female huia (ngutu huia), Whanganui district, 1865.

George V came to New Zealand as Duke of Cornwall and York in the year 1901, a great wave of patriotism swept the country, and when the Duke was presented with a huia feather to wear in his hat as a sign of chiefly rank, every Maori of importance demanded a huia feather for himself. So great was the onslaught on the already limited huia population to supply this demand that the birds never recovered.

Greenstone Pendants

The straight greenstone pendants worn in the ear were termed kurukuru while those curved at the lower end were known as kapeu. The flat variety was called kuru papa. However, many other names were applied and all very important pendants would probably be given proper names.

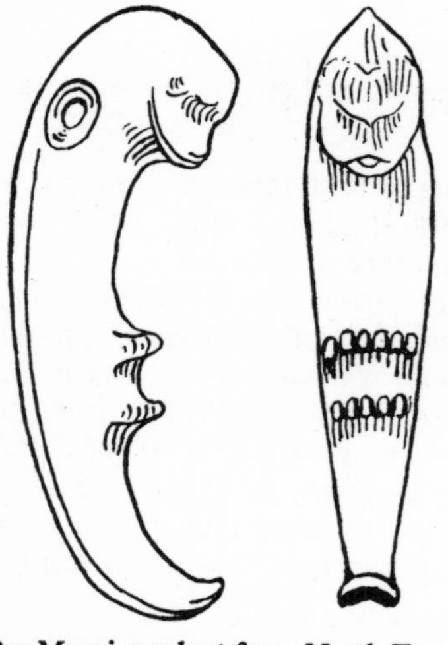

149. Pre-Maori pendant from North Taranaki.

From North Taranaki comes a pendant of most unusual type with a shape resembling some of the southern and other pendants. Here there is a human head above bent forward with downcast mien, while beneath the pendant is also bent inwards, seeming to indicate a possible development from a curved or crescentic type. Two small horizontal rows of notches across the body towards the lower surface are an unusual feature. This object appears to have belonged to the pre-Maori Moa-hunter Polynesians.

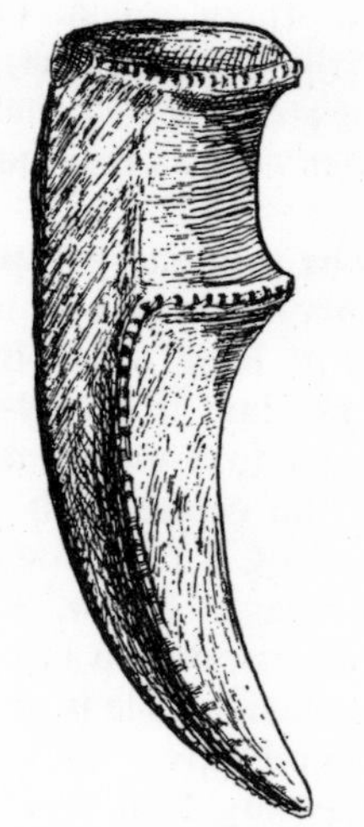

150. A restoration of a type of amulet from Nelson.

The upper portion of a pendant from Nelson is more or less semi-circular, with the flattened portion at the back. It is much broken below and the lower part is missing. Two raised serrated ridges cross the upper portion of the convex front, the lower ridge turning downwards to run parallel to (or join) another serrated line running along the

151. Moa-hunter amulet, Maungamanu, Kaikoura.

posterior margin. Dr R. S. Duff describes similar forms from Kaikoura. In regard to the raised notched ridge he notes "the common existence of the raised notched or serrated ridge as a characteristic ornamental device in ancient New Zealand, in modern Samoa and related groups, and in the Chathams within historical times".

A type of pendant from Kaikoura is seen in a sketch by R. Parsons, Maungamanu, Kaikoura. It is made from bone and consists of a somewhat curved back portion, more or less square in cross section. From this, horizontal and rounded appendages run outwards from its inner concave surface. These are attached anteriorly to a vertical and concave bar which is a part of the whole object as are the appendages. All edges of the body of the pendant as well as the frontal concave bar are notched. This may fairly obviously be judged as belonging to the era of the Moa-hunter.

22

MATS, BASKETS, AND PLAITS

Floor Mats

There were two kinds of plaited floor mats, one fine and one coarse. They were in general use in former times, but are now less common in many localities. The coarser were the more common ones and were quickly and easily made from raw flax. Each blade was divided into six strands or wefts, three running forwards and three backwards, each strand in plaiting passing over two others.

All mats were termed whariki, but the coarser ones were tuwharu and the finer ones takapau. Various techniques used in making the finer mats cannot be explained here, but like the coarse mats they were made from raw flax wefts. Sometimes various patterns were incorporated.

Men were the art specialists of old New Zealand, and it was they who plaited fine floor mats with coloured designs, black, yellow and brown. (It was men also who attached the green-hide dogskin strips to cloaks and in some instances carried out taniko work.) The designs used on floor mats were naturally rectilinear, usually rows of black, yellow, or brown lines defining squares or diamonds in parallel groups of three. Sometimes rows of verticals lines with alternating transverse lines or a draught-board pattern runs across the surface. In others a chevron design composed of three lines makes it appearance.

Baskets

Baskets were of various kinds, an openwork type used to hold various foodstuffs being the most common. They were made hastily as required, those plaited from the leaves of the cabbage tree being stronger than those made from the common flax. Ornate baskets were rarer, being reserved for special articles or for sweet-smelling herbs. A basket termed kopa provided with a flap was often a substitute for a pocket. The common basket was termed kete.

Some years ago we were interested in ordinary kete and the method of their manufacture. On one occasion, at a small kainga near Taupo, enquiries were made in regard to varieties there in use. Several kete were shown and their uses enumerated. The householder who handled them said: "Kete – yes; the Maori lives by kete." This sounded strange at the time. Now it seems reasonable enough. At that period, life was often a problem for large families, and all extra food was carefully conserved in the kete. The ancient Maori collected the kumara and all other products of cultivated land as well as the food of the forests in kete. From sea-shore, sea, rivers, lakes, and streams all that could be utilised as food was collected in the kete. The sandy soil for the kumara plantations was transported in kete load by load from the seashore, and today on many hills and ancient pa sites, ramparts and embankments remain as evidence of the earth-transporting kete.

Two kinds of lacebark tree are recognised by Te Kuiti Maoris. They are known as the houere and whauwhi. The latter is preferred for the value of its bark. Hats (potae) and kits (kete) have always been made from the bark of these trees, but the hats had no brim and the kits were little known. In former times the bark was also used for bandages, particularly for the newly born infant and (as lacebark is said to be stronger than flax) as a bait line for eels. Many yards of kopare plait were made from lacebark and used to make kete. This was easier than the method of utilising large numbers of flax strands, particularly when, as in bush localities, flax plants must be especially grown while lacebark trees were plentiful. We have collected evidence that formerly this type of kit was made in many parts of New Zealand, but it seems to have been regarded with disfavour by experts. The kopare plaits were strung into the correct shape for the future kit, and sewn each to each. The base of the kit was oblong in shape, with an extra strengthening outside kopare plait. In former days the sewing of the kopare kete may have been done with a bone needle. However, the resultant basket was a most efficient and serviceable article of use.

A modern-looking kit of kopare make is in the Dominion Museum, and belongs to the series of lacebark items collected at Moeraki, Otago, by Augustus Hamilton. This is to be seen in an accompanying illustration, but the actual plait has been covered over with numerous ornamental lacebark loops. The loops are made on a three-plait base and swung around the outside of the basket in three lines, the loops being much flattened.

152. Kopare kete, Moeraki, Otago.

A needle has been used to sew the base of the three plait to the outside of the basket. Both at Gisborne and in the King Country, rapaki (kilts) of lacebark were occasionally fashioned for special purposes, and this was continued down into last century.

Headbands

About the year 1896, Augustus Hamilton secured from Moeraki, Otago, a number of kilted garments made by local Maoris from the bark of the lacebark tree. Among these was a headband of this material, a little over two inches deep and twenty-two inches in circumference. It was entered in our register as pare of tiwhere, the latter term evidently being a southern name for the lacebark tree.

153. Headband of lacebark from Moeraki, Otago.

The design on it is of considerable interest for it is the tara (peak) design of the side notching in carving called taratara a kai. The criss-cross work inside each peak is exactly similar to that on pieces of old bone whistles or flutes still to be found on beach middens of Otago. It is therefore apparent that here on this headband we have a glimpse of old southern ornamentation of pre-Pakeha days.

The bark loops and the tassels give a modern touch. There are in all twenty loops, held in position by a somewhat circular base, also of lacebark. Thread is used to attach a number of loops of plaited muka, flax fibre, to the centre of the ornamental bow.

Some time before the year 1899, on the suggestion of Augustus Hamilton, a basketry strip of ten patterns was made by Te Ikapuhi of Ngati Pikiao. Recently we have had the patterns drawn for us and with a little re-arrangement it will be seen that the designs fall readily in three groups. The first four in the series belong to an alternating line group. The next three, Nos. 5, 6, and 7, illustrate a group in which the triangle (5), the diamond (6), and the hour glass (7), become dominant features. The related elements of this group are clearly evident. Lastly are three designs in which a zig-zag line makes its appearance, leading to the sacred step design of Te Arawa, No. 10. (See overleaf.)

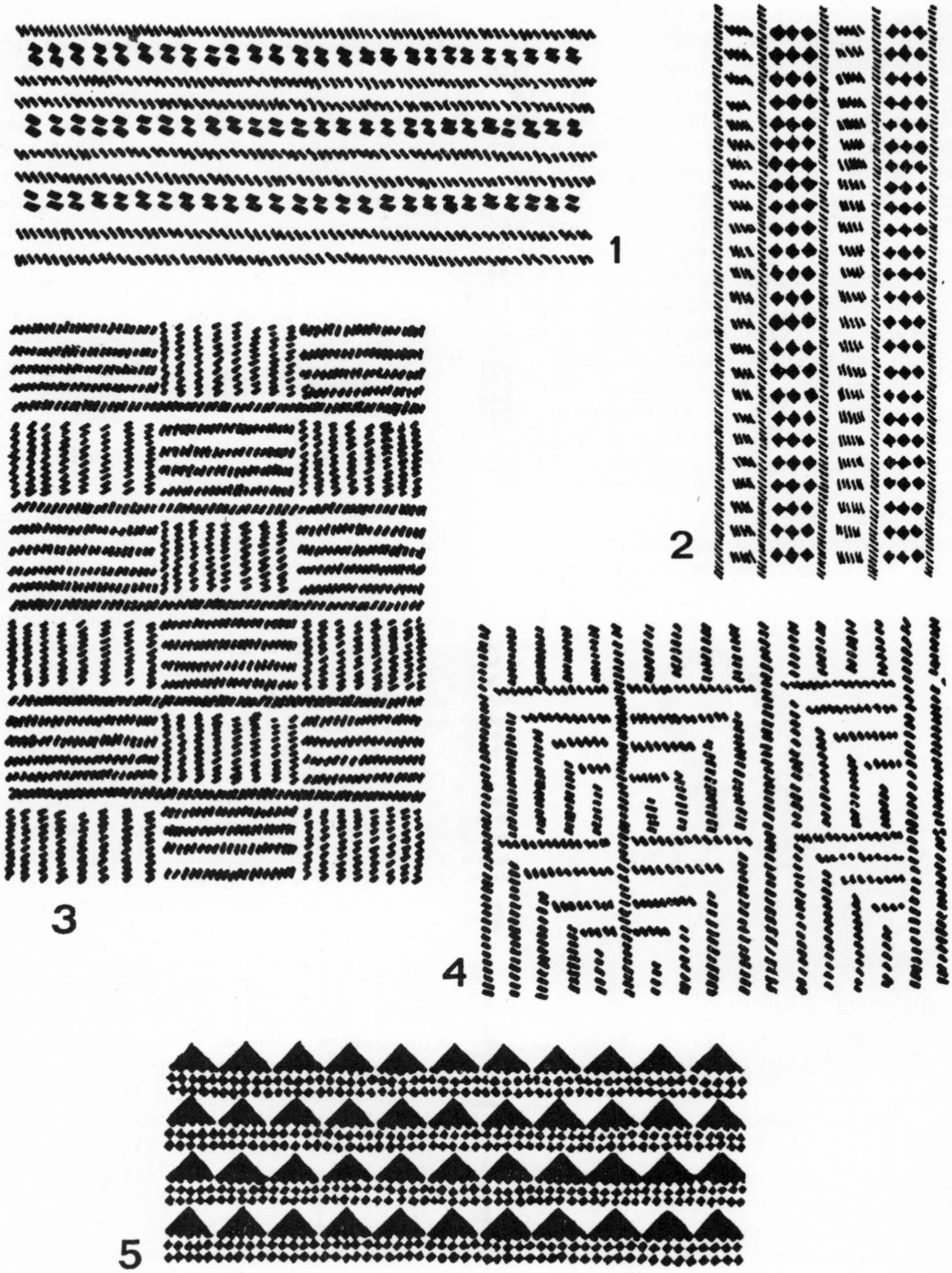

154. Basketry patterns.

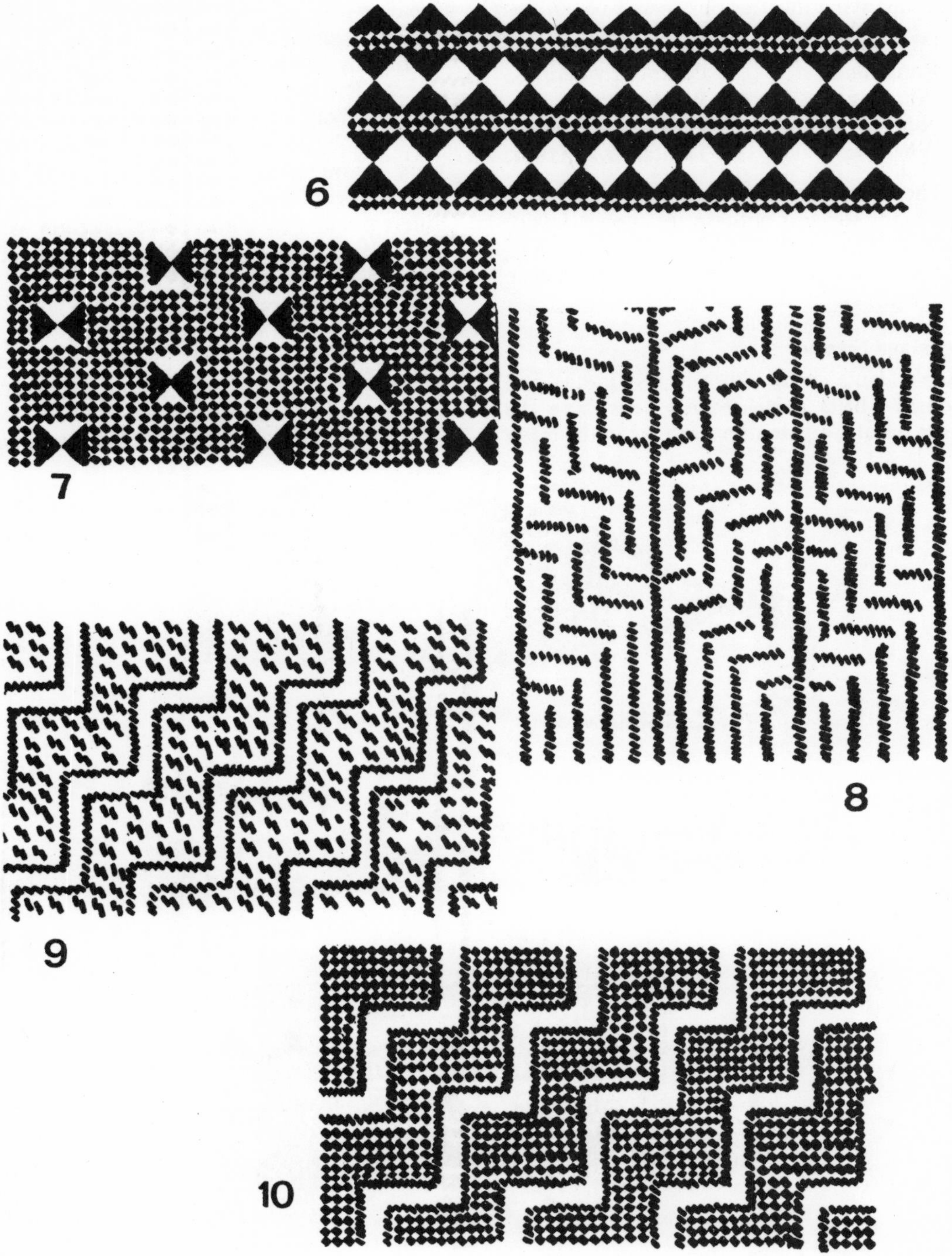

155. Basketry patterns.

A list of the names of the patterns seen in the accompanying illustrations (pages 148-9) are:

1. Poutama
2. Raukumara
3. Whakatutu
4. Niho-taniwha
5. Whakanihoniho
6. Torakaraka
7. Purapura whetu
8. Whakakanae
9. Kowhiti-whakakoki
10. Takitahi-whakakoki

The above names are by no means universal, and many variants of these are known outside Bay of Plenty and Te Arawa. For example, the step design is known as poutama in many places.

Belts and Straps

Men's belts were known as tatua and women's belts as tu. Men's belts were the more ornate, a common form being the tatua pupara in which the plaited fabric was doubled over and the two edges loosely sewn together – another task for the bone needle. Ordinarily men's belts were made of undressed flax leaf with some strips dyed black, and the belt exhibiting patterns similar to those on baskets and mats. Women's belts were more simple, being composed of twisted or plaited strands of flax fibre in different colours, some being fragrant with sweet-smelling grasses such as karetu and maurea.

Maori pack straps (kawe rapa) are now out of date, but once were very common, judging by the large collection in the Dominion Museum. We have seen none in Maori hamlets in the past forty years. It is possible that the necessity for carrying burdens long

1

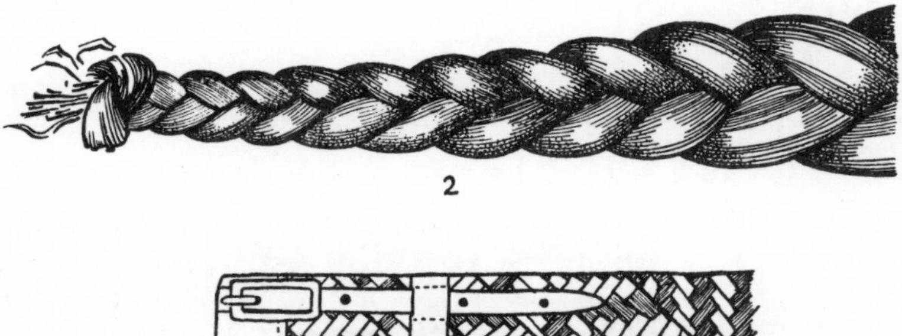

2

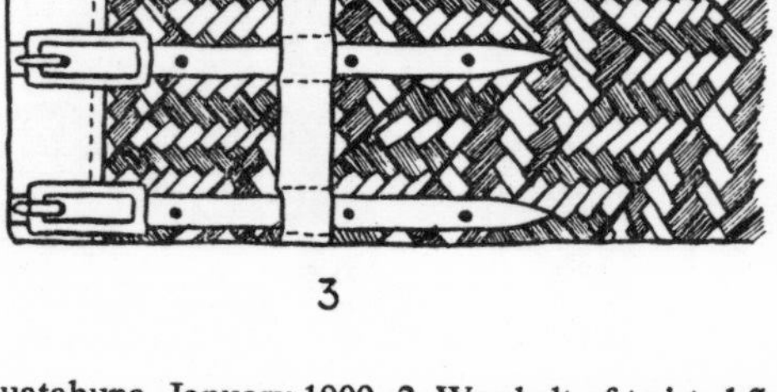

3

156. 1. Pingao belt, tatua pupara, Ruatahuna, January 1900. 2. War belt of twisted flax strands. 3. Modern belt of woven flax, European buckles affixed.

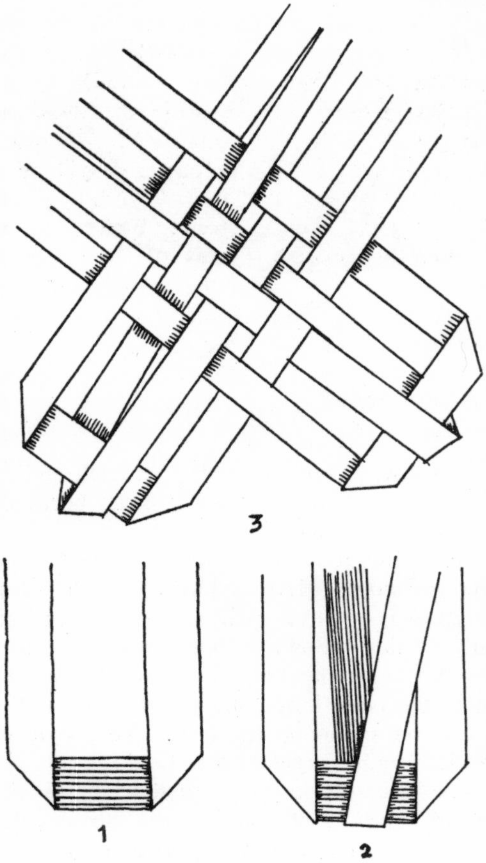

157. Alternative method of making a sandal.

distances became unnecessary with the ownership of horses.

A kawe or burden carrier was used by the Maori partly to replace the balance pole (amo) of their old home. The burden was carried in the kawe in much the same manner as in a soldier's knapsack. It was of somewhat the same construction as the old swag straps used by swaggers in the writer's boyhood. The kawe was a product of the land and was unknown outside New Zealand. Rough bush tracks were impossible for the amo or balance pole, so the backs of women and slaves bore daily burdens tied in the kawe or carried in the kete.

Judge Maning tells us of a dilemma that once occurred in the case of the last canoe to set out on an expedition. All the slaves and commoners had gone on ahead, but there yet remained certain food supplies to be carried to the canoe. Not one of the aristocratic chiefs could carry food on his back, but the trouble was overcome by the chiefs carrying the food burdens down in their arms. Thus was the tapu of head and back retained inviolate.

Sandals

Sandals were in universal use in the South Island, but were less common in the North Island, and on the East Coast seem to have been quite unknown. Sandals were used to protect the feet from frost, splinters, and rough stones. It is even recorded that from five to twenty pairs were sometimes carried by each individual when on the march over rough country. Naturally these sandals, made of raw flax with the sole usually consisting of one layer only, wore out very quickly. A double-soled sandal called torua has been recorded. This was said to last several days. When journeying in Canterbury in 1844, Shortland suggested that the sandals "owed their invention to the necessity of protecting the

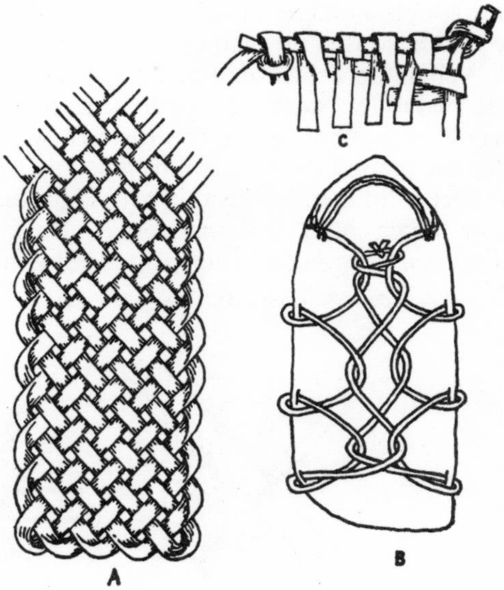

158. Sandal or paraerae: A. The method of plaiting with strips of raw flax; B. Outline of sandal with laces in position, heel band above; C. Half method of completing the heel. (After Buck.)

159. Flax sandals from Otago (after Angas).

feet from the snow, and the small sharp prickles of the small shrub tumatakuri". James Robertson of Martin's Bay was an expert Maori sandal-maker in the 1880s of last century, as my mother, Amy Phillipps, used to tell me.

The sandal has been well described by Sir Peter Buck.* By a study of his diagrams, the student should be able to follow the method of procedure without much effort. The heel portion is represented by the free wefts above. Buck adopts a different manner of completing the heel from that in use on the west coast of the Wellington Province, where a special heel strap, large or small, is used. This is set upright in a curve to encircle the free wefts when the desired length is completed. Around this heel band each weft end in turn is tucked below much after the manner of Buck's illustration, free ends being plaited into the sole below. A tie is necessary at each end of the heel strap which on this coast becomes the laces. (See page 151.)

Transactions of the N.Z. Institute, 54, 1924, p. 357.

According to Angas, it would seem that the Otago sandal differs in having a heel strap composed of three plaited bands attached only to side loops for lacing. Separate laces commence at the ties and cross the feet to enter the back loops and cross again at the heels and so on up the ankle. This style of sandal was formerly used at Otaki.

The illustration given below shows the Maori method of making the ornamental fillet or headband known as kopare or tipare worn on festive occasions, partly to hold the hair in place and partly to support feathers for the hair. The method is well illustrated in the diagram prepared by Mr J. McDonald, and a brief detailed instruction should be adequate.

Two blades of flax of equal width are taken.

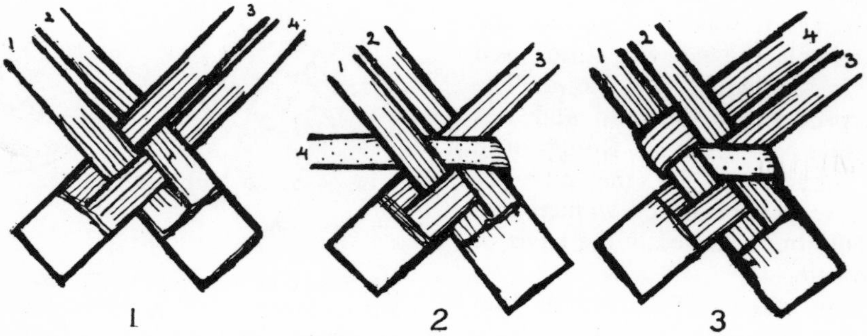

160. The Maori headband.

Bend the flax blades sharply about one and a half inches from the base. Then split each blade into two as far as the bend. This bending of the flax blade, called "he tope" at Otaki, will prevent the wefts splitting to the base of the blade. These two sets with four wefts are interlaced as in figure 1. Study figures 2 and 3 and watch how weft 4 has been woven to bring the four wefts back to the original position, two parallel on each side. Actually, the whole plait is a repetition of this; but in figure 3 we commence with weft 1 and bend it this time from left to right, and then right to left, obliquely upwards, and so on. The headband or kopare plait is very close to our own straw-hat plait. Mr McDonald states: "The Maori says it is an old plait; and the Ngati Porou Tribe of the East Coast call the plait itself mekameka."

A modification of the kopare plait comes from Gladstone near Masterton. With the words, "I will now show you the headband as my people make it," Mrs Pera Ihaka, Ngati Kahungunu tribe, made a sample which is now described. This method of making the headband consists of bringing the right outside weft across all other wefts round the edge of the third weft from the right, under it and up over the weft on the inner side of it to lie parallel on the inside of the single weft on the right. This procedure is a modification of the method shown in illustration 160.

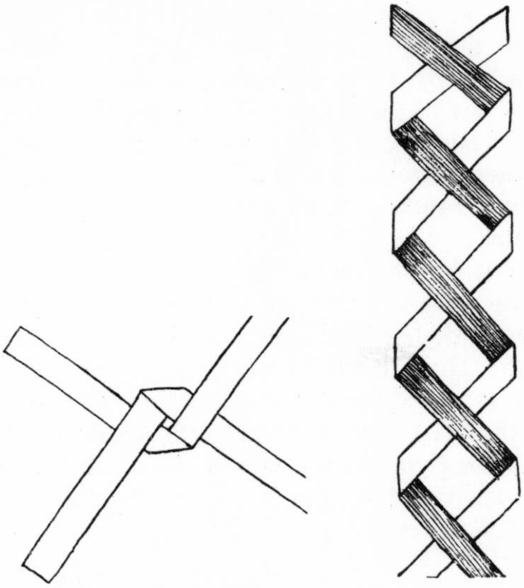

161. Two plait, construction obvious.

One evening we visited Mr Rikihana, Sen., Otaki, carrying a letter of introduction from Mr Elsdon Best. Neither Rikihana nor his wife could speak English so Mr Wills kindly acted as interpreter. We asked whether any knowledge of plaits or plaiting remained. Mrs Rikihana informed us that she had a knowledge of a Maori plait which she called whiri kawe, but no others were known to her. Later Mrs Rikihana was able to show us exactly how this plait was constructed. Mrs Rikihana had learned the art from her mother

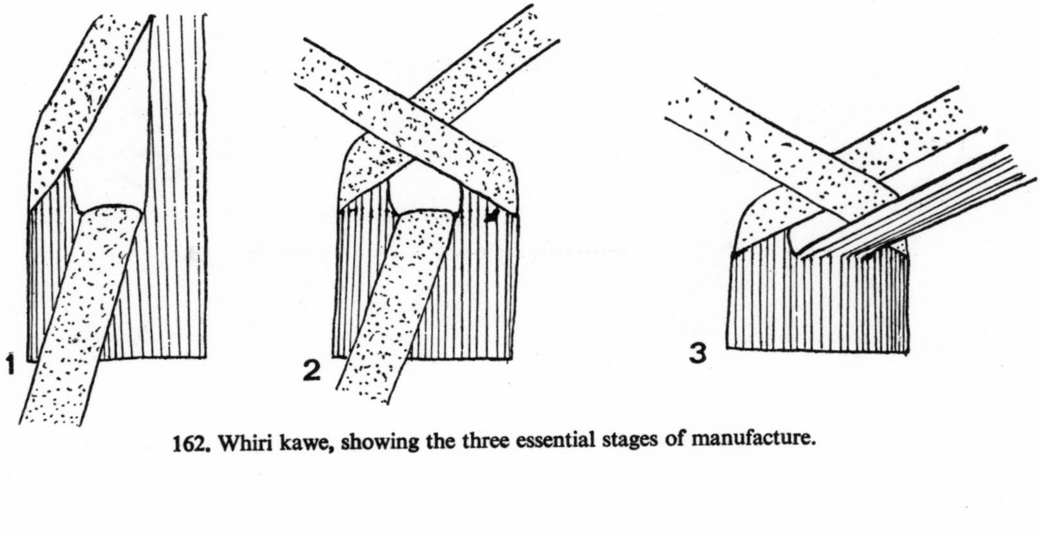

162. Whiri kawe, showing the three essential stages of manufacture.

when very young. At Awanui we found later that the same plait was used for basket handles by Maoris in that locality, though very few of them knew the name of the plait. At Rangitukia this plait was also widely known among the older generation. This three-stranded plait was esteemed for its beauty.

It is simply and readily made as follows: three parallel wefts are taken. They are represented still attached to the butt in the figure. Hold the butt towards you. The centre weft is pulled towards the operator. The weft on the left is turned so that it ranges alongside weft on right. Turn weft on right over weft from left and we get No. 2. Weft originally pulled towards operator now goes over on the right. Repeat this process which is – pull centre weft towards you, weft on left an inwards twist, weft on right over this twist, weft which is towards you down on the right. This plait is still used for basket handles but not for headbands. Well made, it is somewhat elastic.

The small size of the wefts in the sample as first made was a surprise, as was the thinness of the resulting headband; and, through the interpreter, we asked why the headband was made relatively small. The reply received was that in the old days it was always so. Both Rikihana and his wife agreed that the wide headband was modern. In other places several notes indicate that whether the kopare as now plaited is modern or not, in former times the headband was usually quite narrow. As a plait for basket handles the kawe is, of course, made wider.

Knots

Maori knots were of many different kinds. Some were peculiar to the individual, who tied his knots in a manner known only to himself. Any tampering with such knots on a storehouse or other receptacle would immediately be recognised. But there were a number of knots common to all over a fairly extensive area. One such knot is still used by the elderly people of Te Kuiti where it is termed here taniwha. It is unlikely that this knot would emanate from European sources. We were assured that it was an old knot which never slipped.

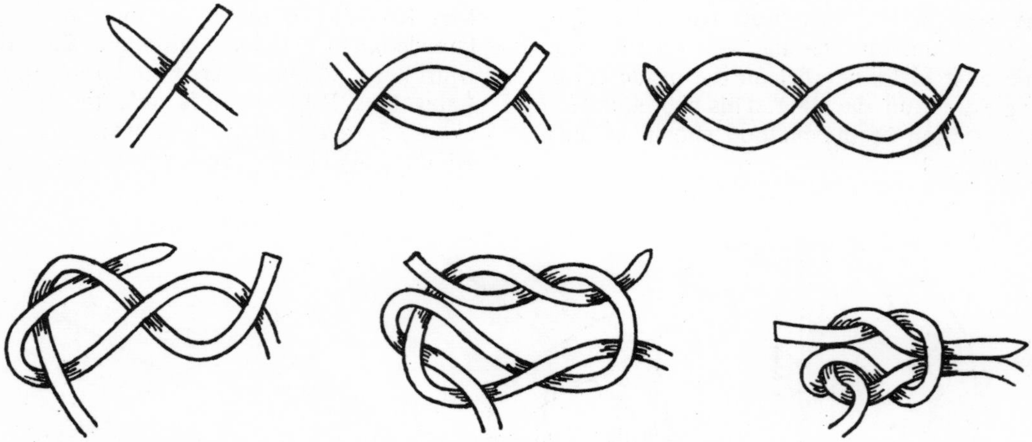

163. A common knot at Te Kuiti – here taniwha.

23

SONGS AND MUSICAL INSTRUMENTS

Songs

In songs and melodies the Maori expressed his innermost feelings and sentiments. Their number ran into thousands, though many would be peculiar to the locality of their origin. Elsdon Best once mentioned his Urewera friend Paitini who, during a single winter, recited to him a thousand songs. Deaths were responsible for the composition of many songs and laments, such as that of a mother expressing her grief for a dead child or a widow yearning for her husband. But any event of importance might be the subject of a song or ditty, sometimes gay, sometimes humorous, or simple lullabies for children. Through many ran a cadence of love and sincerity which would reflect credit on a much more advanced people.

Waiata is the general term used to cover all songs and chants, but there are many different kinds of waiata recognised by descriptive terms. Some of these are: waiata karakia, a ritual formula; waiata aroha, a love song; waiata whaiaipo, a sweetheart song; waiata popo, a lullaby; and waiata tangi, a lament.

Tau is a term often used for ceremonial songs, for example when hauling a canoe the tau waka was chanted. When a tohunga or seer discloses the prophetic utterances of his god or familiar, he sings a divinatory chant known as kite or mata. The pioi is the song of victory sung by a raiding party. There are many others.

Maori songs and chants usually covered a range of not more than one and a half notes, but inside that range there were half and even quarter tones. However, there was a recognised method adopted whereby all could raise their voices to a higher pitch. On still evenings before sunset or at dusk, selected groups would gather in open spaces near certain large trees. Such a singing tree still stood near a homestead on the way to Mahia Peninsula (1924). Here a group gathered to chant their melodies until in the air above the circle a kind of echo would sound, enabling them to lift their voices to higher notes. The general belief was that the

164. Hauling a canoe to tau waka chant.

voices of long past dead were joining with the living. This phenomenon was termed iri-rangi. The reason for it is obscure, but whatever the cause it seems to be part of a belief in the presence of ancestral spirits who returned from the far-off regions to the world of man.

An interesting account of a chant is written by Best:* "In a lament composed by Tamairangi, a famed chieftainess of the Wellington district in the early part of the 19th century, we encounter these lines:

Ko te ngaro pea i a Tuhirangi ki roto
Kaikai-a-waro
I waiho ai koe e Kupe hei rahiri waka rere
i Te Au-miti
I raru ai Potoru.

Take the first line: 'Concealed perchance like Tuhirangi within Kaikai-a-waro.' This falls meaningless on our ears until we are told that Tuhirangi is the Maori name of Pelorus Jack, the famous dolphin of French Pass, and that Kaikai-a-waro is the name of a cave or depth in which he is supposed to live. The next line: 'Left by Kupe to welcome canoes sailing by way of Te Au-miti.' Te Au-miti is the Maori name of French Pass, and the reference to Kupe opens up a long story of old-time Polynesian voyagers and their doings. The last line: 'Where Potoru was baffled' refers to another voyager from Polynesia, whose canoe, Te Ririno, was wrecked at French Pass."

Some years ago when the new carved house, Tama te Kapua, was opened at Rotorua, I wrote the following lament in Maori style in memory of the former carved house, an earlier Tama te Kapua. Tama te Kapau was the great chief who was in charge of the Arawa canoe. The lament has been included as a further example of how a song or chant might contain the whole history of the subject. In explanation, Nga Oho was the old name of the Te Arawa tribe, Te Ao Kapu Rangi was a high-born chieftainess of Te Arawa who climbed on the roof of a still earlier Tama te Kapua on Mokoia Island, all who entered the house coming under her protection. This was when Nga Puhi attacked the island. Te Taupua and Te Hauiti were two of the original carvers. Pango Ngawene was the leading tohunga at Ohinemutu. His hip tattoo was copied for one of the rafter designs, the painters being Hamuera and Poniwahiao. Many of the carvings from the original house were transferred to Owhata and Awahou.

Child of Te Arawa, offspring of Whakaue.
Love of Nga Oho cherished of our parents
This new temple is not you; maybe my
eyes are misty.
In peace were you builded, a memory of
Te Ao Kapu Rangi
Our mother who bestrode the tahu, and so
were Te Arawa saved;
Saved on Mokoia and guns of Nga Puhi
were silent.
Te Taupua and Te Hauiti, what say you?
Tama the great is fallen; Tama, the old, is
gone.
Whither shall we journey, perplexed and
grieved.
Pango Ngawene, priest and sage, you are
the roof.
On the sacred heke your puhoro is out-
lined
By the brush of Hamuera; by the brush of
Poniwahiao
Across your sacred paepae mighty and
great of the earth
Have met to pay you homage, homage to
you, O Tama!
Homage to Te Arawa. Your sacred roof is
gone,
Your mana is no more. With tears my eyes
are dim.
Owhata and Awahou restore again the
limbs:
The heart remains: Goodbye, farewell,
O Tama!

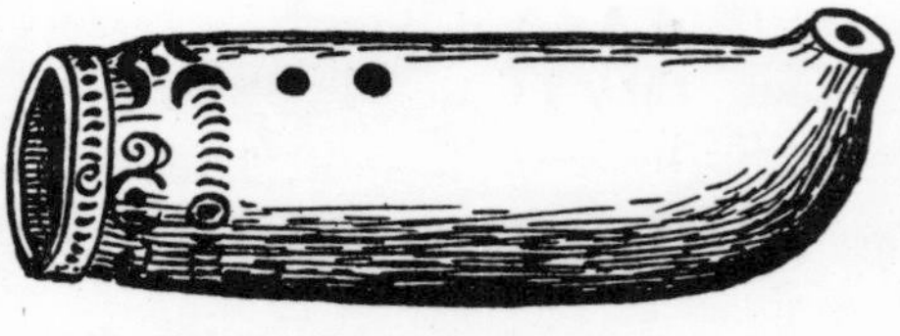

165. Nguru, plain (after Rev. R. Taylor).

*Dominion Museum Bulletin, No. 8, 1925. p. 107.

166. A nose flute (Oldman Collection). About six and a half inches long.

Musical Instruments

Stringed instruments were unknown until Europeans arrived. One early visitor has left it on record that the Maori disliked the violin, so he would play it to get rid of unwelcome guests. Simple melodies appealed most, and a noisy drum also gave them pleasure. Their perception of musical time was accurate.

When Tasman came to New Zealand he was greeted by Maoris who blew several times on an instrument of which the sound was like that of a Moorish trumpet. This was either a shell trumpet or a long wooden trumpet. Captain Cook noted two or three sorts of trumpets and a small pipe or whistle. He found their songs harmonious enough, but

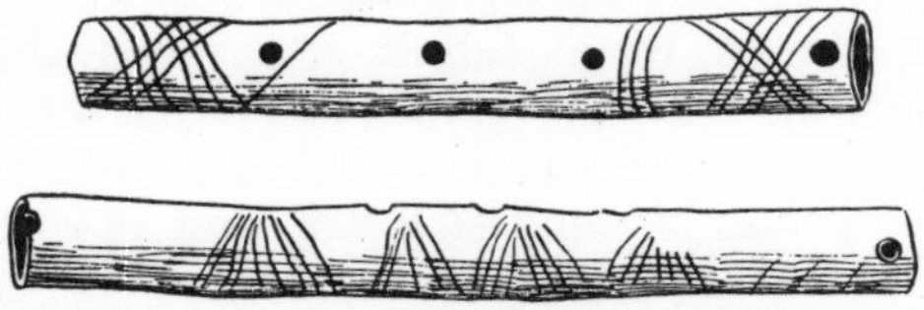

167. Flutes from wing-bone of albatross, Warrington, (after J. Edge Partington).

very doleful to a European ear. The pipe or whistle was evidently the bone or wooden whistle usually termed koauau. These flutes usually have two or three holes and were apparently the most common musical instrument of former times.

Nose Flutes

Nose flutes or nguru differ from koauau in being shorter, relatively thicker and curved at one end where there is a small hole. This small end was held close below or against the right nostril while the left nostril was closed with the left thumb. The nguru was manufactured of stone, bone or wood. There is no record of how the hollowing out process was carried out, but in the case of stone nguru it would have been a long task. Most nguru have two holes along the length to give some modulation to the sounds produced. A wooden specimen in the Hancock Museum, Newcastle-on-Tyne, is unique in still having the suspension cord in the form of a narrow strip of dogskin. The nose flute was once also used in India, and there is also said to be a record of its use in South America.

Pu Torino

The pu torino has been described as resembling a flageolet or piccolo (see page 160). The mouthpiece is at one end, the other end being either open or closed. A bulge in shape appears in the centre of the length, where there is a relatively large hole. This often takes the form of a human mouth. Some detailed carving is usually present. The pu torino is made in two halves neatly fitted together and bound with ake vine. The sound is said to be harsh and shrill, though one writer has described the sound as like water running into a gourd when dipped in the creek. It may here be mentioned that the term pu denotes any long tube or hollow cylinder. When first introduced this was a general term for firearms.

168. Wooden nguru (Hancock Museum, Newcastle-on-Tyne).

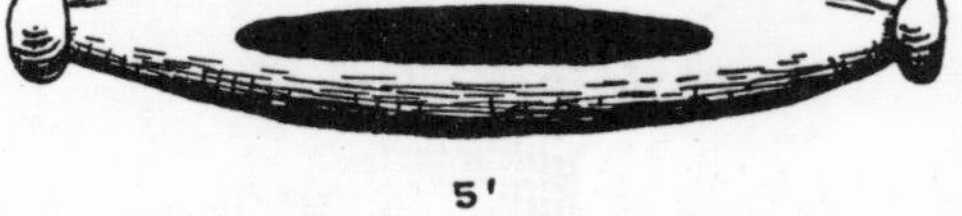

169. Pahu or wooden gong, Ruatahuna (after Best).

Trumpets

The shell trumpet known as pu tatara, was formed from Triton shell formerly found at low tide on beaches of the North Island. Such shells were fitted with a wooden mouthpiece, usually carved, the apex of the shell being first cut off neatly. The call of this shell trumpet was a loud bellowing blare which could be heard over a considerable distance. The call was often a signal for war parties to assemble.

The wooden trumpet (pu kaea) was, like the shell trumpet, used to assemble war parties and assist in sounding the alarm. Relatively few of these have been preserved. This trumpet was made in two halves from selected wood such as the matai. Each of these was fitted carefully together with the bark outside, and usually lashed firmly in position. At the terminal end a bell-shaped mouth was usually constructed. This was either hewn out of the solid or composed of short pieces lashed to the tube. Inside the pu kaea is a tongue or valve which is said to add greatly to its shrillness and power.

The flax bugle, or tetere, was essentially a children's toy which on occasions was used by adults for signalling or heralding the arrival of visitors. Many years ago we were given an account of the flax bugle as used at Otaki, the account being supplied by the late Mr Rawiri Rota Tahiwi. He stated that about the year 1870 he was one of the senior boys attending Otaki school, and at this time it was his duty at 9 a.m. and again at

170. Striking the war gong (after Angas).

171. War trumpet bound with split vine (after J. Edge Partington).

1 p.m. to blow the tetere to summon the children to their classrooms. His model of a flax bugle quickly perished.

Again, in 1933, information was supplied by Mrs Wai Whitinui, Aupori Tribe, Awanui, North Auckland, who stated: "A soft inner blade of flax termed ko rito is taken and rolled around the index finger, crossing at the tip. The rolling is continued in a spiral manner until a tube nine inches long is produced. Another larger blade is taken and commencing at the tip wound tightly round the wide end of this tube and the winding continued until about twelve inches is added. This process is again repeated until a tube three feet long is made. A small piece of flax is taken to secure this wide end."

Another type of bugle was described at Awanui by Mata Tupi and her daughter, Mary. They stated that this bugle was of much importance in former times, for it was commonly used to send messages for some distance. It was also made of flax, but twisted at intervals in process of manufacture. It was made over three feet long and there was a recognised code system of blows which had recognisable meanings. This bugle was likened to a goat's horn.

Gongs

The Maori gong (pahu) was made of wood. It was of two kinds, the first being canoe-shaped and hollow in the centre. When struck with a wooden mallet, it is said to have emitted a sound heard in still weather twenty miles off. An early writer has left us a record of the gong on the platform inside a pa. Here

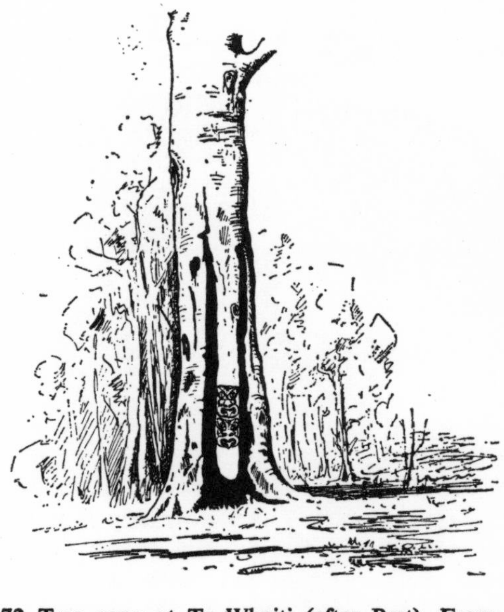

172. Tree gong at Te Whaiti (after Best). From a sketch by Capt. G. Mair in 1869.

the striking stick is shown inside the slot. It may have been used in this manner on occasion, but it is more reasonable to suppose it would be struck on the edge or from above. Thor Heyerdahl has recently told us that a slit drum appears in South America.

A drum made by a Ruatahuna Maori in 1899 was a tree gong where a tongue of wood manufactured from the substance of a hollow tree descended nearly to the ground. The vibrations from this gong were said to have been "tremendous".

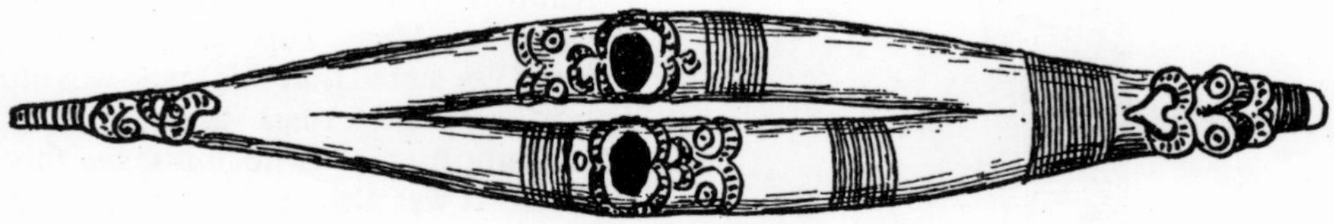

173. Pu torino (after J. Edge Partington).

24

TOYS AND PASTIMES

IT WAS IN AUTUMN and winter that the Maori found time for the arts of pleasure – for pastimes and playing with toys, often in a spirit of competition, and a desire to stand well in the community. A good-natured being of old named Takatakaputea, who dwelt on earth among the seventy children of the Sky Father and the Earth Mother, was one of the main authors of pleasure and the "patron saint" of amusement down the ages.

174. Moari or giant strides (after Sir George Grey).

Pastimes and toys would seem to belong chiefly to the domain of children, but in many games adults participated and held their own competitions. The full range of games in which Maori children and adults indulged regularly was as large as that of many favoured and civilised groups of society. The games included the following: kite flying, wrestling, spinning tops, foot races in couples (taupiripiri), mu tore (a game like draughts), whai (cat's cradle), swings (moari or giant strides), teka (dart throwing), surf riding, swimming, toboganning, riddles, memory games, poi dance with small ball and haka (a posture dance), as well as many other amusements.

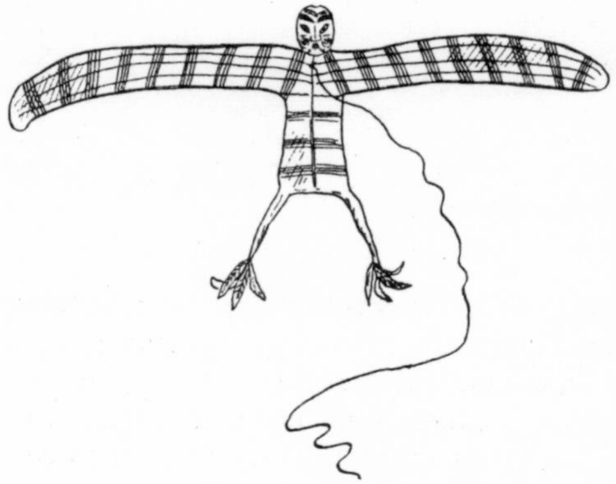

176. Maori kite, British Museum (after J. Edge Partington).

175. Children's kite, manu taratahi (after Best).

Swings

First of all we will discuss swings, of which there were several forms. Sometimes a seat would be attached to a trailing vine. A favourite swing was the moari or giant strides, where a number of ropes were attached to the summit of a tall pole erected on undulating ground or on the edge of a river bank. Each rope would have a person clinging to it and everyone joined in the chanting and merriment. As will be seen in the illustration (page 161), a younger child sits on an improvised seat while the rest hang on using both arms.

Elsdon Best has left us the following chant sung by Ngati Porou moari players:

Ka rere au, ka rere au
Ka rere au i te morua titi,
E kohera, e kohera po,
Ki roto wai titi.

Kites

Kite flying was a favourite pastime of children and men. The kites (manu) made by children were easily manufactured of common materials such as raupo (bulrush), while those of the men were more elaborate and of large size. Kites were of two main types, those

177. Bullroarer with whizzer above (after A. Hamilton).

with tails and those without. The tailed types were usually triangular or of a shape that gave some balance, while the kites without tails had human features and bird form, the general shape somewhat resembling a monoplane. The kite was used not only in play, but also sometimes by adults in ritual and divination. We have shown a delicately made specimen consisting of flowering stalks of the toetoe together with cross pieces of raupo sewn neatly across them; also a bird man form in the British Museum.

Darts

From Mr Ray Humphries, of Titahi Bay, comes a Maori game in which a blade of flax was cast as much as 200 yards by somewhat the same method as the sling spear (kopere) used in warfare. A blade of flax was taken with a good butt end and cut off short near its apex. From the midrib a strip was partly detached, its free end being tied to a long handle. Swinging this in the appropriate overhead manner, Maori children were able to send a flax blade flying through the air a

178. Slinging the flax blade.

remarkable distance. When thrown the mid-rib would strip from off the blade before it became airborne. This game was first observed in the 1890s in the Wairarapa by Mr Les Gaskin of Martinborough. The throwing stick had to be long, as long as possible, nine, ten, or even twelve feet. We have seen this game demonstrated, and Mr Humphries, who tried it many times, states that the longer the pole the better the result. Mr Patu R. Ranapia of Te Kaha also assured us that it was common in the Bay of Plenty.

The Manchester Museum owns a long carved pole which may have been used for slinging flax blades or darts. It is well carved all over except for the short pointed end. Janus-like figures appear on the upper stem. A remarkable feature is the reduction and apparent weakening of the pole in the lower half of its length. This may have been a deliberate contrivance for hitching the string for throwing purposes.

Bullroarers

A bullroarer (purerehua) was used by Maoris in many parts of New Zealand. It consisted of a relatively thin, elongate piece of wood pointed at the ends and attached to a cord which varied in length according to the size of the wooden slot. At its free end the cord was usually attached to a handle, much in the same manner as a crude fishing line. The user held the handle end and vigorously swung the bullroarer into action. In Otago schools, 1900–6, this game was commonly played by children (perhaps derived from Maori

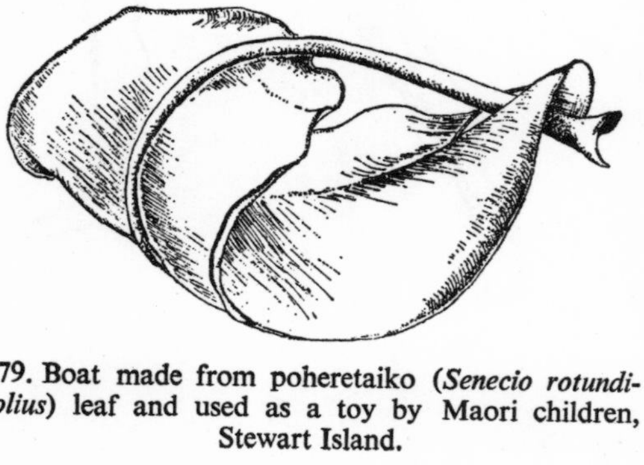

179. Boat made from poheretaiko (*Senecio rotundifolius*) leaf and used as a toy by Maori children, Stewart Island.

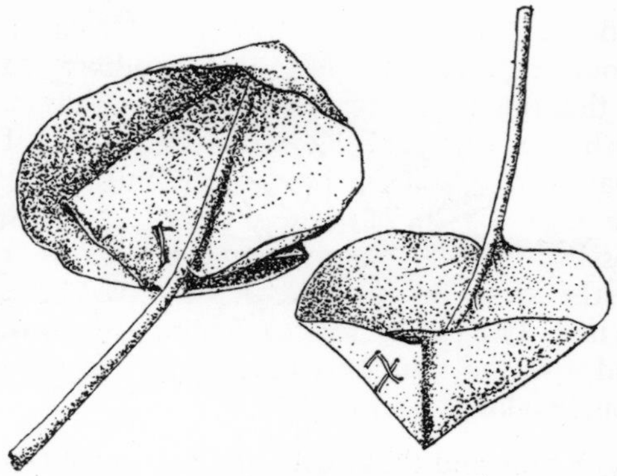

180. Leaf cups from Stewart Island.

sources), some skill being required to get the correct sound. The shape of the wooden slat, length of cord and length of handle, were all regarded as matters of importance. Augustus Hamilton tells us that on the west coast of the North Island the bullroarer was used in certain funeral ceremonies.

Cat's Cradle

A game in which children as well as adults excelled was usually termed whai, and is known to us as cat's cradle. It is a pastime which is found in every land. In the long winter evenings the construction of string figures of various patterns was regarded as a useful pastime. It trained both the brain and the fingers. Any child who was quick and clever at learning whai was deemed worthy of being taught higher things. Several people would collaborate in setting up the more complicated figures, and contests in proficiency at string games were not uncommon.

Leaf Cups and Boats

Recently, through the courtesy of Mr R. H. Traill, we have had presented to the Dominion Museum two small leaf cups as formerly used by children on Stewart Island. Leaves of the puheretaiko tree, *Senecio rotundifolius*, were taken and a section of the leaf folded inwards to make a large cone at one end of it. This fold was secured by one or more ties. The stalk was held in the hand while drinking. The puheretaiko leaf grows to a large size and is somewhat leathery. Mr R. H. Traill had the cups made by Mrs Dawson, Half Moon Bay, Stewart Island. A modification of this toy comes from Mr Rongo Halbert, Gisborne, who said that sixty years ago leaf boats were a common toy used by children on the East Coast. They were blown as far as possible from the shore and then taken over by the wind. Rongo Halbert's sample shows an inner tying of the leaf, as in our illustration, and also the stem tied inwards to the same point making a rolled leaf.

Tops

The whipping tops of the Maori are divided into two main classes, the potaka-takiri, or common whipping tops, and the potaka-whawhai, which may be described as fighting tops. The potaka-whawhai, like the common whipping top, was spun furiously by means of a whip of flax which had a wooden handle with strips of flax tied to it. Contests were generally arranged and performed by adults, the tops being spun in some cleared space or along well-known top-spinning routes. Sometimes these fighting tops were of large size.

However, we are concerned here with a group of whipping tops of moderate size collected by the late Captain Bollons, mostly on middens around New Zealand coasts. They were probably made and used by children. In all, the collection consists of six tops which vary in length from one and three-quarter inches to two and three-quarter inches. Pumice tops would probably require constant sharpening if used to any great extent, but as pumice was very common it would be possible to fashion new tops or shape old ones as required.

Windmills

The drawings on page 167 illustrate the toy windmill. The first shows the method of manufacture. Two blades of flax of equal width are taken and these are crossed as seen on the back of the completed toy. Then we bend each blade in the shape of the letter N, the ends being fitted one into the other. The ends are now pulled tightly together and the

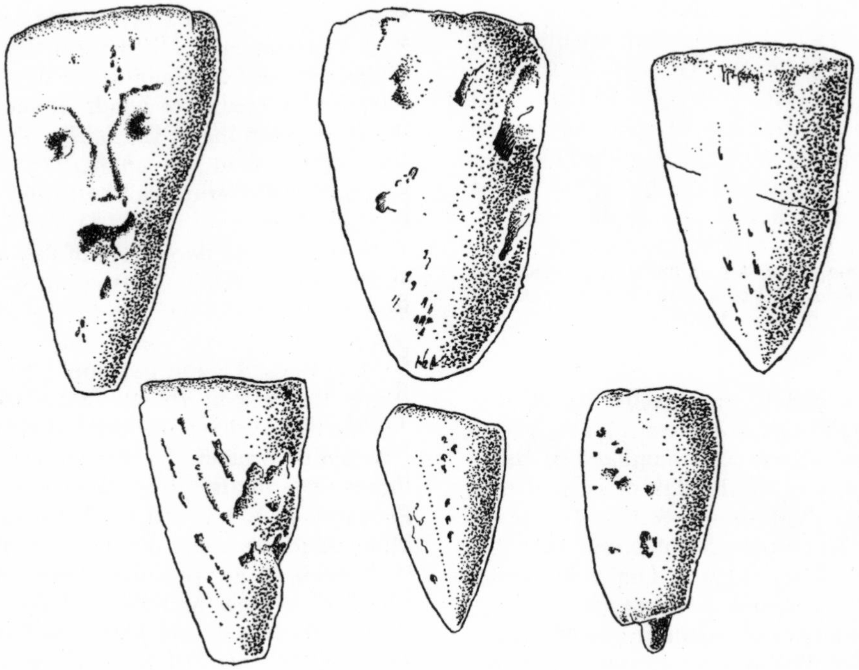

181. Maori tops.

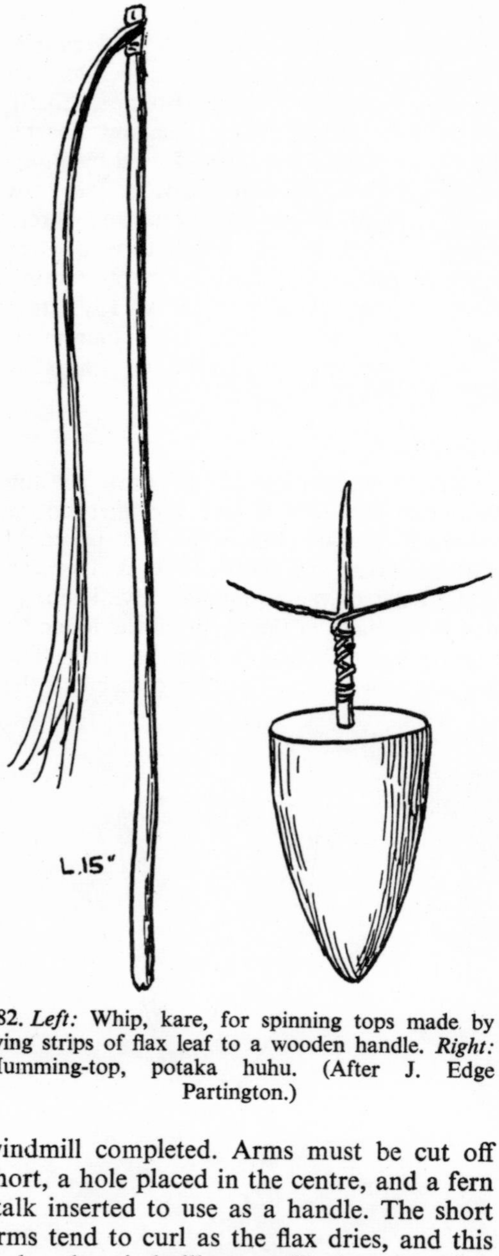

182. *Left:* Whip, kare, for spinning tops made by tying strips of flax leaf to a wooden handle. *Right:* Humming-top, potaka huhu. (After J. Edge Partington.)

windmill completed. Arms must be cut off short, a hole placed in the centre, and a fern stalk inserted to use as a handle. The short arms tend to curl as the flax dries, and this makes the windmill more effective. For some time there was much doubt about this toy which was first recorded at Otaki. However an identical windmill is made of coconut leaflets in Niue Island, according to Mr J. M. McEwen. Later is was ascertained that the windmill was known as tititi parerera, and was correctly made of raupo. As they used this toy the children used a charm addressed to the god of the wind to make their windmills turn: "Homai ra he hau motaku titi parerera".

Miniature Canoes

A boy who lived in Dunedin in the 1860s found that toy boat racing was an important pastime of Maori youths. As they were taught by their elders, they constructed flax boats in large numbers. They were sailed in and around Dunedin. In the year 1931, Sir Alfred Robin, the young boy of the 1860s, constructed a flax boat for the Dominion Museum, and from this the illustration has been drawn. Later it was ascertained that similar toy flax boats were made by Bay of Plenty children.

In the series of drawings supplied we can trace the manner in which the toy craft is constructed. A fairly wide blade of flax is taken and cut obliquely from the midrib upwards at a point near the butt end. A length long enough for the intended boat is then cut, and the open ends of the flax perforated and sewn together neatly by means of a fine piece of flax, the sewing being done by deft movements of the fingers. Three pieces of flax are used as miniature seats. These are attached by means of bends at each end of the seats. Sections of the fabric of the inner sides of the boat are uplifted so as not to penetrate the exterior and these hold the three seats in place.

To erect a sail, two pieces of flax are cut as in diagrams 2 and 3; 3 is the sail stay, and is bent at the point H, the lower part being placed beneath the seat and upper part holding the sail (2) in position. The property which flax has of rolling in on itself as it commences to dry holds the sail securely.

When first made, the claw or V-like sail of these tiny boats gives them an unusual appearance. Small strips of flax are often attached to the upper points of the sail to aid in holding it in position. Below they are attached to bow and stern. Vessels with a claw sail have been recorded from Santa Cruz, while "half-moon" sails have been recorded from Hawaii and the Society Islands.

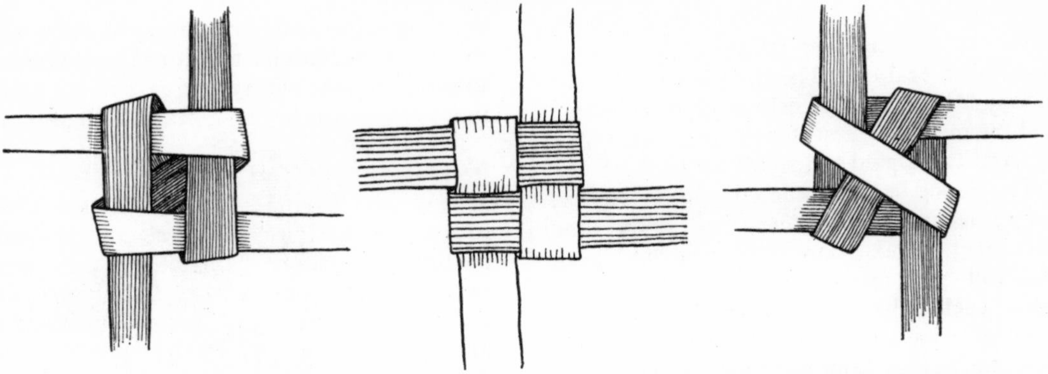

183. Making a Maori windmill. *Left:* Construction. *Centre:* Completed front. *Right:* Completed back.

Dances

Two dances were the haka and the poi. The haka was for the most part a posture dance, vigorously performed by men, originating from the many gestures of defiance and contempt hurled at an enemy on the eve of battle. Sometimes even a sham fight was sufficient to provoke such a dance, and one early writer tells us that the dance was conducted with so much fury on both sides that at length he became quite horrified, and for some time he could not divest himself of

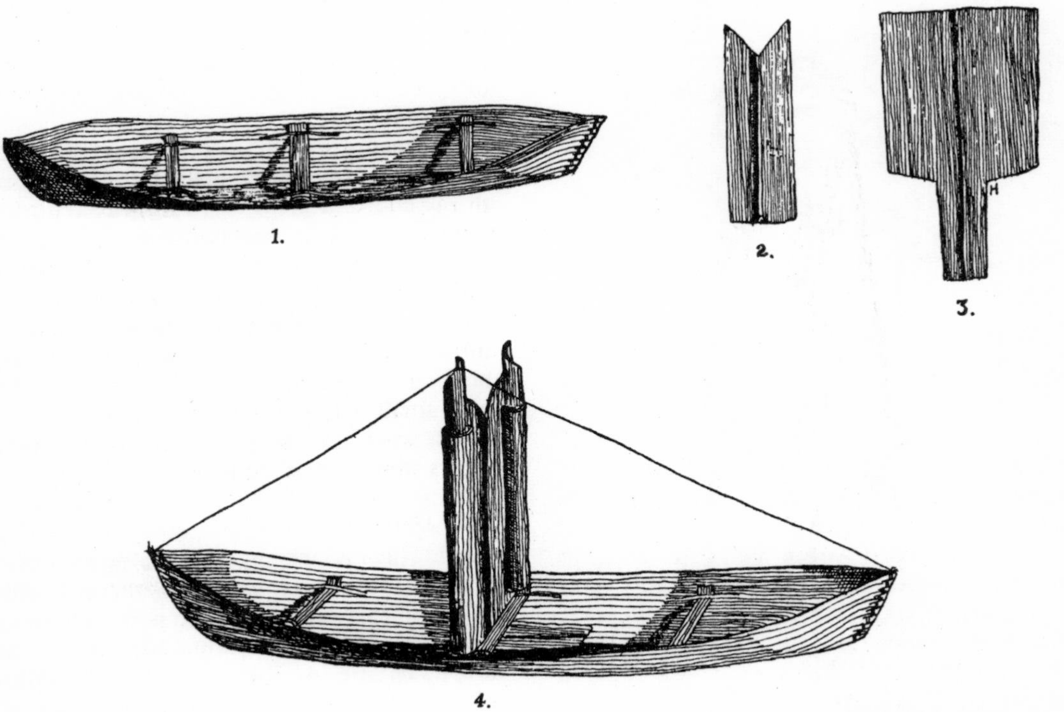

184. Toy canoe of the type used in Dunedin in the 1860s made by Sir Alfred Robin. 1. Upper oblique view. 2. The sail. 3. Stay for sail. 4. The completed canoe.

the feeling that the performers were playing false, so closely did this mock combat resemble a real one. The dreadful noises, the hideous faces, the screeching of the women, and the menacing gestures of each party were expertly calculated to inspire terror.

The dance today, while still full of vigour, cannot recapture the intensity of the old-time performers. Haka dances have always been and still are practised on ceremonial occasions, each tribe jealously guarding its own series of haka and training its performers over long periods. A famous Hawke's Bay haka, said to have been one of the best of its kind, was dictated by Mr Hore Kawhe, in July 1946, at Te Karaka, Waiohiki:

Ko te korou ano te kaha taua
Aha! ha!
Ko taku paataka ko te Waiohiki (*repeat*)
Ko kitea i reira te hanga ne te tangata (*repeat*)
E hiwaha, hitarera, hou! he! ha!

Apparently this haka was composed for the opening of a well-known pataka built at Waiohiki by Tareha te Moananui, M.P., in the '50s of last century.

185. Elongate raupo-type poi ball.

186. Circular poi, Waitara, Taranaki.

Poi Dances

The other form of posture dance, which has survived to the present, is the poi. Here a ball on the end of a piece of string was kept in a regular twirling motion by the performers, all acting in perfect unison. It is usually played only by women. A common type of ball was either oval or nearly circular and made of raupo, while special balls were larger and more carefully made. Here we must record a quite small ball with piupiu attached used by parties when travelling in Taranaki. Songs or chants were sung during the performance.

Hand Games

Another game which trained the eyes and muscles to act in complete accord was matimati, played by young and old alike, and esteemed as a vogorous exercise of the body. The late Mr Rikihana, Sen., of Otaki, a kind and genial man who was master of many avenues of Maori learning, demonstrated the manner of its performance. At

Otaki matimati was played as elsewhere with five movements: both hands slap thighs; movements (both hands) to right; movements to left; movements to breast; and movements above the head. Competitors face each other and with hands on hips one commences with a toro totonawa, then a ngahi ngahiono, then whituwani, then a te iwa haka, then a hurimai, the winning cry. Meanwhile the hands have been in fast motion, one competitor endeavouring to keep up with his opponent. Matimati was the term often used at the commencement when facing each other with hands on hips.

In 1933 Tu Manahi supplied the Arawa version of this game. There are, in all, five actions which are as follows: 1, slap thighs; 2, hands right; 3, hands left; 4, hands slap chest; 5, hands above head. To commence: 1. E mate ra (hands on hips) or Mate rawa, mate rawa; 2. E ma or E mate (hands as desired); 3. E mate (loser starts); 4. E hingi (previous winner replies); 5. E hingi ona (winning cry); 6. E whiu (previous loser); 7. E whiu waru (winning cry); 8. E te iwa (loser starts); 9. E te iwa haka (winning cry); 10. E tuku (loser starts); 11. E tuku mai (final winning cry).

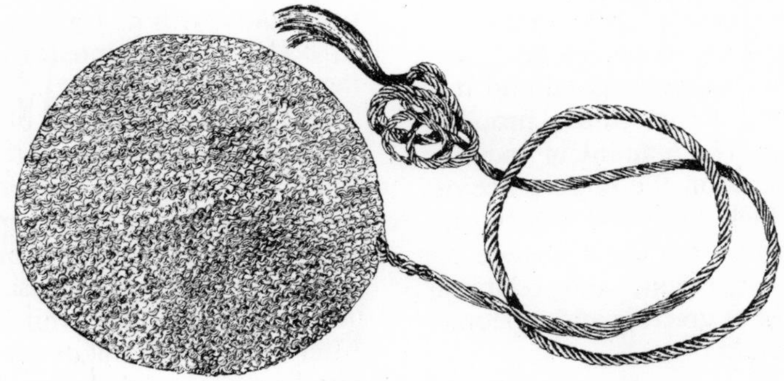

187. Long poi with outer netted covering of muka fibre and stuffed with raupo down.

25

THE LIFE CYCLE

MAORI MOTHERS AND THEIR BABIES

The Newborn child

The birth of a child was regarded as an important event. The mother and her attendant were moved to a small building which was known as the nest house or whare kohanga, when certain signs were observed. The building was tapu and set apart from the village. The mother remained there for a week or more after the birth of her child. Then came the day when relatives arrived and the mother sat in front of her house proudly exhibiting her baby. The amount of speech-making would depend on the importance of the family into which the child was born. Presents of some sort were usually made to the mother and her infant, and relatives came with a message of greeting and welcome to the newly born child.

Baptismal Ceremony

The grandparents were sometimes responsible for the upbringing of grandchildren whom they claimed during babyhood. Ordinary children had a short baptismal ceremony in which mother and nurse accompanied the tohunga to a stream. In the case of high-born infants this ceremony was greatly extended, and concluded with the child being placed at a favoured spot beneath the window or on the porch of the large assembly house, surrounded by tribal treasures and weapons.

Massage

Information relating to the traditional manner of treating babies in the Urewera has been provided by Mrs Peter Beckett. During the first day of the baby's life, the baby's head was held firmly at the back with one hand and pressure exerted gently with the other, which was held as flat as possible on the forehead of the child. This was in order to flatten the forehead and prevent bulging. It was essential that this should be done on the first day of the baby's life. It was important that, when not being fed, cleaned, or massaged, the baby should be wrapped tightly with its legs in a straight line with its body. This was intended to prevent bandiness.

The happiest moments of a baby's life were the periods of massage. All mothers did this, being instructed by those of an older generation. The baby's feet were gently shaped with the right hand, from toes to heel. Some kneading was necessary. The toes were held in the left hand while treating the heel. After washing the body, the legs were massaged on the outside with a little oil. Before being put to bed at night the child was massaged on the trunk, front, and back, as well as on the arms. It is said that the feet could be shaped correctly only on the day after birth.

The statement that the baby was wrapped tightly in a band of lacebark or a cloak for the first three weeks of its life was verified at the Bay of Islands and elsewhere. It was described as being wrapped "stiff as a poker". It was found that a number of Maori mothers had actually practised massage on their own offspring. In particular, Mrs Waioeka Brown, of the East Coast, stressed the importance of this for babies and growing children. She used three distinct motions: mirimiri, short strokes with the fingers; tukituki, an up-and-down pounding; and romiromi, the kneading motion used generally in massage.

Sir Peter Buck has written: "I remember my mother looking at my legs approvingly and saying, 'My hands made your legs what they are.' There is a saying which counsels mothers: 'Stretch the legs of your daughter that she may walk with grace across the courtyard before the assembled people.' "

Clothing

Warmth was one of the first essentials for the newly born baby. A coating of large leaves was heated slightly and plastered around the body. An ancestor of a leading Gisborne family was known as Tapipi, which was the name given to the custom of plastering leaves around the body for warmth. In the interior of the North Island it was customary to tie a well-beaten bandage of tapa, prepared from the bark of the lacebark or hohere tree, around the body of the baby. This custom appears to have been common in many places but is now forgotten.

Near Taihape, the diaper consisted of a fine moss known as kohukohu. The baby was enveloped in this, and at intervals the soiled, wet portions were removed for washing and new material added. A wrap known as kope was placed around it. On the East Coast, only fine muka scrapings known as kuka were used for the newborn child. The usual term for these was kukukuku, kuku being the mussel shell used in the preparation of the fibre. At Hokianga the moss, waiwaikoko, gave off a pleasing perfume, and when dry it was used in place of diapers. The same was true of the fern mangemange.

When the baby was old enough, it was often placed in some sort of receptacle containing its covering of moss or muka fibre. The muka fibre has great lasting qualities. In the north there is some evidence that muka fibre which had served the parents was also used for the children, having been washed many hundreds of times. On the

188. Common kete used to hold small baby immersed in muka fibre.

East Coast a coarse basket was used as a container, and the baby was immersed in muka fibre, remaining there for part of the first year of life. Other informants have told of the occasional use of the basket for the baby, but not on the permanent basis employed on the East Coast, where this custom obtained until late last century. It is probable that many babies survived the crowded wharepuni at night because of their immersion in a basket which could be tied to the wall or rafter.

Kope is the usual term for a baby's diaper of today. In the past this seems to have been the wrap which enveloped the baby and held the kuka, or kukukuku, in position. The present North Island term for a baby's cloak is generally whariki, while kope is reserved for the actual diaper. Rope is a similar term used in Northland.

Pokeka was a well-known southern generic term for a fine cloak for babies. Tiny children appear to have become used to the state of nudity at a very early age unless the weather was cold, as in Southland. When learning to walk Maori babies were sometimes held in a supple-jack frame or pakokori.

About the year 1875, an English child named Florence Rogers was born at Ohanga on the east coast of the North Island. Her parents engaged the services of a local Maori woman to act as nurse, a gentle person named Heterina. Heterina was greatly honoured to have charge of the child and, to show her esteem for it, she decided that it must have a wrap. It was to be no ordinary garment, but a wrap which was fit only for a high-born infant. The weaving must have its appropriate poka, or shorter weft rows, to make the wrap fit more snugly around the small body. Warmth was not essential to a child who had other tiny garments, so the open-work technique of the ornamental basket, kete whakawaitara, was used. Lastly, a fringe of European wool was added.

The wrap was used on all the important occasions during the first year of the baby's life. It was then carefully stored away, until Florence Rogers, no longer young, presented the garment to the Dominion Museum.

Carrying the Baby

When the Maori mother went abroad and wished to take the baby with her she carried it on her back. In some localities a kawe, or swag strap, made from the bark of the lacebark tree and pounded to make it soft, encircled the baby's body so that it could not fall to the ground. This had the advantage of leaving the mother with both hands free. An enveloping cloak, generally a korowai, was placed round it. No examples of this kawe have been preserved, though it is possible that these were once in general use.

In some localities Maori girls from the age of nine or ten upwards carried the babies on their backs. The load was lifted only at infrequent intervals during the day and the girls had of necessity to be spectators in the games rather than participants. In addition to bearing children, the mothers were required to perform many other duties which were usually undertaken by men. Special food-producing duties, building, canoe making, and fighting were the main tasks of Maori men. All the rest, including the drudgery of collecting firewood, cooking, assisting with agriculture, the treatment of fish and birds for food, collecting shellfish, etc., was the lot of the average Maori woman. Widows of middle class or inferior families were sometimes given the task of the daily collection of firewood for the umu, the preparation of food, and other menial tasks.

MARRIAGE CUSTOMS

Maori Marriages

Maori marriages were of several types, the least important being, perhaps, what has been described as the "customary marriage". This type of marriage was common among the lower classes. It usually consisted of a brief courtship and a decision to live together as man and wife, without consulting anyone. Such marriages sometimes led to troubles if members of the upper class dared to defy convention. The second form was the marriage of people belonging to the middle classes, who contracted social marriages or concurred with the arrangements which had been made for them in childhood or adolescence, marrying for social position, land, or to cement the links between hapu, families, and sub-tribes. The third form of marriage was that contracted by the aristocracy and higher grades of society. Such marriages would be the result of long tribal discussions, and would be accompanied by some form of religious ceremony. For political reasons it was considered desirable to marry inside the hapu.

There was some variation in these forms of marriage, according to tribe or locality. The second grade marriage, termed pakuwha, was more common in some tribes than in others, and consisted of a formal handing over of the bride to her husband. The amount of ceremonial in such a marriage often depended on the economic status of the people concerned and their social standing in the community.

According to South Island records, it seems that the custom of infant betrothal, taumou or tapui, was almost universal. Young people who disagreed with their parents would often choose to elope with someone else. This breaking of an old custom sometimes led to wars and disputes. In the North Island infant bethrothals were less common, though they were sometimes regarded as necessary to link tribal groups or distant relatives more closely together. Betrothals could take place at any time during childhood, and much formality is said to have accompanied betrothal requests, particularly if the infants were of chiefly rank.

Marriage Feast

The marriage feast was known as the umu kotore, and this might also apply to the bride's younger sisters, otherwise they might become barren.

It was usual for a woman who married a man from another tribe to live with and claim allegiance with her husband's tribe after marriage, but sometimes, when the woman was the stronger personality, the husband would leave his own tribe and live among his wife's people. In this case the husband would be required to surrender his land rights, and was sometimes regarded as a nonentity in his wife's tribe. Most men married only one wife, though common consent enabled the man to marry a second if the first wife proved sterile. A chief of high lineage usually had several wives, and it seems to have been an accepted axiom that the senior wife had a position of authority over the others, particularly if she was the mother of a first-born son. A first-born child would have land rights and privileges over the other children.

Early contacts with missionaries led many Maoris who had adopted Christianity into church marriages, but this system broke down during the internecine wars of last century. Customary marriages with little celebration or ritual became common, and these were legally recognised in the Maori Land Court and elsewhere until early this century. Under the Marriage Act, 1910, it became necessary for a formal marriage between Maoris, or between Maoris and Europeans, to be contracted in a recognised manner.

DEATH AND BURIAL

Tangi

When a death occurred, the Maori people unashamedly gave way to their feelings. The period of mourning, which is now limited to three days, was known as the tangi (weeping). To a European observer, the tangi is something inexpressibly sad and forlorn. The death of one person affects everyone. Others have who passed to the spirit world are again remembered and mourned. Wailing and lamentation by women continues at intervals day and night until the burial takes place.

Death means the arrival of visitors from

far and near to join in the general mourning, and to partake of the hospitality of the bereaved. This entails an immediate demand for large quantities of food and adequate shelter for all. In all communities there was usually individuals who could exercise control in such emergencies, and deal with the problems as they arose. Visitors were welcomed with speeches and salutations, after which came the hongi, a nose-pressing ceremony, which in some instances included an embrace.

Visitors usually brought with them some treasured possession, such as a cloak or a greenstone mere, as a gift for the dead. After their respects has been paid to the dead food was served to everyone. Relatives, particularly women, wore a symbolic wreath of kawakawa, or some other sacred tree. Some even wore chaplets of seaweed, symbolic of the journey which the spirit must make when it plunges into the sea at Cape Reigna to cross the great ocean westwards to the land of spirits.

Formerly, when a great chief died, he might lie in state with his weapons and prized possessions forming a fitting background to his last appearance before his fellows. His famous deeds, his great battles, or his work as a food provider, were recalled and retold. Reference would be made to his high and ancient lineage, and his great ancestors would be named, particularly if they had founded co-lateral lines. Funeral dirges would be sung, and certain chants suitable to the occasion would be intoned.

When leaving the presence of the dead it is customary to back away with the face still towards the departed. This is said to be a very old custom dating from early times. In addressing the dead it was customary to explain that the wairua must now depart from the haunts of men and cross the great ocean of Kiwa to be with those who have departed this life. There was a customary belief that the spirit was permitted to remain in its familiar haunts for a period of nine days, after which certain rites were taken to ensure its departure.

One beautiful echo of the tangi is the remembrance and appreciation of the dead which is a part of the greeting when old friends meet. Before ordinary courtesies are exchanged, visitors stand apart while an orator bewails the loss suffered by the passing of relatives and friends. After this come the greetings – in particular the hongi, consisting of a nose-pressing ceremony, already mentioned, which is sometimes simply a caress with the side of the nose.

After the sacred ceremonies performed during the tangi, it was necessary to observe a whakanoa ceremony which would remove the tapu of the close relatives of the deceased, and also to relieve the tensions which had arisen. The ceremonial observance known as takahi was employed throughout the North Island with the exception of Northland. Essentially it consisted of stamping through the house where death had occurred, thus driving spirits away from the dwelling, and even to send the wairua of the deceased, which may have been held to his home by bonds of affection, on the long journey to the Reinga. By observance of the takahi, which removes the tapu not only from the close relatives but also from the house itself and all its chattels, normality returns to the place of death; this is celebrated by a final hakari or feast.

An important part of the ceremony was the sprinkling of water where the body had lain and elsewhere in and around the house, which substantiates the definition of the verb takahi in the latest William's *Dictionary of the Maori Language:* "Perform a ceremony, involving stamping on the ground, for producing water." (This goes back to the time of Ngatoroirangi of Arawa fame.) There is also a reference to a karakia.

No record of a stamping ceremony has been left to us by any of the great writers of the past, possibly because it was an intimate ceremony in which a limited family group was concerned. It is even more astounding that such a ceremony has persisted into the present century without being recorded. Mr M. R. Jones has reported that he has attended the ceremony several times amongst his Waikato and Maniapoto people and referred particularly to the karakia which was chanted by an elder relative as he preceded the family through the house. Modern prayers are sometimes substituted for the karakia.

The following karakia takahi had been supplied by Mr P. te H. Jones of Taumarunui. It is one of two often used in the Waikato which he had memorised. It will be seen that the karakia is really an extension of the tangi and is an exhortation to the spirit to take its departure to the Reinga and the new life of of the spirit world.

He Karakia Takahi

Ka hura tangata a-uta
  Ki tangata a-uta;
Ka hura tangata a-tai
  Ki tangata a-tai.
Pera hoki ra te korepe nui,
  Te korepe roa, te wahi awa;
Te totoe awa whakamoea.
  Whakamoe tama
I araia te ara!

Kauraka tama e uhia
  Tukua atu tama
Kia puta atu
  I te ta-whangawhanga
He putanga ariki
  Ki te whei-ao
Ki te ao-marama
  Tihe!
Mauri ora!

A Purificatory Incantation

Men of the land bewitch
  Men of the land;
Men of the sea bewitch
  Men of the sea.
Hence the parting of the many,
  The long parting, the parting by [water;
The parting, alas, with the doomed [now asleep.
  O son, now sleeping
Arise betimes, and be on your way!
Let our son go free,
  Let him go onward
Until he emerges
  And goes forth o'er the bay.
Let him go forth like a high chief
  Into the dawn,
And onward into the world of light!
  Sneeze lustily!
'Tis the breath of life!

Burial

To some extent the disposal of the dead varied with the locality. While the head was often retained in some convenient spot, the disposal of leg and arm bones, as well as certain other larger bones, was a matter of deep concern to close relatives. The trussed-up skeleton might be placed in the branches of a tree, or in a cave. Common people were usually buried in the ground, or in the sand hills by the seashore. In the case of the leaders, the bones were well concealed lest an enemy might find them and use them in the manufacture of bone fish hooks, to taunt the tuhe of the departed chief. In communities which felt themselves secure from attack, a burial house was sometimes made to hold the bodies of famous men. Such a burial house was once situated not far from Manutuke, near Gisborne. In his study of the early Polynesians who settled at the Wairau bar, Blenheim, Dr R. S. Duff found that selected individuals, probably chiefs, were buried with their main treasures, adzes, and necklaces, as well as with food for the spirit journey, in the form of moa eggs.

Monuments to the dead were common. The body of the deceased might remain in such a monument for a short period, perhaps a year, and then be removed and buried elsewhere. These monuments were erected to commemorate great men. One of the most common was the canoe cenotaph. It apparently embodied the old idea of a spirit journey across water after death. When a great chief died his canoe was cut into two parts, the prow being erected as his memorial. Sometimes a great deal of decorative skill was lavished on these monuments, and a few were carved. In fact some of the most exquisite carved pieces which have found their way into museums may have once belonged to monuments erected for the dead, an instance of this being certain of the group of Te Kaha carvings in Auckland Museum.

Tombs and Chests

In the monuments to the dead as portrayed by G. F. Angas, the first and upper tomb is described as "mausoleum of Tohi, mother of Rauparaha, on the island of Mana in Cook Strait". This richly ornamented tomb is constructed of wood, painted and decorated with feathers. The border of a kaitaka mat is seen depending in front of the papatu papaku, or box for the body, within which the body was originally placed in a sitting posture. All the ground within the outer rail is strictly tapu. The second and fourth figures are canoe cenotaphs, one from a small pa in Tory Channel and the other from Te Awaiti, Cloudy Bay, while between these is figured a carved tiki in an old pa near Lake Roto Aira. To the left of the lower face on which the man's figure stands is a little elevated whata or box for holding the bones of a favourite child. The last and lower figure is a monument to three children near Te Awaiti, Cloudy Bay.

A small group of old carved chests shaped in human form have been found in caves in the Hokianga district, and at Raglan. Elsdon Best always believed that owing to their "un-Maori-like" carving, and the fact that at the time of their discovery no Maoris in that vicinity had any tradition concerning them, they belonged to the pre-Maori era preceding 1350 A.D. There seems good reason to think that they go back to the days of the Moa-hunters. A feature of several of these chests is that they are carved to represent the human form, some having the head bowed forward and the chin sunk on the chest in the manner which a corpse would assume in a sitting burial. Each has a wing-like arm, and some have webbed feet. Large hands, when present, are termed haohao, and they have skeleton fingers, as of a bird.

A Dominion Museum photograph shows two heads of burial chests and one small chest. In the central figure we note with interest the use of a dividing snake tongue, which is also seen on certain tiki, and was first pointed out by Dr H. D. Skinner. In this figure we have also the use of webbed feet and a blind eye, the latter being a curious feature of several museum burial chests. Chests such as these did not hold the complete skeleton but only certain bones (scraped) such as leg and arm bones and vertebrae. Some small chests held the bones of children.

Genealogical Staves

To the old-time Maori death was by no means the end of the personality. The departed lived on, both in visible symbols and in the whakapapa, or genealogical table, committed to memory and recited on all important occasions. Sometimes, as an aid

189. Burial chest – side view (Dominion Museum).

to memory, genealogical staves termed rakau whakapapa were used. They were pieces of wood carefully wrought with a series of prominent knobs running along one side. One of these, together with an ancient Maori skull and some spring flowers, was figured by the late Augustus Hamilton. In the skull the teeth are worn flat with long usage. The ancient Maori seems to have suffered very little from tooth decay.

INDEX